Marketing and Entrepreneurship in SMEs

Marketing and Entrepreneurship in SMEs: An Innovative Approach

David Carson, Stanley Cromie
Pauric McGowan and Jimmy Hill

University of Ulster at Jordanstown

FINANCIAL TIMES
Prentice Hall

An imprint of **Pearson Education**

Harlow, England · London · New York · Reading, Massachusetts · San Francisco · Toronto · Don Mills, Ontario · Sydney
Tokyo · Singapore · Hong Kong · Seoul · Taipei · Cape Town · Madrid · Mexico City · Amsterdam · Munich · Paris · Milan

10045848695

Pearson Education Limited
Edinburgh Gate
Harlow
Essex CM20 2JE
England

and Associated Companies throughout the world

Visit us on the World Wide Web at:
http://www.pearsoned.co.uk

First published 1995

© Prentice Hall Europe

Typeset on $10^1/_2$/12pt Ehrhardt
by Mathematical Composition Setters Ltd, Salisbury, Wiltshire.

Printed and bound in Great Britian by 4edge Ltd, Hockley, Essex.

Library of Congress Cataloging-in-Publication Data

Marketing and entrepreneurship in SMEs : an innovative approach /
   David Carson ... [et al.].
      p.   cm.
   Includes bibliographical references and index.
   ISBN 0-13-150970-5
   1. Marketing—Management. 2. Small business—Management.
   I. Carson, David.
HF5415.13.M3447 1995
658.8—dc20   94-43999
                                                                    CIP

British Library Cataloguing in Publication Data

A catalogue record for this book is available from
the British Library
ISBN-10: 0-13-150970-5
ISBN-13: 978-0-13-150970-2

10 9 8
08 07 06 05

Contents

Figures and Tables

Foreword

Marketing and entrepreneurship largely determines the fate of business owners and SMEs around the world – their success, their growth, their profitability. And the creation of employment by SMEs is the economic engine driving the global quality of life.

Research has shown that venture capitalists often see marketing as the most highly rated component in new enterprises, along with the management team and financing. The identification and evaluation of market opportunities, combined with their strategic and tactical pursuit, are at the heart of entepreneurial success. This is indisputable.

It has also become evident that as the largest corporations downsize and re-engineer, they are seeking the entrepreneurial behaviour of successful SMEs. It was widely assumed in academia, even five years ago, that SMEs just required a simplified version of the more 'sophisticated' marketing practices used by the largest companies. Now it is becoming apparent that marketing is often fundamentally different and more successful in SMEs than in large firms. This is partly because marketing implementation can be more important to success than planning and strategy.

What some may not consider, however, is that marketing and entrepreneurship are also an integral part of the world history that is unfolding before our eyes. Numerous countries in Latin America, Asia and Europe are for the first time fully embracing the market system. Inherent in the system is a marketing philosophy, and entrepreneurial spirit that has contributed to many millions of new business births.

Marketing and entrepreneurship can both be viewed as fundamental philosophies – ways of seeing and responding to the business world. Studies have shown that these orientations are intertwined and consistent with one another. Yet they are too often not combined. Overwhelmingly, marketing books today still teach planning and analysis for large corporations rather than the dynamic process which intermixes entrepreneurs' qualitative and insightful comprehension of a market-place with good judgement and action. This book provides a refreshing and landmark change by bridging the marketing discipline with the entrepreneurship field. Marketing is treated as the externally oriented and dynamic function that it truly represents. Good marketing is inherently entrepreneurial. It is coping with uncertainty, assuming calculated risks, being proactive and offering attractive innovations relative to competitors. And good entrepreneurship is inherently marketing oriented. A customer focus by everyone in the enterprise is a way of life. And the implementation of marketing strategies that generate customer satisfaction is essential to survival.

'Small business', from a research perspective, is quite simply the enterprise size variable. Entrepreneurship is at least partly represented by the early stage of the business life cycle. But to begin to fully understand SMEs and entrepreneurship, we must study many related variables such as few, if any, economies of scale, severe resource constraints, a limited geographic market presence, a limited market image, little brand loyalty or market share, little specialized management expertise, decision-making under even more imperfect information conditions than in larger firms, a sheer scarcity of time per major management task, and a mixture of personal, non-maximizing financial goals. Just as a child is not a little adult, a new venture or SME is not a little Fortune 500 firm. In firms where several of these conditions exist, one could expect that the marketing function could both be viewed differently and performed differently than in larger firms.

It has been observed that, several decades ago, marketing teaching was more entrepreneurial – in recognition of the uncertainties inherent in coping with customer and competitive environments. But there has been very little research regarding marketing and entrepreneurship (including new ventures), since the inception of the *Journal of Marketing* in the 1930s. Three related bodies of literature, however, include new product research, diffusion of innovation studies, and marketing strategy writing. The entrepreneurship field began to evolve substantially in only the 1970s, although considerable progress has been made. And then the first research meeting on marketing and entrepreneurship was held in 1982, with the first annual University of Illinois at Chicago/American Marketing Association Research Symposium on Marketing and Entrepreneurship in 1987. Eight volumes have appeared since then, including a recent book on research opportunities for faculty and PhD students. An Entrepreneurial School of Marketing Thought is evolving which could fundamentally change the way we understand marketing.

This book will be seen as an important historical contribution because it is the first to integrate the unique knowledge that interrelates entrepreneurship and marketing into a form for use by professors, students and practitioners. Also, there are many important perspectives, conceptualizations, and outright practical and useful methods never before presented. The very concept of entrepreneurial marketing, for example, with its attention to networking and competency development is a major contribution to marketing and entrepreneurship thinking. The authors are pioneers. The reader will be richly rewarded for the time devoted to studying this book.

Gerald E. Hills
Coleman/Denton Thorne Chairholder
in Entrepreneurship and Professor of
Marketing, University of Illinois at Chicago

Preface

The disciplines of marketing and entrepreneurship, if that is what they are, have a long history. Their origins can be broadly located in management, marketing, entrepreneurship and small business. But herein lies a problem for the student, researcher, theorist or practitioner: when considered together, marketing and entrepreneurship are always marginalized in the context of any one field. This marginalization is compounded further when reviewing the literatures of management and entrepreneurship and management and small business. The consequence is that, if one wants to research and study marketing and entrepreneurship, one has to search widely across a range of often diverse literature.

Of course, this problem is not limited to the student or researcher alone. Practitioners are also faced with this minefield of multidisciplines if they wish to explore more formally the theoretical foundations of what they actually do. Further, most theories and approaches appear (to the practitioner) more suited to large companies rather than to small and medium enterprises (SMEs). More often than not, the onus is on practitioners to *learn* concepts rather than being able to *use* them to suit their unique decision-making requirements.

If these arguments are accepted, then one can see that a text is needed which addresses marketing *and* entrepreneurship. This is what we have attempted in this book. The text adopts an innovative approach, while acknowledging the foundation of the accepted and established theories, a scholarly approach and practical applications. To this end, Part One is devoted to reviewing aspects of the disciplines of management and marketing as a foundation for the innovative approach. We have assumed that the reader has some prior knowledge and appreciation of these disciplines, at least to the point of understanding some of the standard jargon.

The main thrusts of the text are an emphasis on the importance of *adapting* the traditional approaches to marketing and how such adaptation can lead to marketing that is appropriate to SMEs. The pivotal influence of the entrepreneur on an SME is acknowledged and approaches are proposed which show how this influence can be harnessed while recognizing the innate characteristics of the entrepreneur. This leads into an emphasis on the aspects of networking and competency development that are used to develop SME marketing, an approach that is essentially *entrepreneurial marketing*.

The text is intended to be used both as a study guide and as a self-learning tool. That is, it is intended for students of entrepreneurship and marketing and also for practising entrepreneurs. Entrepreneurs will benefit from an insight into the foundations and processes inherent in their decision-making, which in turn will enable them to engage in marketing more effectively. This marketing is not simply entrepreneurially speculative; rather it allows for entrepreneurial freedom of expression but channels its processes through appropriate strengths afforded by aspects of adaptation, networking and competency development, a combination we call 'entrepreneurial marketing'.

To bring together the key elements of entrepreneurial marketing the text has been divided into three parts. Part One consists of six chapters. Chapter 1 describes the broad overview of marketing and entrepreneurship, outlining its origins and background and underlining its importance. Chapters 2 and 3 focus on management and marketing. The topics themselves are not defined; rather, the concentration is on those major developments that have occurred recently and that are currently developing. Chapter 4 introduces the concept of entrepreneurship and outlines the factors that make up the entrepreneurial character. Chapters 5 and 6 return to the topics of management and marketing but this time in the context of SMEs, by addressing how SME owners and managers carry out management tasks and the way they can perform marketing activities. In short, Part One is the foundation on which the rest of the text is built.

Part Two interweaves the topics of management, marketing and entrepreneurship and introduces the new concepts of 'marketing competencies' and 'networking'. Chapter 7 examines and defines what is meant by management competencies and focuses on those most appropriate to marketing. Chapter 8 considers the scope of marketing management decision-making, while Chapter 9 introduces the notion of managerial relationships which are fundamental to Chapters 10 and 11 which consider the interface between marketing and entrepreneurship and entrepreneurial management respectively. Part Two completes the progression towards the innovative approach of Part Three.

In Part Three, Chapter 12 sets out a general framework for developing entrepreneurial marketing, emphasizing the importance of adapting the traditional management and marketing concepts and combining this with appropriate competencies and the effective use of networks. Chapters 13 and 14 examine in more detail what is meant by marketing competencies and marketing networks and how they can be developed and used by entrepreneurs. Building on these chapters, Chapter 15 sets out how to develop a marketing plan from the perspective of the entrepreneur. Self-completion worksheets are referenced in this chapter and are set out in Appendix A. In Appendix B the text concludes with four case studies of entrepreneurial marketing. Each case describes the integration of all the component parts, but emphasizes different aspects. This appendix concludes with a short overview of the purpose and value of the text.

Part One

Chapter 1

Marketing and entrepreneurship: an overview

Objectives

After reading this chapter the reader will have an understanding of the origins, evolution and progression of the concepts of marketing and entrepreneurship. The chapter reviews the broad domains of these distinct disciplines in the context of small and medium-sized enterprises (SMEs).

Introduction

What does marketing and entrepreneurship in SMEs mean? This is an intriguing question from many perspectives, especially so when one considers that marketing as a discipline is long established and has a strong empirical base founded on management concepts. Further, entrepreneurship has long been recognized as the catalyst for business development, innovation and growth. And in the broader sense, SMEs as an entity are generally acknowledged as the seedcorn for industrial and

3

commercial development in most capitalist economies. So we have three strong, well-established components to answer the question posed above. This suggests that a mix of these components will yield a powerful approach to doing business. But this will only be true if we can harness the strengths of these dimensions and organize them into a cohesive mechanism. To this end we must consider what is actually meant by each of the dimensions. This involves examining the origins and evolution of the dimensions, thereby evaluating their characteristics. We can then determine the context in which they can be brought together for effective business development.

At first glance there seems little in common between marketing and entrepreneurship. In general, they can be seen as two distinct areas of study, both with a wide spectrum of specific interest topics. Indeed, the research history and origin of marketing and entrepreneurship have been traced back to what is primarily marketing on the one hand, and what is primarily entrepreneurial management on the other. Marketing and entrepreneurship have two quite different and distinct origins, and as a consequence, it could be argued that there is an inherent dichotomy between them.

Let us consider, by way of example, marketing planning. The nature of marketing planning is essentially that of a managerial process, which explores what marketing actually does, the process by which marketing operates. But how can marketing planning be described and explained? The principal stages in the process involve companies conducting an internal audit of all their activities relating to marketing and an external audit of all factors impacting on marketing activity; devising a strategy; and implementing and controlling the marketing activities. This definition suggests that planning is a formal process.

The importance of marketing planning is a point that is well made in much of the literature. The broad characteristics of formal marketing planning can be listed and described as follows:

- *Structured*, in that it adheres to rigid frameworks and processes designed to generate knowledge and known outcomes.
- *Sequential*, in that the structure will follow sequential steps designed to move progressively along a clear course of action.
- *Disciplined*, whereby adherence to the sequential structure is essential to the successful completion of the activity.
- *Systems-oriented*, because formal marketing needs to be built around systems, so that all those involved in using it know where their actions fit within the overall system.
- *Short-, medium- and long-term* decisions in marketing, like any other business discipline, require to be taken over time. The time-scales involved are not only short-term but, by necessity, must also include medium- and long-term time dimensions for certain courses of action to come to fruition.

Some measure of the dichotomy between formal marketing planning and entrepreneurship is highlighted by considering some of the fundamental characteristics of entrepreneurs. It is generally accepted that entrepreneurs are generalists rather than focused individuals, task-oriented, ambitious, domineering, inspirational and adaptive, autocratic and charismatic, creative and opportunistic, with a high degree of self-esteem and self-fulfilment. These traits obviously have an impact on small firms in a wide variety of ways, but particularly in relation to marketing. But this impact is often at odds with the formality of the process outlined above.

However, even though we can demonstrate a clear dichotomy between the two disciplines, there is a stronger argument for considering marketing and entrepreneurship as closely related. After all, both are inherently and explicitly concerned with doing business. By this we mean that essentially they are about making things happen for the benefit of all parties involved in an exchange. Both are concerned with identifying opportunities in the marketplace and determining the feasibility of finding, making or procuring the components or parts necessary for an end-product that satisfies the perceived opportunity.

So what is the catalyst or linkage? Both will involve strong elements of *management* in the form of decision-making activities. As we shall see later, such management can span a spectrum of styles, which may be extremely informal and flexible at one end – typically that which pertains in very small firms – and extremely formal and rigid at the other – typically where larger firms operate.

Let us first consider management in the context of entrepreneurship.

Entrepreneurship and management

The literature originating from both these areas can be grouped into two categories. The first category can be described as historical and conventional, and describes research concerned with validity and confirmation. Research here will carry out reciprocal and replicating studies designed to validate previous research studies. Research topics within this category are likely to focus on the managerial dimensions of entrepreneurship by considering principles of management and decision-making, structures of management and organization, and managerial processes. Research is focused on the formal aspects of management as the dominant perspective on entrepreneurship.

The second broad category tends to be more progressive, with a primary focus on new concepts applicable to the area. The research activity is concerned with the micro-dimensions of entrepreneurship. That is, the understanding of what happens within the firm in relation to entrepreneurship. Research topics are likely to focus on the characteristics and style of decision-making, behaviour and relationships, personal contact networks and entrepreneurial competencies – indeed, any new concepts applicable to the area. This outline is illustrated as a broad continuum in Figure 1.1

This research perspective can of course apply equally to the marketing domain, so let us now consider management from the perspective of marketing.

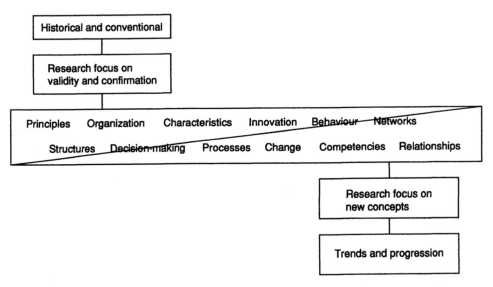

Figure 1.1 Research linkages and emphasis; marketing management and entrepreneurship.

Marketing and management

The marketing function, especially in larger organizations, can be seen as an adjunct of the broader management function of any enterprise that involves elements of organization and planning. The organization structures of management in an enterprise are most likely to be reflected in its marketing function. Indeed, the management processes, style and culture of a marketing function or department will reflect that of the enterprise as a whole.

Research in relation to management and marketing has traditionally centred on larger organizations in a variety of market sectors, although, generally, management thought and theory in the past have tended to centre on large *industrial* organizations, while marketing thought and theory have centred on large *consumer* organizations as a result of the interest in consumer behaviour.

Marketing also attracts researchers from many disciplines. Much of the focus is on the definitions and understanding of the marketing process, the managerial dimensions of marketing decision-making, the interaction between organization and customer and consumer satisfaction. It is easy to see the relationship between marketing and management. But if management is central to considerations of marketing and entrepreneurship, it is not difficult to see a connection between marketing and entrepreneurship.

We have suggested that management approaches can be informal and flexible, or formal and rigid. We can also consider management in two other ways: first, as a system for doing business, and second, as a context in which business will be performed. Management systems involve *organizing* work through the coordination and integration of activities and *formalizing* organization systems into hierarchical superior/subordinate positions and relationships. As management activities have been organized and formalized, and as this will mean that they must occur in the right sequence over time, management must incorporate the notions of *sequentiality* and *progression*. That is, management systems tend to be organized and ordered in such a way that they have a clear order in which they occur, and the sum total of these events progresses towards a cumulative whole end-result.

As an organization grows and develops, it begins to create *specialist* functions, activities and tasks. Individuals become specialized in one function, activity or task to the point where they become experts in that area. But they must still perform to a management system. Our earlier description of marketing planning serves to illustrate this process within a specialist function.

So far we have described the internal systems of management, but we must also recognize that management will be performed in some kind of *context*. Obvious management contexts are represented by the strong environmental influences of the market, in terms of geographical specificity or market segment. Such environmental influences, in fact, determine the focus and resources of management within an enterprise. For example, an enterprise that is solely concerned with a domestic market will have different management and marketing needs from an enterprise that has a wider international focus. Equally, an enterprise that is concerned with industrial markets will perform in a different context from an enterprise that is concerned with providing a service.

Marketing, entrepreneurship and SMEs

The concept of *context* allows us to bring into consideration the important context of small business. There is a substantial literature on the principal managerial component of SMEs, namely, entrepreneurs and entrepreneurship. Entrepreneurship attracts researchers from many disciplines. Much of the focus is on the concept of small business management and entrepreneurship, the characteristics of entrepreneurship, the characteristics of small business and management and entrepreneurship. The central dimension to this interface between small business and entrepreneurship is management, in the broad sense of the term.

While it is acknowledged that marketing and entrepreneurship are often seen as two distinct disciplines, it is important to emphasize that the emergence of marketing and entrepreneurship into a single discipline stems from strong common roots. As we have stated earlier, this commonality is inherent in *management* dimensions. Let us consider some of these in more detail from the perspective of *marketing management*, and then consider how this leads naturally to the context in which entrepreneurship thrives most; that is, in small firms.

Perhaps the strongest link between marketing and entrepreneurship is that they both have markets and customers as their central focus. It is generally recognized that the greatest difference between the marketing function and other functions within an organization (e.g. finance and personnel) is that marketing must perform *outside* the organization, that is, in the marketplace. The marketing function is the organization's interface between its internal systems and its customers; it is the bridge between the organization perspective and the market and customer perspective. This external focus is a natural dimension of entrepreneurship, since entrepreneurship is essentially about exploiting the market. An entrepreneur is only marginally concerned with mechanisms internal to the organization, and only then in terms of making change happen within the internal systems. An entrepreneur's interest will naturally be stimulated by what is perceived as a market opportunity which offers exploitation of a circumstance and/or stealing a march over competitors.

Marketing and entrepreneurship: separate or integrated?

The separate perspective

Marketing and entrepreneurship attract scholars from common backgrounds – psychology, organization behaviour and behavioural sciences in general. Currently, however, the research outputs of the combined area of marketing and entrepreneurship are only of general, if not peripheral interest to existing disciplines from any of these areas. That is, the entrepreneurial discipline is only marginally interested in the specifics of marketing. The majority of researchers are more interested in the *management* of entrepreneurship as it affects the *whole* of a business operation; few researchers are interested in the marketing dimensions of entrepreneurship. Entrepreneurship is viewed as an all-encompassing business activity and as such, it is seen as not belonging to any one business discipline or function. Entrepreneurs are generally viewed as not being good at, and therefore not getting involved in, organizing, planning, etc.; rather, they are seen as concentrating on issues more concerned with business opportunities and development.

Equally, most marketers, who may be interested in marketing dimensions of entrepreneurship, are unlikely to consider current entrepreneurial literature and research as a main source of information; their attention will more probably focus on the mainstream marketing discipline. Marketers have a strong base in processes and techniques. There are proven and accepted ways by which marketers can carry out their marketing activities. Often, these approaches and techniques seem to have no correspondence with entrepreneurship. Indeed, for the reasons outlined above, entrepreneurial literature makes little reference to marketing as a discipline or function. Consequently, marketers interested in entrepreneurship are frustrated by having to trawl a largely peripheral literature on entrepreneurship to find only occasional useful references.

The combined perspective

As we have indicated, however, marketing can be viewed as an integral part of entrepreneurial activity; in this context, the importance of marketing to entrepreneurship − or, indeed, entrepreneurial marketing − is obvious. All firms need to grow or adapt in order to survive and growth and change are marketing-led dimensions, since both rely on new sales, either of new products or from new customers. Entrepreneurial style, activities and concepts, such as innovation, creativity and idea generation, are all fundamentally intrinsic to and compatible with marketing philosophies. Consequently, the importance of marketing within entrepreneurship is inherent.

The domain of marketing and entrepreneurship

What are the implications for SMEs in applying marketing through entrepreneurship? To what extent do the tried-and-tested methods used by professional managers from larger companies need to be adapted? Is adaptation sufficient, or is a totally new and different approach required? These are the issues that management in SMEs needs to address and has been addressing over the past few years, though with varying degrees of success. Much of the early initiative has been in general management, but increasingly the problems of decision-making in specific business functions, such as finance and marketing, in the context of SMEs have become a focus.

However, when it comes to an understanding and knowledge of *marketing planning*, there is still some way to go. Indeed, it has been noted that SME owners/managers have a limited knowledge of marketing planning practices. Any attempts at formulating marketing plans using recognized marketing theory and terminology would seem to be limited and dependent on the depth of experience and knowledge of the owner or manager. In many SMEs, marketing planning activity may be limited to planning for selling within a narrow industry perspective. The broader scope of marketing planning seldom features understanding or relevance, perhaps because of lack of knowledge. Inadequate marketing is a commonly identified reason for SME failure and is recognized as a weakness of SMEs generally. Typically, inadequacies in marketing can be traced to the lack of a planned marketing approach.

If these assertions are accepted, then there is a real need to increase the awareness of SME owners/managers to the importance of a planned approach to marketing. Equally, there is a need to consider how marketing in SMEs can be improved. Arising from these considerations, marketing planning might be concerned with the practical implications of how SMEs plan their marketing. In understanding *how* SMEs do this it might be useful to explore in depth marketing in SMEs on the basis that marketing has, for a number of years, been focused on what to do in a given marketing situation, and has largely ignored how to do it within company, competitor and customer constraints.

Over the past decade significant research in the area of marketing and entrepreneurship has been situated on some kind of continuum between two categories (see Figure 1.1), that is, as represented by historical and conventional approaches on the one side and new concepts on the other. To consider this further, Figure 1.2 indicates that specific interest has occurred in some aspects of the following:

- *Base perspectives, overviews and insights.* Theorists and practitioners have begun to examine the suitability of some theories and techniques from the joint perspective of marketing and entrepreneurship. In addition, there is an examination of broad descriptions and definitions and analysis of their meaning in the joint context and its likely future direction.
- *Research issues.* There is much work concerning the appropriateness of research approaches and whether more innovative research techniques should be employed. There is some indication of this in the continuum outlined in Figure 1.1
- *Technology, growth and innovation.* Considerations in this area stem largely from historical research in entrepreneurship.
- *International issues and viewpoints.* There is a growing realization that the domain of marketing and entrepreneurship is international in perspective and that it does not belong to any one country or culture.
- *Marketing operations, forecasts and trends.* Considerations in this area stem largely from historical research in marketing.
- *Strategic issues and management decisions.* Considerations in this area stem largely from historical research in management.
- *Education and training.* Educators and trainers have long grappled with the difficulties of addressing marketing concepts to entrepreneurs and entrepreneural concepts to students of marketing.

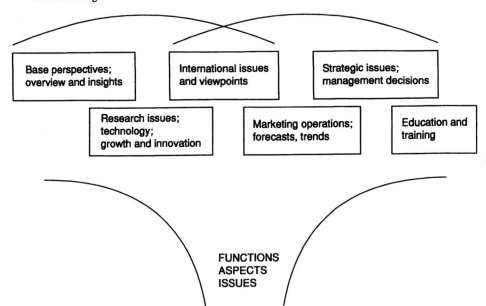

Figure 1.2 Significant research in marketing management and entrepreneurship.

Much of the research has examined the management functions of SMEs, the aspects of marketing and entrepreneurship and issues of marketing and entrepreneurship. In future, it is likely that these distinctive categories will continue to develop as the research area as a whole matures. It can also be expected that there will be increasing cross-fertilization between the two categories as well as further new concepts such as marketing and business or enterprise development and entrepreneurial cultures, and so on.

As stated in the introduction to this chapter, marketing and entrepreneurship in SMEs represents three strong, well-established components. This chapter has shown that, together, they have the potential to yield a powerful approach to doing business, but there are significant problems to be faced.

Established marketing approaches and techniques are built on operating systems that are framed around relatively rigid, progressive and sequential processes. That is, they tend to follow conventional management approaches. This standard marketing does not seem compatible with entrepreneurship when it is considered that entrepreneurs are inherently flexible, *ad hoc* and informal in their decision-making. To this must be added the limited resources of SMEs both in financial and human terms. These limitations mean that much of the standard management and marketing approaches are inappropriate for SMEs. The problem is compounded by the strong entrepreneurial influence in the decision-making, since entrepreneurship is equally incompatible with formal approaches.

It is these issues that are addressed in this text. That is, how to overcome the incompatibilities, gel the strengths of all three components and, by so doing, offer an innovative approach to harnessing these strengths successfully to create more effective entrepreneurial marketing in SMEs.

Summary

Research and the ensuing literature on marketing and entrepreneurship have seldom overlapped. As a result both have evolved along distinct paths and those interested in marketing have been concerned about issues of marketing and those interested in entrepreneurs have been concerned about issues of entrepreneurship. It is possible to think of marketing and entrepreneurship as two quite distinct disciplines, even to the point of there being a divergence between their fundamental characteristics. Where thought processes have converged it has been on aspects of management, that is managing marketing and managing entrepreneurship. When considering management aspects such as decision-making and exploitation of opportunities and making a profit, it is easy to see the common perspectives of marketing and entrepreneurship. These perspectives are seen most often in SMEs and here the notion of entrepreneurial marketing can be perceived.

Learning questions

After reading this chapter, the reader should be able to answer the following questions:

1. What are the research linkages between marketing and entrepreneurship?
2. What are the common areas of research of both disciplines?
3. Why is there a dichotomy between marketing and entrepreneurship?
4. What is the primary common focus of marketing and entrepreneurship?

Chapter 2

Developments in management

Objectives

After reading this chapter the reader should be able to appreciate why organizations need managers, and should have an overview of the classical approach to the subject. The reader should also realize that, while the managerial functions of planning/decision-making, organizing, coordination, control and motivation are fulfilled in all organizations, the methods by which they are utilized in entrepreneurial ventures will differ significantly from those used in large bureaucratic concerns.

In entrepreneurial firms:

1. Planning is a flexible process.
2. Decision-making is only partly rational.
3. Tasks are less specialized and departments tend to be organized on *ad hoc* lines.
4. Coordination is achieved through cross-functional integrating teams.
5. Control is less intrusive than in bureaucracies and leans towards self-control.
6. Managers motivate their staff by offering enriching work.

All these aspects are discussed in more detail in Chapter 11.

It should also be recognized that power, influence and politics are everyday aspects of business life. Uncertainty allows managers (and others) to modify their power by political means. In addition, in view of the complexity and ambiguity in modern businesses, some managers consider that empowered employees are more effective than rigorously controlled ones. Finally, readers should also be aware that a range of behaviours, knowledge and personal attributes are essential underpinnings to the effective performance of managerial duties. These underpinnings are essential in any debate on competence.

Introduction

Marketers and entrepreneurs actively seek business opportunities but these opportunities are realized and exploited through the production of goods or services which satisfy human wants. The production of goods and services normally takes place within organizations, and the complexity and fragmentation of organizational life make it imperative that the processes of transforming raw inputs into meaningful outputs are managed. Managerial involvement is important, therefore, if the entrepreneurial process is to achieve its full potential. However, while there is an implicit recognition of the importance of management there has been a vigorous debate on the nature of management, with no clear agreement about the components of the job. In this chapter we shall consider briefly why management is regarded as an indispensable activity, examine the basic managerial functions and focus on those aspects of management that are appropriate in expanding profit-oriented entrepreneurial organizations.

Let us consider first why organizations need managers. It has been suggested that managers are those people who are in charge of organizations or their sub-units. They are responsible for determining the purpose of their organization or department in the present and the future. Having established goals or objectives, managers are then responsible for ensuring that activities are carried out to ensure that organizational ends are attained. They allocate tasks, delegate responsibilities and ensure that activities are completed to a satisfactory standard. But managers perform another key role. Many people contribute to the functioning of organizations and managers make sure that shareholders, managers, suppliers, employees and others receive sufficient rewards for the contributions they make. Managers reconcile the requirements of the various interested groups. They also ensure that organizations have links with key institutions and contacts in their environment and therefore determine that the organization functions as an open system.[1]

Classical views on management

These activities would be regarded as important by many students of management, but while there is some agreement on the basic purposes of management, there is far less agreement on what the day-to-day aspects of the job entail. Classical writers on the subject consider that all managers perform the basic functions of planning, organizing and controlling. One prominent writer has recently described management as encompassing 'planning/decision making, allocating, motivating, co-ordinating and controlling'.[2] There are those who are very critical of this definition but, as we shall see, while their criticism has some validity with respect to how the managerial process is conducted, it is less convincing as a comment on essential managerial functions.

Classical management writers view the managerial process as a rational, logical and well-ordered practice in which managers take the initiative and plan activities. They do this by conducting a considered analysis of the opportunities and threats posed by the business environment, by reviewing the internal capabilities of the venture together with its ability to acquire resources and, in the light of the values and preferences of senior managers, choose a strategic direction for the organization. Once agreed, it is assumed that objectives can be broken down easily into measurable aims, schedules and activities which will determine the behaviour of all employees.

Activities are then divided into routine, repetitive, specialized tasks, which are allocated to individuals and then coordinated by means of the creation of suitable work constellations. These work-groups are under the direct supervision of a manager, and the activities of these functional work-groups are coordinated by middle managers. We can see, therefore, that organizations become both horizontally and vertically differentiated. The myriad of tasks individuals and machines perform are not marketable in themselves; it is only when they are combined with the activities of many more individuals that a product capable of giving consumer satisfaction is produced. These individual outputs must conform precisely to specifications if they are to be usable, and consequently organizations expend enormous effort to ensure that employees do precisely what they are supposed to do. They are told what to do, how to do it and when to perform duties, and they are given precise instructions on the routeing of their work once it is completed.

This explicit delineation of duties has led one author to describe organizations as 'structures of control' with managers playing a key role in the process of control.[3] How is this control exercised? It has been suggested that when recruiting staff, managers are concerned to ensure that the new entrants will easily accept the values and culture of the organization and therefore select individuals who will fit readily into the system. Once inside the organization employees must conform to numerous administrative and technical controls. Rules and procedures abound, production targets are set and employees must work at a speed controlled by machinery. In many organizations decision-making is centralized and managers exercise social control over their staff. These and many more mechanisms of control restrict the discretionary element of work and ensure that what is supposed to happen does in fact occur. Classical writers concluded that managers had the right to command employees and to expect compliance, but they recognized that incentives were necessary to motivate staff and gain their commitment. They felt that cash incentives were most appropriate for this purpose and supported the introduction of payment by results schemes. Classical writers argued in favour of fair wages but considered that sanctions should be applied if performance was substandard.[4]

The classical image of the managerial process is one of order, predictability and control. Plans, schedules, standardized jobs and regular flows of materials and information are the order of the day. Centralized decision-making ensures effective coordination and the proliferation of rules, procedures and formalized behaviour ensure that organizations run smoothly.

This is a reasonably accurate description of the managerial process in some enterprises. Large, long-established organizations employing non-sophisticated, non-regulating technical equipment and operating in a simple, stable environment often employ many classical principles.[5]

Alternative approaches to management

Even in the rapidly changing, complex world of today there are still many organizations that function in the conditions just described; entrepreneurial organizations do not. Theirs is a rapidly changing world in which creativity, innovation, flexibility and change are the norm. However, even in this kind of environment the basic managerial functions need to be performed, but the manner in which they are carried out will be different from the approach in bureaucratic businesses. The management of SMEs and entrepreneurial ventures are addressed directly in Chapters 5 and 11, but here we shall review the basic managerial functions and suggest how they might be carried out in future-oriented entrepreneurial businesses. Let us begin by examining aspects of the planning process.

Planning and decision-making

All organizations must consider their goals and determine those objectives that must be achieved to accomplish those goals. The classical management theorists considered that these activities would be characterized by: (1) being directed from the top of the organization; (2) adopting a logical and formal approach; and (3) rational economic decision-making.

There are those who argue that this top-down approach to planning is an oversimplification. In many large, entrepreneurial firms individuals regularly approach management seeking approval for projects they have developed and to which they have a strong personal commitment. Many good ideas emerge from within businesses and managers need to decide whether to support them and commit resources to them. In general, senior managers will normally support those projects that are consistent with or advance the strategic goals of the organization.[6] If we accept that plans emerge from within organizations, then we must also accept that plans are not inflexible but are subject to a degree of fluidity.

In support of this argument John Kotter reveals a less certain planning world in which informality coupled with relationship skill is indispensable. Kotter shows that fragmented, varied and disjointed behaviour is instrumental in allowing managers to achieve their objectives. The managers he observed spent a great deal of their time with others, had short, inconsequential conversations with them, asked lots of questions, rarely appeared to make major decisions and spent quite a lot of time discussing seemingly trivial issues.[7]

In contrast with classical opinion, Kotter's sample did not set aside time for contemplative planning, but their informal behaviour allowed them to decide what their organizations were to do, and to work, through people, to make sure that necessary things got done. Kotter's managers rarely had detailed plans but they did develop agendas, that is, lists of targets they felt they must meet in the short, medium and long run. Knowledge of the business allows managers to ask questions when gathering informal information which is pertinent to their agenda. Agendas are not carved in stone; they set out basic intentions and are altered or stabilized regularly in the light of up-to-date information.

Once formulated, agendas are implemented through a network of collaborative relationships with people who can deliver the agenda. In Kotter's study, managerial contacts ranged far and wide and were to be found at various levels both inside and outside the organization. The managers influenced others by persuasion and manipulation and built on known staff relations to draw up a network of individuals who would implement agendas with little or no resistance.

It is rather surprising to note, given the authority and status of these managers, that they rarely resorted to coercion or intimidation. These methods were used sparingly and normally only when requests, negotiation or coaxing had failed. The better managers utilize many contacts and 'ask, encourage, evoke, praise, reward, demand, manipulate, and generally motivate others with great skill in face-to-face situations'.[8] Kotter points out that the 'questionable' behaviour of having lots of short, unplanned conversations with a great many people on a wide range of work and non-work issues makes sense in terms of developing agendas and networks. In addition, the managers were building relationships, and concerns for families, enquiries about golf handicaps and general chit-chat are part and parcel of forming a relationship. Finally, scheduled meetings take time to organize and these managers gleaned the requisite information by viewing every chance meeting as an opportunity to obtain highly relevant information from contacts.

Henry Mintzberg, in his study of managers at work, reached similar conclusions to John Kotter. His sample worked at a rapid pace and their work was characterized by diversity, uncertainty and fragmentation. His managers were not reflective planners, and interpersonal competence, along with the ability to collect data through face-to-face contact, was an essential attribute.

Kotter and Mintzberg have been extremely influential in enhancing our understanding of the means by which managers carry out their duties.[9]

Kotter's work is influential in indicating how managers develop and implement plans, and there is evidence to show that they seldom adopt an entirely rational stance when making their decisions. This is not to imply that managers are irrational. Rather, it has been suggested that they have a limited approach to rationality. Complete rationality, of the type developed in economic models of the firm, assumes that the organization's goal is to maximize profit, that there is unlimited access to information, that all alternative approaches to a situation are known and that the manager will choose the alternative that brings optimum profit. In the everyday world these conditions do not obtain. Decisions must be made with incomplete information because people do not have the capacity to assimilate all relevant information and evaluate all outcomes. Even if they had the capacity, the necessary time and cost are excessive. Herbert Simon suggests that managers make satisfactory not optimum decisions. In the light of the information at their disposal and the objectives they have set, managers make reasonably effective rather than perfect decisions. Once a promising solution to a problem emerges, it is likely to be implemented.[10]

Joint decision-making

Other matters limit the rationality of managers in their decision-making. Rational and economic theories of organizations suggest that profit-maximization is the dominant organizational goal and that all individual and group behaviour is directed towards meeting this objective. Through the division of work, specialized individuals and groups concentrate on aspects of the overall objective, but collectively all effort combines to produce goods or services for profit.

However, the act of organizing creates a situation in which individuals and groups depend on one another. Work done by one department becomes an input for another. In an ideal world information and products will move smoothly between units, but organizations are complex entities and operations do not function like clockwork. Problems in acquiring resources from suppliers, substandard work, machine breakdowns, etc. cause disputes between interdependent departments and people. In resolving these disputes the parties acknowledge their interdependence but they also pursue their own goals. They want associated units to provide them with what they need with the minimum disruption to the smooth working of their own operations. But each department has similar goals. Consequently, we have a network of interacting units which are concerned to contribute to the overall aims of the organization and to pursue their own, independent goals. In resolving these disputes the parties will implicitly adopt a joint decision-making or a negotiating stance.[11]

Making plans and decisions and implementing them are important processes, and styles can vary from the programmed approach of management scientists to the unstructured, fragmented and messy orientation of those who manage in very uncertain conditions. Personal preference, environmental conditions, available information and the complexity of situations, not to mention the type of organization under consideration, will determine the type of planning and decisions that managers carry out.

Organizing

Once a decision is made on what to produce managers have to face the matter of how services are to be provided or products made. It is feasible for a person — a marketing consultant, for example — to complete all aspects of the work a client needs. They can plan their approach and personally provide a range of marketing services. However, it is much more common for individuals to specialize and complete part of the requisite work. Some individuals will be responsible for securing contracts, others will carry out marketing research, product innovation, advertising and distribution work. Specialization is economically attractive in that: (1) individuals become expert in their working methods; (2) few opportunity costs are incurred in the process; and (3) activities can be carried out concurrently and production bottlenecks can be avoided.

Grouping of tasks

Organizations divide tasks into their component parts but these components are not marketable. It is only when tasks are linked together meaningfully to produce complete goods or services that organizations realize the fruits of their labour. In other words, the individuals who perform tasks, while they may perform their work independently, are dependent on others to provide a viable product or service. However, individuals need one another for a variety of reasons. If people who perform similar business or managerial functions are located side by side, they can learn from one another and may develop new, innovative services. For example, skilled craftworkers may benefit from discussing production problems with one another. It is useful, therefore, to have all workers who perform the same work process in close proximity and managed by someone who is an expert in that process. The craftworkers depend on each other to resolve production problems and, even though a firm produces a variety of products, they might feel that the interaction between them is fundamental to producing high quality products. This is called functional departmentalization and was favoured by the classical management writers.

Alternatively, it may be beneficial to have all activities concerned with producing a particular product, serving a specific market or meeting the needs of a particular kind of customer located in the same department. For example, a company that produces carburettors, ignition systems and engine monitoring systems may decide to house all work concerned with each product in the same physical location under one manager. In manufacturing carburettors, diecast workers will produce a metal shell, this will then pass to drillers who drill a number of holes in the body, and then certain metal surfaces will be polished. Concurrently, a press shop will produce the range of metal parts needed in the carburettor. Finally, these pressed parts and the carburettor shell will flow to an assembly-line where floats, springs, etc. will be added and the carburettor will be assembled. By having all the steps in the workflow in close proximity and managed by one person, it is easy to focus attention on the product. If there is a problem in the diecast department, it will have a knock-on effect on the assembly operation; but if both these operations are in close proximity under one boss, this will make it easier to sort out the problem.

Grouping work activities together facilitates interdependence but it performs another useful function: it allows managers to manage a reasonable number of people. The managerial span of control will vary depending on the type of work that is performed in a department, but there is a limit to the number of people who report to one boss.[12]

Let us comment further on these key organizing concepts of specialization and the creation of organizational departments.

All organizations require their personnel to specialize, and in bureaucratic businesses this specialization is extensive. However, while this system offers considerable economic advantages, specialized work tends to be boring and individuals are rarely committed to it. Research reveals that if individuals are allowed to: (1) exercise a degree of independence in their work; (2) practise a range of skills; (3) make a self-contained or complete product; (4) produce something that society values highly; and (5) receive regular feedback on their performance, they will be more likely to be motivated at work. Such work will combine processes of planning, organizing and doing. The tasks will be composite ones, which require discretion by workers, not a robotic following of instructions. In general, greater specialization in work will reduce the likelihood of employees experiencing autonomy, etc., with a greater likelihood of unpleasant work experiences.[13].

Organization requires managers to address the issue of how to divide work and then to consider how to coordinate the disparate activities. The creation of work-groups, under the direction of a manager, is a basic step in achieving coordination, and we have seen that grouping by business function or market section is a fundamental method for creating work constellations. Which is the more appropriate approach in a market-led entrepreneurial firm? Gathering together individuals who complete aspects of the same business function has cost advantages but it has one major disadvantage: the focus of employees is on a business function, not on customer needs. In a functional arrangement there can be an inversion of means and ends. The primary purpose of businesses is to give customer satisfaction and this is more likely to occur in a market grouping of activities. In this arrangement the majority of tasks required to satisfy customer needs are grouped together and administered by a manager. Individuals can more easily make the connection between their activities and the satisfaction of a customer's needs. However, while this criterion for grouping activities focuses attention on customers, it will be most effective when those customers' requirements are reasonably predictable. In those situations where rapid changes in technology, knowledge and markets are common or where client needs are not predictable, different organizational arrangements are more appropriate.

The tasks performed by innovative organizations are non-routine and complex and are best accomplished by temporary project teams. These project teams may diagnose the problem faced by their clients and decide what skills are needed to meet their needs. However, because the solutions may be quite novel, it is impossible to plan in detail how the jobs will be done. As the work progresses, adjustments to the plans become necessary, and this will normally be accomplished in face-to-face discussions. The complexity of the tasks means that decision-making must be decentralized to experts. Rules and procedures will be absent or general, specialists will work side by side and focus on the needs of the client. A senior manager or project leader will be in charge of activities but discussion and participation, not the issuing of orders, will be the management style of the senior manager. These *ad hoc*, temporary teams will form and reform as new projects are taken on and problems are solved. Conflict and disagreement may be quite common but the source of the conflict is different from that in bureaucracies. Professionals and experts will disagree over courses of action and the project manager must be skilled at discussion, negotiation and politicking to get the best out of these contributors. In reality, these *ad hoc* structures are far removed from highly differentiated, formalized and centralized bureaucratic structures.[14]

Coordination

To facilitate coordination, organizations place managers in charge of departments and require them to take an overview. Managers take a broader perspective than those who report to them and by their physical presence they coordinate by direct supervision.[15]

If the manager's department has dependent relations with other departments, face-to-face contacts will be used to make sure that the work and information flow easily between the units. While it is difficult to surpass the brain of the overseeing manager as a coordinating device it is also possible to achieve coordination by preparing plans and schedules to link various interdependent activities.

The managerial hierarchy is the primary coordinating mechanism. Additional mechanisms include direct contacts between managers and planning schedules. In a stable environment with few innovations firms may compete on quality, price and customer service. In this stable environment the managers at the top of the hierarchy will understand fully what is happening within the functional departments and will be able to coordinate matters between them. An illustration of this scenario is provided by Lawrence and Lorsch's study of an organization manufacturing metal containers.[16]

Alternatively, where the overall environment is turbulent and complex, the situation faced by Lawrence and Lorsch's plastic manufacturers, the functional departments of production, marketing and research may face quite different sub-environments. The research sub-environment may be very changeable and complex, while the production department may be much more stable and simple. Marketing, on the other hand, may face an intermediate situation. As a result, individual departments will have quite different structures, time-horizons, leadership styles and orientations. However, such a firm will need to generate frequent innovations to remain competitive and this will require the functional departments to work cooperatively. Organizations will need to take coordination seriously, if they want to facilitate joint decision-making between discrete departments.

The managerial hierarchy, direct managerial contacts and plans may be used, but two additional integrative devices can be introduced: (1) an integrating department; and (2) permanent integrating teams comprising members from the functional departments and the integrating department. In the latter, the functional managers need not be drawn from the top of the hierarchy. Some representatives may be senior managers but others may be local managers and still others may be independent individuals or group leaders. Members of integrating teams may be drawn from the hierarchical levels which offer them the knowledge to make a meaningful contribution to joint decisions. Such cross-functional teams are effective because all the functional contributors' views will be given serious consideration, irrespective of their hierarchical status, and differences will be dealt with openly.

In general, innovative, growth-oriented entrepreneurial ventures, which have developed a degree of functional specialization, will need to expend energy in coordinating those activities needed to sustain market-oriented innovations.

Control in organizations

To assist with coordination and to make sure that the organization achieves its stated purpose most ventures develop a range of controls. Let us reiterate the rationale for organizational control. Organizations are often complex entities whose goals are constantly broken down into sub-goals, programmes, schedules and tasks, which are carried out in dispersed locations. These tasks are of little consequence unless the personal output of disparate individuals combine to produce something that provides consumers with satisfaction. Therefore, it is essential that individual and group behaviour is appropriate and can provide products and services of the correct quality at the right time and in the necessary quantities. In most organizations, if one person produces substandard products, it will have a knock-on effect on many other people. In addition, much of the work of organizations is routine, boring and resented by employees. For this reason close surveillance is often kept on many personnel.

Methods of control

Most organizations feel they need to control their employees, and bureaucracies employ an extensive range of control mechanisms. However, excessive control can create serious problems. Most people resent being controlled, many resist it, and consequently organizations seek less intrusive methods. Indoctrination is useful here. If employees believe in the organizational mission or share the beliefs and values of managers, they are likely to behave in an appropriate manner. Therefore visionary managers seek out and select individuals who, through their family background, schooling or training, have acquired appropriate attitudes. Once individuals are inside organizations they are also socialized in its culture. Their regular associates let them know, directly or indirectly, how they are expected to behave and if they refuse to comply, they will be punished.

Output control is another useful approach. Rather than insist on how jobs are to be done, managers say how much output, by what time and of what quality they want. Individuals are then given discretion to achieve the results. If it is relatively easy to measure performance, then this approach can be effective. Similar results can be achieved by setting the parameters within which individuals must act or by the control of information which is used for decision-making.

If a department or division is an economic entity with easily attributed costs and revenues, then the unit may be given financial targets and considerable discretion in achieving targets. Top management are saying, in effect, that they are not concerned about how objectives are achieved provided they are met. Decision-making is delegated to employees. They are assigned tasks, delegated authority and held accountable for their performance. Senior managers will monitor performance at pre-scribed intervals and offer feedback to keep things moving.

The kind and type of control that is used in organizations is often a matter of choice. Managers will make their choices by considering their own preferences, the nature of the work and the likely consequences of control. However, in many countries individuals are less willing to submit to control and there are those who advocate that working groups, with the assistance of their managers, should set their own targets and develop their own plans. They argue that individuals will be much more motivated to achieve these kinds of target and that the quality of their work will improve. Individuals will exercise self-control in achieving the goals they themselves set.[17]

Motivation

Individual behaviour can be influenced by external controls, but if the individual is motivated to behave appropriately, it will avoid much of the resentment that control engenders. Because managers rarely make products or provide services themselves, much of their work being accomplished through people, it is important that they understand what motivates individuals to act. Motivation comes from within, but managers can create the conditions that give rise to superior job performance.

Motivation is a complex subject and we shall address the matter briefly. It has been suggested that when needs are not fulfilled, individuals experience unease and engage in behaviours that lead to the fulfilment of needs. If one accepts this approach to motivation, then it is incumbent on managers to discover what a person wants and to create the conditions that allow these needs to be satisfied. While few people underestimate the importance of motivation, it is rather difficult for managers to treat people as individuals and they often assume that money can meet many needs. By offering monetary rewards for effective behaviour and withholding rewards, or threatening to remove an employee's means of livelihood through dismissal, managers adopt a crude approach to motivation.

Individuals do respond to monetary rewards but an over-reliance on money as a motivator can create problems for managers. Money is useful in meeting security needs but less effective in meeting ego and social needs. It has been argued that if employees are allowed more discretion in their work, this will let them meet their higher-order needs; various organizations have initiated job-enrichment schemes to accomplish this objective.

Management as a political process

We have discussed how the characteristics of organizations lead managers to modify the classical approach to management and to recognize: (1) the complexities and unpredictability of organizations; (2) the network of interdependent people and work units within businesses; and (3) the socio-technical features of firms. These realities created a challenge for classical management theory, but yet another challenge has since emerged. Their explicit focus on economic rationality precluded them from recognizing that, while individuals and groups do endeavour to meet organizational objectives, they also pursue their own ends even if these are in conflict with organizational purposes. Let us explore how and why such behaviour occurs by utilizing Mintzberg's views on power in organizations.

Let us consider, by way of example, the difficulty in converting goals and objectives into measurable sub-objectives. It may be the goal of an enterprise to increase the level of customer satisfaction, but how is a manager to know whether customers are satisfied or not? It could be argued that the number of complaints received in a week, the speed with which complaints are satisfactorily dealt with, the number of goods returned or the number of accolades afforded to the organization by a consumer watchdog are indicators of levels of satisfaction, but they are only approximations. Managers who have a poor record, as indicated by these criteria, will argue that the indicators are merely surrogates for consumer satisfaction and that it is not fair to assess them using such rough-and-ready measures. They will use their power and influence to get the indicators changed to include measures on which they score well.

If objectives are not easily measured, the uncertainty allows managers to use all their skills of influence, persuasion and manipulation to define objectives, make sure that their department is indispensable in accomplishing them, demand additional resources to accomplish tasks, convince top management that the projects they favour should be incorporated into the strategy of the enterprise, and generally bend the rules to increase the power, status and rewards which are allocated to their own department.

This scenario offers a very different perspective on management from the classical view. Beneath the façade of permanence and regularity an undercurrent of tension, challenge and uncertainty flows. Managers have to reconcile actual outcome with planned events; differing opinions on objectives and their measurement; organization and individual opinions on what constitutes good work; and individual and departmental means with organizational ends. Management is therefore likely to be a somewhat chaotic, problematic process, characterized by uncertainty and the exercise of political skill. Managers will think of organizations as a network of interdependent parts which, to some extent, recognize their mutual interest and the benefits of cooperation, but they will also pursue their own ends and compete with their associates. Relationships between individuals and departments will be influenced by power/dependency, the exercise of political skill and the resolution of differences through negotiation.[18]

Managerial power

In the face of this uncertainty managers utilize a variety of power bases to accomplish objectives. Hales suggests that these include: physical power, economic power, knowledge power and normative power.[19] Others have added personal power. This power may accrue to a role incumbent or an individual. For example, legitimate authority is given to the manager as a role incumbent, but economic power, together with some knowledge and normative power, also accrues to office-holders. Managers control the disbursement of economic resources and their status allows them access to privileged administrative and technical information which is useful to others. They may also understand fully the history, mission and key events in the organization's development and successfully imbue others with the organization's key values and beliefs. However their presence may allow them to bully others physically or verbally; technical knowledge, which they have personally acquired over time, may confer considerable influence; and strongly held personal beliefs might persuade others to behave in a prescribed manner. In addition, the managers' charisma may induce others to follow them.

Managers must: (1) know what people want; (2) produce or provide something others value; and (3) be able to give (or deny) individuals what they want in order to influence them. This is not an exact science. Many assumptions are made, misconceptions are common and unexpected outcomes occur when managers influence others. What is more, the power relationship is not static. A production department may depend heavily on computing to keep its automatic machines running, but an advance in technology may allow production staff to run their own systems and dispense with the services of the computing personnel.

An understanding of the needs of others and one's power base are useful guides to behaviour, but two more issues enter the equation. It is generally agreed that coercive power will elicit alienative involvement, renumerative power will evoke calculative involvement and normative power will bring about moral involvement. In other words, individuals respond in predictable ways to the power base and associated method of influence which a manager uses. Responses to influence will also depend on the perceived legitimacy of managerial action. If those being influenced consider that managerial action is reasonable, they may willingly cooperate; if not, they may grudgingly acquiesce.[20]

To elicit willing cooperation managers use a repertoire of power bases and methods of influence, and they often depersonalize their instructions by emphasizing the technological or economic imperatives for their decisions. Reference to imperatives is a useful means of influence for the manager, but Hales notes that the final stage in the depersonalization of managerial power is the embodiment of power in the structural features of organizations. A significant number of the power sources available to managers are derived from organizations, and managers emphasize the existence of rules, procedures, reporting relationships, hierarchical realities, resource constraints and many other organizational matters when managing. The fact that organizational structures and procedures are designed, developed and implemented by managers will not be mentioned when instructions are issued. The importance of these and other structural features of organizations for the managerial process has led Hales to coin the phrase 'management through organization'.[21]

A radical approach to management

We have described managers as responsible people who perform a number of activities in the managerial process, but there has long been a debate about who should perform these managerial activities. In our discussion so far it has been implicitly assumed that managers plan, organize and control, and that non-managers complete operational activities. In other words, managers do the thinking and non-managers perform routine duties. However, it is quite possible that the planning, organizing, coordination and control of jobs can be done by those people who actually provide products or services.

While they did not refer to empowerment, the organization development movement in the late 1960s and through the 1970s recommended the creation of self-correcting work-groups who would learn to solve their own problems and manage their own affairs. These writers advocated the development of trusting interpersonal relationships, together with a challenging, questioning atmosphere among employees. They recommended the decentralization of decision-making to experts and group training methods to initiate a culture in which employees would feel responsible for organizational goals. In general, they favoured group rather than individual involvement in work tasks, advocated proactive, planned approaches to change and recommended collaboration rather than competition within and between organizations. In this situation the manager is much more of a coach or facilitator than a director of operations.

Organization development (OD) practitioners regarded human resources as the most valuable and flexible of all the resources and bemoaned the fact that many organizations failed to get the best out of their staff.[22]

Transformational leadership

While few writers today recommend the leaderless groups that were supported by some OD protagonists, several authors recommend that organizations need transformative leaders, not directive managers. Transformative or transformational leaders are adept at communicating a vision to employees and securing their commitment in the pursuit of this vision. The transformal leader shows a concern for the intellectual development and other needs of staff and emphasizes that through collaboration leader and followers have the ability to solve problems and transform the organization.

These approaches to leadership or management are unlike those advocated by the classical writers, it is therefore helpful to make some comparisons between these directive managerial approaches and transformative ones. To do so we draw on a useful table developed by Alan Bryman[23] (see Table 2.1).

If we examine the statements on the left-hand side of Table 2.1, we can see a strong resemblance between them and our description of the classical approach to management. They recommend that power is retained at the top of the hierarchy; that formal communication channels dominate; job tasks are allocated precisely; written rules, procedures and contractual regulations are fully utilized; and above all, that managers exercise rigorous control. In this kind of work environment calculative or even alienative involvement by employees is the norm.

Table 2.1 Themes in New Leadership literature

Less emphasis needed on:	Greater emphasis needed on:
Planning	Vision/mission
Allocating responsibility	Infusing vision
Controlling and problem-solving	Motivating and inspiring
Creating, routine and equilibrium	Creating change and innovation
Power retention	Empowerment of others
Creating compliance	Creating commitment
Emphasizing contractual obligations	Stimulating extra effort
Detachment and rationality on the part of the leader	Interest in others and intuition on the part of the leader
Reactive approach to the environment	Proactive approach to the environment

Source: A Bryman (1992) *Charisma and Leadership in Organisations*, London: Sage, Table 5.2, p.111. Reproduced with permission of Sage Publications Ltd.

In contrast, transformational leaders are less concerned with directing and controlling their staff and are much more concerned with creating the conditions which will release the enormous potential individuals have to contribute to the future development of the organization. Transformative leaders strive to create commitment, interest and motivation from workers in pursuit of a vision to which they subscribe. In a modern world where change in knowledge and markets, together with a demand for individualized service by customers, is so common, rigid controlling bureaucracies are much less likely to meet consumer needs than flexible, empowered transformative ventures. Calls for an organizational and managerial approach akin to transformational leadership are not new, but they have a greater sense of urgency in today's rapidly changing, competitive world.

Managerial skills and competencies

In this chapter we have traced some major developments in management and have presented it as a process characterized by the planning, organization, coordination and evaluation of work. Whether these functions are performed by directive managers, persuasive networkers or empowered employees they must be carried out. We can consider these major management functions as the domains that must be mastered if managers are to perform effectively, and success in these domains will come about if managers perform a number of key roles. An important empirical study of managers at work by Mintzberg concluded that the crucial roles of the manager could be grouped under the headings of handling people, processing information and making decisions.[24]

Managers work through people to get things done. Management is also dependent on the gathering, interpretation and dissemination of volumes of information which is indispensable for planning, decision-making, coordination and control. Managers are forever making decisions. Managerial decisions range from strategic ones to rather mundane operational decisions. However, managers must be aware of the procedures and dynamics of the decision-making process if they are to perform this role effectively. Managers must make entrepreneurial decisions about the future of the organization, but they are regularly required to resolve disputes between individuals, groups and organizational divisions. The network of people and units within organizations who depend on one another for instrumental, resource-related, emotional and political reasons invariably interpret matters differently, and managers have to intervene to resolve conflicts. Managers also decide on the allocation of resources to competing ends and in many of the situations they face their lack of absolute power forces them to engage in joint decision-making.

A basic model of managerial competencies

Superior performance in key domains and the taking of important roles are necessary for managerial effectiveness, but the latter will only occur if individuals behave appropriately. Therefore, if we are to uncover the skills which enable managers to excel in key domains, we must search for those behaviours and activities that underpin important roles and domains.[25]

A skilful individual can develop the capacity for appropriate behaviour through experience or training, but while skill can be developed this will not occur unless an individual possesses key personal characteristics. In addition, knowledge is a crucial ingredient of competency. Competent managers will possess a reservoir of necessary behaviours but they must know when and how to use them. Knowledge of business realities, management theories and environmental affairs will allow the manager to set in motion a sequence of actions which lead to superior performance.

To conclude our discussion on management let us consider the knowledge, personal qualities and skills which endow a manager with the capacity to accomplish managerial objectives. In the first instance let us present a simple model in Table 2.2 to illustrate our approach.

In other words, we suggest that a range of personal characteristics, basic knowledge and behaviours will underpin those clusters of activities which contribute to the effective performance of managerial roles and functions. By way of illustration let us comment on the key managerial role of negotiation. Negotiation skills are vital in achieving the basic managerial functions of coordination. To be effective, negotiators must be self-confident but they must also understand the nature of negotiation. It is a joint decision-making process and negotiators must resist attempts by aggressive individuals to conduct negotiations in a unilateral decision-making mode. Key skills for negotiating include interpersonal attributes such as communication and perception, the ability to evaluate a mass of information and the creativity needed to invent options for mutual gain. Negotiation is a vital process in allowing managers to display competence in one of their major domains.

In Table 2.3 we have applied this approach across the board and in it we present a somewhat eclectic schema, based on a review of the material examined in this

Table 2.2 From management behaviours to management functions

		Managerial Goals		
Plan	Organize	Motivate	Control	Coordinate

		Managerial Means		
Leadership	Deciding	Negotiating	Allocating	
Visioning	Empowering	Changing	Agenda-setting	
Inspiring	Networking	Problem-solving	Communicating	

Managerial Skills
A broad range of abilities, knowledge and skills

Table 2.3 Managerial competences: those personal qualities necessary. Knowledge, exhibited skills and essential activities for competent performance

	Plan	Decide	Organize	Control	Coordinate	Motivate
Key Activities	Develop vision Develop agendas Develop schedules, targets and tasks	Clarify objectives Set alternatives Evaluate action Choose course Evaluate	Agree tasks Assign duties Group activities Relationships Work-flows	Know objectives Monitor Evaluate Feedback Correct	Assess differences Assess interdependencies Design MIS Lateral links	Understand staff Assess needs Offer rewards Assess impact
Key Skills	Manage information Entrepreneurship Intelligence Network Analyze Conceptualize Influence Liaise	Manage information Entrepreneurship Liaise Analyze Allocate Network Create	Allocate Delegate Manage conflict Analyze Lead Schedule Communicate	Manage information Monitor Dissemnate Lead Influence Manage conflict	Manage information Liaise Network Lead Politick Negotiate Manage conflict	Lead Coach Empower Persuade Reward Communicate Facilitate
Key Knowledge	What is possible Environmental conditions Organizational strengths and weaknesses Resource	What is possible Detailed knowledge of organization Nature of organization's goals Culture of organization	Aware of contingencies Aware of forms of organization Aware of limits of formal organization	Financial awareness Organizational procedures Methods of control Reaction to control	Knowledge of total organization and its operation Methods of ensuring integration	Knowledge of people Theories of motivation Available rewards
Personal Qualities	Open-minded Adaptable	Open-minded Determined	Logical thinker	Impact Presence	Tolerance of ambiguity	Social orientation Charisma

chapter, of the personal qualities, knowledge and skills which lead to the successful performance of managerial functions.

Robert Quinn and his colleagues[26] allow us to set our ideas in context. Quinn *et al.* examined the approach taken to management by the classical, human relations, open systems and contingency writers, and formulated a single framework for the study of management which draws on all four approaches. They then argue that the world of the manager is characterized by constant change and effective performance will only occur if managers utilize a range of skills or competencies. In their opinion '*competency* is the knowledge and skill necessary to perform a certain task or role.'

A detailed discussion of management and marketing competencies is given in Chapter 7, but this preliminary discussion lays a firm foundation for it. Management is action–oriented and certain functions must be performed for organizational effectiveness. However, an amalgam of knowledge, experience, personal attributes, attitudes and behaviours are necessary for competent managerial performance.

Summary

In summary, management is a ubiquitous activity which is indispensable for the effective performance of activities and the functioning of organization. In this chapter we have addressed aspects of the why, what, who, how and underscoring elements of management.

Managers afford a sense of direction to people in organizations and design the essential regulating features of businesses. They are the responsible people, those in charge, who make sure that what is supposed to occur does in fact happen. In pursuing these objectives they have to be conscious of the need to think about the direction they want their organizations to take and the means by which to get there. With a sense of direction and an image of their means managers must ensure that essential tasks are assigned to individuals, that responsibilities are recognized and that sufficient supervision is in place to ensure that requisite activities in the furthest reaches of the organization are accomplished. Through planning, organizing and control organizational tasks are coordinated to provide marketable products and services. Managers work through people to get things done and they must get the best from their human resources.

How they achieve their goals is a matter of choice. Detailed plans may depict what needs to be done and precise written procedures may inform individuals of what, how and when they must perform their tasks. Alternatively, employees might be afforded discretion in choosing the most appropriate methods and timing for their duties. The management functions can be accomplished by directive or non-mandatory means.

The chosen method will depend on the values of the manager and on certain organizational contingencies, but the likely impact of managerial style on individuals and groups must be taken into account. Managers must elicit appropriate behaviour from their peers and employees in situations where their power is rarely absolute. An understanding of the political reality of organizational life and the power at one's disposal are vital if managers are to direct, negotiate with or empower their staff.

How they perform their job will depend on these matters and on the skill and knowledge managers possess. A recognition of the essential competency domains, the skills and knowledge and the capacity to improve the latter is essential for effective managerial and organizational performance.

Learning questions

1. 'Entrepreneurs and marketers are action oriented individuals and the mundane managerial process will inhibit their effectiveness.' What is the validity of this statement? Suggest ways by which the entrepreneurial and managerial processes might be made compatible.
2. In the absence of detailed plans, precise organizational structures and tight control it is impossible to coordinate organizational activities. Discuss.
3. It has been suggested that political skill is a crucial managerial asset. Why might this be so? Examine the means by which managers can enhance this aspect of skill in an entrepreneurial venture.
4. Some writers suggest that it is the duty of the manager to manage. Prepare a set of working notes which will assist you in a forthcoming discussion with a manager who is resisting attempts to empower his employees.
5. What do you consider to be the essential personal attributes, knowledge and skills that the manager of an innovative SME should possess?

Notes and references

1. Mintzberg, H. (1973) *The Nature of Managerial Work*, Englewood Cliffs, NJ: Prentice Hall. See pp. 94–6 for a discussion of the manager's basic purpose.
2. Hales, C. (1993) *Managing through Organisations*, London: Routledge, p. xviii.
3. Salaman, G. (1979) *Work Organisations: Resistance and Control*, London: Longman, p. 107.
4. Taylor, F. W. (1947) *Scientific Management*, New York: Harper & Row. Taylor advocated the use of monetary incentives to individuals to stimulate employee productivity.
5. Mintzberg, H. (1979), *The Structuring of Organizations*, Englewood Cliffs, NJ: Prentice Hall. See p. 314 for the conditions in which machine bureaucracies thrive.
6. Mintzberg, H. (1989) *Mintzberg on Management*, New York: The Free Press. See chapter 2, pp. 25–42 for a discussion on planned and emergent strategy.
7. Kotter, J. P. (1982) 'What effective general managers really do', *Harvard Business Review*, November–December, pp. 156-67.
8. *Ibid.*, p. 163.
9. Mintzberg (1973), *op. cit.* See pp. 28–53 for a discussion on the characteristics of managerial work.
10. Minkes, A. (1987) *The Entrepreneurial Manager*, Middlesex: Penguin Books. See chapter 5, pp. 69-83 for a discussion on rationality in decision-making.
11. Mastenbroek, W. F. G. (1993) *Conflict Management and Organisation Development*, Chichester: John Wiley. Mastenbroek views organizations as networks of interdependent sub-units.

12. Mintzberg (1979) *op. cit.* See chapter 8, pp. 104–33 for an examination of the criteria for grouping activities.
13. This approach to job design is based on a model developed by Hackman, J. R. and Oldham, G. R. (1980), *Work Redesign*, Reading, MA: Addison-Wesley.
14. For a detailed description of adhocracies, see Mintzberg (1979) *op. cit*, pp. 431–65. For a lively summary, consult Robbins, S. P. (1990), *Organization Theory*, Englewood Cliffs, NJ: Prentice Hall, pp. 147–54.
15. Mintzberg (1979) *op. cit.* discusses co-ordination by direct supervision on pp. 3–5.
16. Lawrence, P. R. and Lorsch, J. W. (1967) *Organization and Environment*, Boston, MA: Harvard University Press, chapter 3, pp. 54–83.
17. For a general discussion on control see Mintzberg (1979) *op. cit.*, pp. 148–60. An original source on self-control is McGregor, D. (1960), *The Human Side of Enterprise*, New York: McGraw-Hill.
18. See Mastenbroek (1993) *op. cit.*, pp. 12–19 for an examination of types of interdependency.
19. Hales (1993) *op. cit.*, pp. 17–46 on power, influence and authority.
20. See Etzioni, A. (1961) *A Comparative Analysis of Complex Organizations*, New York: Free Press for responses to influence and Hales (1993), *op. cit.*, for a discussion on legitimacy.
21. Hales (1993) *op. cit.*, p. 47.
22. See, for example, Bennis, W. G., Benne, K. D. and Chin, R. (1969) *The Planning of Change*, London: Holt, Rinehart & Winston.
23. See, Bryman, A. (1992) *Charisma and Leadership*, London: Sage; and Popper, M., Landou, O. and Gluskinos, V. M. (1992), 'The Israeli defence forces: An example of transformational leadership', *Leadership and Organisational Development* 13, pp. 3–8.
24. Mintzberg (1973) *op. cit.*, pp. 54–99.
25. Lindsay, P., Stuart, R. and Thompson, J. (1993) 'Development of the top team: The definition of a competence framework to small and medium sized firms'. Proceedings of the *EFMD European Small Business Seminar*, Belfast.
26. Quinn, R. E., Faerman, S. R., Thompson, M. P. and McGrath, M. R. (1990) *Becoming a Master Manager*, New York: John Wiley.

Further reading

For a presentation on classical approaches to management see Brech, E. F. L. (1965) *Organisation: The Framework of Management*, London: Longman.

For an authoritative discussion on control in organizations and the depersonalization of management, see Thompson, P. and McHugh, D. (1990) *Work Organisations. A critical introduction*, Basingstoke: Macmillan.

The notion of work specialization receives excellent treatment in Litterer, J. A. (1965) *The Analysis of Organizations*, New York: John Wiley.

The attractions of different means of departmentalization are fully discussed in Jackson, J. H. and Morgan, C. P. (1978) *Organization Theory – A Macro Perspective for Management*, Englewood Cliffs, NJ: Prentice Hall.

Change strategies and resistances are thoroughly examined in Wilson, D. C. (1992) *A Strategy of Change*, London: Routledge.

For a readable examination of power and influence, see Handy, C. (1985) *Understanding Organisations*, London: Penguin Books.

Carroll, S. J. and Gillen, D. J. (1987) 'Are the classical management functions useful in describing managerial work?', *Academy of Management Review* 12, pp. 38–51 is excellent for seeking common ground between classical writers and the work activity school of management.

On negotiation, see Hayes, J. (1991) *Interpersonal Skills*, London: Harper Collins, chapter 8; and Fisher, R., Ury, W. and Patton, B. (1991), *Getting to Yes*, New York: Penguin Books.

For a discussion on need theories of motivation and Frederick Herzberg's theories of job enlargement and enrichment, see Mitchell, T. R. and Larson, J. R. (1987), *People in Organizations*, New York: McGraw-Hill, pp. 158–62 and 172–4.

Mintzberg, H. (1983) *Power in and around Organizations*, Englewood Cliffs, NJ: Prentice Hall, pp. 171–217 has a detailed discussion on the emergence of political behaviour in organizations.

See Daft, R. L. (1983) *Organization Theory and Design*, St Paul: West, pp. 297–309 for a discussion on types of information in organizations.

Chapter 3

Evolution and development of marketing

Objectives

This chapter briefly reviews the origins and evolution of marketing. It identifies and describes the major developments of marketing throughout the 1980s and into the 1990s and speculates on future trends. We introduce the concepts of marketing in context, particularly the context of small business and the concept of industry-specific marketing, whereby SMEs must conform to industry marketing norms.

History and evolution of marketing

It is interesting to observe that marketing as a discipline has a long history, dating back to the late nineteenth century. The need for marketing arose from the need to stimulate demand for growing surpluses in items such as commodities. These surpluses occurred as a result of improvements in production technology stemming from the industrial revolution. As technological improvements widened into other consumer types of products, the need for marketing also widened. This period of marketing evolution, driven by emerging institutions with production or technological expertise, was dominant until the 1940s.

In the late 1940s and early 1950s marketing activity evolved and tended to emphasize advertising promotion and buying and selling. This was the period of the great expansion in the availability of consumer products, fuelled by rapid industrial expansion and greater disposable income. Consumers were responsive to glossy advertising messages and sophisticated sales arguments built around new and exciting and, most significantly, previously unattainable products. This period in marketing evolution consisted of a functional orientation, which in turn led to the managerial focus of the 1960s onwards.

As markets grew and ever-increasing numbers of consumers from widely diverse backgrounds demanded products to meet their new lifestyles, marketing too had to adapt. The 1960s and 1970s saw the evolution of what we now accept as the marketing era; that is, the adoption of the marketing concept. This concept was determined by an emphasis on market research into consumer behaviours and desires. It was founded on a recognition that consumers from different backgrounds and beliefs had different demands. Market research quickly determined that it was possible to segment consumers into loosely homogeneous groups which behaved in similar, but unique ways. This realization led marketers to recognize the need to put the consumer first in any marketing activity. Thus marketing in this period – and indeed, ever since – has been primarily customer-focused.

The late 1960s and early 1970s also saw the widening of marketing's scope. Many argued that marketing was appropriate in any transaction regardless of whether it involved a product or service and profit considerations. Hence the development of non-profit marketing circumstances, which now generally come under the auspices of macro-marketing, which is concerned with the impact between marketing systems and social systems.

Dominance of strategic marketing management

Throughout the 1980s and still today the strategic concept of marketing has dominated. Strategic marketing still emphasizes the importance of understanding consumer needs but takes a wider view, through critical analysis of opportunities for long-term competitive advantage. The extent of this management domination is illustrated by an examination of textbooks focusing on 'principles of marketing' or 'introducing marketing'. In the 1960s and 1970s such texts followed a standard format, beginning with an introduction which would include a brief history and describe the marketing concept and philosophy. Thereafter, chapters would examine various dimensions of the marketing mix, with a final chapter or two on topical aspects of marketing, such as industrial marketing and international marketing. The focus throughout all the chapters was on the foundation principles of the topic. Contemporary introductory texts have evolved so that now there is a strong emphasis on the managerial dimensions of the foundation principles. Thus, texts now describe planning and implementation, analysis and decision-making processes used in marketing. Such descriptions are not confined to separate chapters but are an integral and necessary part of all chapters. Most contemporary texts still have topical chapters, which now cover issues such as global marketing, ethics in marketing, regional marketing and marketing in different contexts such as services and relationship marketing. It might be argued that newcomers to marketing are actually being introduced to marketing management or strategic marketing as a topic rather than to principles of marketing.

In a wider sense there is some criticism of the way marketing texts are presented. Gummesson[1] has summarized objections to traditional marketing textbooks as follows:

Objection No. 1: The textbook presentations of marketing are based on limited real world data.

Objection No. 2: Goods account for a minor part of all marketing, but the textbook presentations are focused on goods; services are treated as a special case.

Objection No. 3: Marketing to consumers dominates textbooks, while industrial/business marketing is treated as a special case.

Objection No. 4: The textbook presentations are a patchwork; new knowledge is piled on top of existing knowledge but not integrated with it.

Objection No. 5: The textbooks have a clever pedagogical design; the form is better than the content.

Objection No. 6: The Europeans surrender to the US and its marketing gurus and do not adequately promote their own original contributions.

The domain of marketing

What now is the domain of marketing? This is a vexed question which has occupied many writers and marketing scholars over many years. It is complicated by the fact that marketing is a dynamic discipline which is continuously evolving. There are many opposing views of what actually constitutes marketing's domain. Frequently, a perception is determined by whether it is based on psychology, sociology,

Table 3.1 Classification of marketing phenomena

		Positive	Normative
Profit Sector	{ Micro		
	{ Macro		
Non-Profit Sector	{ Micro		
	{ Macro		

anthropology, economics or business. Similarly, different perceptions will be determined by whether marketing is viewed as an art, where a much freer and *laissez-faire* approach might prevail, or a science, where scientific rigour and position will dominate the perspective of marketing. Equally, the domain of marketing will be influenced by whether marketing is viewed as an exchange process or whether it has a wider role determined by a marketing behaviour, which may be determined by many other factors as well as exchange.

All these parameters are encapsulated in a classification of marketing phenomena using categories devised by Kotler[2] and Hunt[3] to define the scope of marketing. The three categories are: (1) profit or non-profit sectors; (2) micro/macro-perspectives, represented by individual units of organization and larger groupings of aggregation; and (3) positive/normative perspectives, involving descriptive 'What is?' and 'What ought to be?' perspectives. The cells of the schema are illustrated in Table 3.1.

Meinert et al.[4] have devised a conceptual model of the domain of marketing by way of a consensus view (Figure 3.1). This model brings together a wide range of influences on marketing, ranging from general environmental factors through to the processes for developing marketing thought. The key factor in the model is the interaction and exchange of views and ideas among marketing academics and practitioners that turns on some common consensus on what is an acceptable domain and what is not.

In addition to the conceptual domain of marketing and its acceptable parameters, marketing has developed over the past decade and more into several key, well-defined and specialist areas of conceptualization, definition and operation. The most significant of these areas are: concentration on strategy and planning; global marketing; services marketing; customer care; relationship marketing; ethics in marketing and marketing in different 'specialist' contexts. We have already outlined the importance and development of marketing strategy and planning, let us now review each of the other areas.

Global marketing

The origins of global marketing lie in exporting, which in itself originated in the functional and management era of marketing. In those times firms would primarily

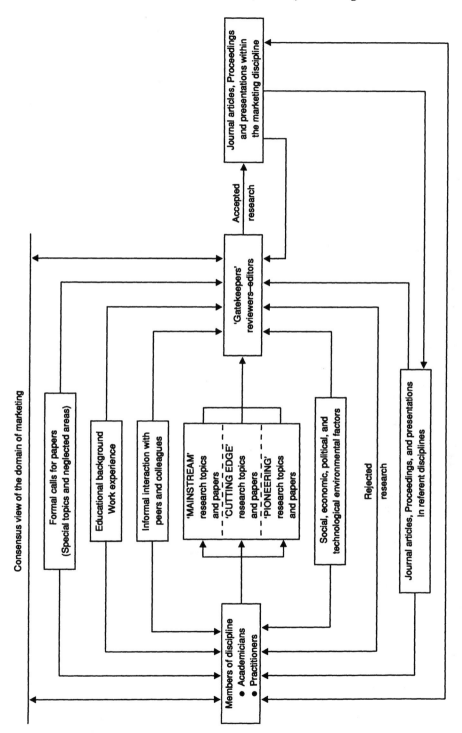

Figure 3.1 Development process: consensus view of the domain of marketing.

export their existing products to foreign countries, without any significant adaptation to suit the foreign buyers' requirements. As foreign buyers began to demand more custom-made products specific to their needs, and as exporters recognized that much larger markets could be reached if they applied the full range of marketing techniques, so exporting evolved into international marketing.

International marketing offered many firms the opportunity to benefit from dimensions of size and economies of scale and costs of investment. But most importantly, firms that had become fully marketing-oriented could apply the principles of marketing orientation to any country or market with considerable success and competitive advantage.

Global marketing results from the merging of markets as they become more internationally interdependent. Also, as national boundaries begin to diminish and become less important to trade, so they develop various commonalities, which marketing can readily exploit. Good examples of this are the European Single Market or European Union (EU) and the North American Free Trade Area (NAFTA). This 'globalization' of markets enables large firms to become not only more efficient but also able to compete in more markets. Global marketing has led to common competition between very large firms operating in most significant markets. It has also led to standardization of component parts and indeed standardization of products, which may serve shared lifestyles brought about by common and standardized communications from these very large firms.

The concept of global marketing has some inherent dimensions. These are summarized by Semenik and Bamossy[5] as follows:

- Fundamentally, the role of the marketing manager for a global firm is the same as the role of a marketing manager in a domestic environment. However, the environment is more complex and dynamic.
- Multinational corporations have unique abilities in developing and executing global corporate strategies which influence the development of marketing strategies.
- Global firms develop global strategies, but firms of all sizes can develop strategies to compete effectively in global markets.
- Global strategies influence the organization structure within firms and the organization structure itself influences global strategy development.
- As countries develop parity with respect to technology, product quality and manufacturing costs, the role of marketing will become even more important for achieving and sustaining competitive advantage in global markets.

Global marketing in the future will continue to develop as markets become increasingly sophisticated. The resultant global marketing efficiencies will increasingly be applied to new markets as they in turn develop. Whole industries will increasingly become global. Good examples of these are the motor vehicle industry, household brown goods (e.g. televisions and videos) and telecommunications in general. Also, consumer-branded products will continue globalizing, particularly as increased competition occurs in established markets for such goods.

Services marketing

The origins of services marketing stem from the developments of consumer and industrial markets, in terms of value, expectation and activity. The growth of the service industry can be attributed to increasing affluence, which has led to a whole range of new dimensions. Greater life expectancy led to a demand for products and services for ageing populations and more leisure time, which in turn led to greater life complexity and a resultant demand for more sophisticated services. More disposable income demanded more choice and variety and a greater sophistication in products and enhanced performance.

Traditional product marketing was essentially myopic to many of these new circumstances. Increasingly, marketing required new concepts, which focused on the added value requirements of more affluent and demanding markets, via enhanced service. In the late 1970s and early 1980s writers such as Shostack and Gronroos recognized that services had unique characteristics which differentiated them from goods, and as a consequence required a different marketing emphasis. Service characteristics are summarized as heterogeneity, intangibility, perishability and inseparability, in terms of simultaneous product and consumption. These characteristics require that services marketing is primarily a process activity which has as its core the buyer–seller interaction. As a consequence of this core the customer becomes a major player in the performance of the service itself.

The concept of services marketing is currently well established and theory and practice have developed markedly in recent times. Current and future developments will concentrate on enhancing the quality of services. Initially, developments in service quality centred on the service product. That is, ways were sought to improve services by improving the tangible dimensions of services, either by offering more by adding value, or by improving the efficiency of a service by providing it more quickly or frequently. This concentration led to a focus on improving the internal systems within an organization. This was manifested in the concept of total quality management (TQM), whereby every function within an organization was viewed as a component part of a complete system whose task is to improve the operational efficiencies that contribute to the quality of a service.

Future developments in services marketing are likely to be concerned with improving further the quality of the service product. In addition, it is increasingly being recognized that such quality improvements cannot ignore the wider dimensions of marketing activity. These will include an examination of other marketing activities, which may contribute to the overall service quality, such as other components of the marketing mix. Thus, the quality of services marketing will incorporate improvements in such activities as communications, customer care, selling, etc. These activities may all be deemed to be internal to service operations, but these operations may expand into what is now called the 'total service concept'. This incorporates service marketing activity at the pre-purchase stage, such as providing stimulating and informative literature or instructions and guidelines on how to use a service. Similarly, post-purchase enhancements may be introduced after the service transaction itself. Improvements in the quality of marketing at all these stages will be required if true services quality is to be achieved.

Customer care

An important dimension of quality in marketing is customer care. Customer care has its foundations in the fundamental concepts of marketing which puts the customer at the core of thinking and activity. The philosophy of marketing is essentially that of customer orientation. The origins of customer care stem from attempts by marketers to enhance the dimensions of after-sales service. As marketing decision-makers became increasingly aware of the advantages of providing good after-sales service, so the concept of incorporating such service into the total product package began. In order to gain maximum impact from such incorporation this concept was marketed as 'added value'. In the early stages of the development of this concept the enhancement of a product through added-value was viewed as providing something beyond the minimum or standard version of a product. Later, this was to lead to the concept of core and peripheral dimensions of customer care.

Today, the guiding concept of customer care, indeed of marketing, is value, incorporating the ideal product in the ideal use. Customer care transgresses all aspects of marketing, whether it be in consumer markets or industrial markets, inter- or intra-industry. A good customer care package will benefit from consistency in task performance and balancing that performance across all the dimensions of marketing. Consistency is crucial in maintaining performance standards. Marketers have acknowledged this by recognizing that customer expectations relate to both hard tangible and quantifiable factors, such as performance and reliability, which can be measured, and soft intangible and qualitative factors such as customer feelings, perceptions, expectations and requirements, which are more difficult to measure. Concentration on the tangible factors may improve customer care, but much of the improvement will be negated by the neglect of the soft, intangible factors.

What are the key component parts of customer care? What is the scope of customer care marketing activity? Much of the explicit focus of customer care lies outside the core of marketing activity. Obviously, there is an implicit dimension of customer care in all aspects of marketing activity. As a consequence, the tangible aspects of marketing, primarily the core product, represent the broader aspects of customer care in terms of meeting customer needs, perceptions and expectations. The core aspects of customer care focus on customer/organization interactions and as a consequence are primarily people related and intangible. In addition to the core, customer care will have a peripheral dimension, that is, factors that are not immediately essential to the service but that may serve to enhance, widen or enrich the core service. This peripheral aspect can be substantial and consists of a wide range of factors and activities, both internal and external to an organization. It is an established view that peripheral factors will eventually evolve into meaningful core aspects in their own right.

Customer care today is concerned with balancing the tangible and intangible factors so that each will complement the other. Customer care has an equally important dimension which is internal to the organization and which involves *all* the employees and their activities. This internal dimension forms part of a wider dimension now generally considered as 'relationship marketing'.

Relationship marketing

This is an area of marketing which is still evolving and which will become increasingly sophisticated. The essence of relationship marketing stems from the increased refinements of customer care, internal marketing and the broader parameters of total quality management. The driving force behind relationship marketing is getting and keeping customers, but it should be recognized that it is broader than just the company/customer interface.

The management of relationship marketing must focus on forging stronger links and building closer relationships between an organization and its customers as well as between an organization's various functions. The essence of this focus is on communication. From a customer perspective good communication signals efficiency and flexibility. Such efficiency and flexibility is manifested in the quality and ease of relationships between people at all points of interaction. This consistent interaction should occur at all stages and in all areas of employee and customer contact. An organization will not only be aware of its core contact personnel, but also its peripheral contact points, as well as its first and last contact points. A weakness in any of these contact points may result in damaging the relationship between an organization and its customers. The prime focus of any relationship contact point should be on establishing sound, one-to-one interactions between company personnel and between personnel and individual customers at a personal level.

So relationship marketing is not only concerned with an organization's relationship with its customers. It is also concerned – indeed, in some cases equally concerned – with relationships between an organization and a whole range of personnel at points of contact and interaction with customers. For example, the interaction between an organization and its suppliers will have a significant bearing on the quality and continuity of materials. Broader interactions may be business associates and key influencers within an industry. All these interaction contact points will be influenced primarily by the activities of an organization's personnel and the relationships that they can engender and develop.

The prime objective of relationship marketing is about long-term customer retention through a diverse range of marketing activities and functions. The emphasis will be on providing product benefits and good quality customer care, with a high degree of customer contact and resultant customer commitment. All this can and will be achieved by bringing together all the activities of an organization into a total concept. This requires that all functions within an organization work together as a cohesive inter-functional team, which has the same fundamental objective: long-term customer retention. It is this notion of relationship marketing that many writers believe will become the essence of marketing in the future.

Ethics in marketing

Ethics is the branch of moral philosophy that deals with moral judgements, standards and rules of conduct. It is essentially individually-oriented perceptions of right or wrong. In a marketing circumstance the need for ethics may arise from factors which are both internal and external to an organization. External factors may be influenced, indeed even determined, by people such as gatekeepers and controllers, vested interests and consortia and specialist interest groups. It may also be influenced by activities such as lobbying and various customs and practices, such as auditing practices or price collusion. Internally, ethics becomes important because of the malpractice of so-called professionals, over promises and deceptions and possibly falsifications, perhaps even bribing and rigging of transactions, or the general aspect of a concern for safety and security.

While all those issues will have an undoubted influence on marketing performance and perception, the role of ethics in marketing derives primarily from the principles of exchange. Essentially, exchange requires equality and equity; a promise principle base; morality of duty and aspiration and trust; responsibility and commitment; stability, sacrifice and loyalty. Much of this, of course, goes further than simple exchange. It is not difficult to see that many of these are inherent requirements of customer care and relationship marketing – indeed, of all marketing.

How does management introduce and maintain ethics in marketing, particularly in a fiercely competitive environment? Advocates of ethics in marketing maintain that it is possible to undertake marketing in such an environment by introducing a number of practices. These begin with creating an ethical corporate culture and instituting ethics as an integral part of employee training. All ethical concepts must also be expressed in all an organization's activities. Periodically an ethical audit should be carried out to ensure standards are being maintained.

However, ethics in marketing is a wider concern than just that of the individual firm. Ethics is a dimension that must transcend an entire industry, but most importantly, the entire marketing profession. The issue of how to introduce and maintain ethics in the marketing profession continues. The marketing profession undoubtedly can be easily infiltrated by less scrupulous individuals and their malpractices. However, as marketing becomes more professional and the quality of marketing performance improves, so the concept of ethics in marketing will grow. A good recent example of ethics in marketing is demonstrated by the groundswell of concern with 'green' marketing, which was a recognition of and a response by marketers to the demand for more environmentally friendly products. Green marketing and ethics in marketing will continue to evolve and grow in line with greater market sophistication.

Marketing in specific contexts

All the above descriptions can be said to be marketing in different contexts. While those described so far can be deemed to be major developments in marketing, there are many other areas which are and which will continue to see developments. Two in particular are not-for-profit marketing and small business marketing.

Not-for-profit marketing has its origins in the debate of the late 1960s and early 1970s about widening the domain of marketing beyond that of exchange transaction. There was a consensus then as now that marketing belongs as much in not-for-profit organizations as in commercial and profit-making organizations. The term not-for-profit is a loose, generic term for an extremely diverse range of activities. While the basic concepts and theories of marketing can apply in any circumstances, they need to be adapted to suit the peculiar circumstances of particular environments. Thus there are many different contexts in which marketing will be performed in the not-for-profit arena. Today, and increasingly in the future, marketing is performed in government departments, health services, charities, non-commercial arts and museums, to mention just a few. In all these examples the marketing emphasis and the tools of marketing employed may be quite different. In government marketing the emphasis is likely to be on education and information provision, in health marketing it will be on meeting public expectations, charities will market to their two client markets of givers and receivers, and arts and museums will focus on stimulating interest. In every case, the underlying philosophy of not-for-profit marketing is market-focused customer orientation and in providing a sound customer service.

Marketing in the small business context has long been recognized as uniquely different. The economic recessions of the 1960s and 1970s sharpened the focus of the role and contributions that small to medium-sized firms played in most economies. Indeed, with 90 per cent of firms in any economy being small to medium-sized it means that most marketing strategies and plans stem from this sector. However, most of the textbook descriptions of marketing have large corporations in mind. The small firm owner/manager is expected to apply basic marketing concepts as they are presented in this way. However, it is now recognized that small firms have unique characteristics, determined by resource constraints and the influential personality of the owner/manager, which dictate the kind of marketing that can take place. As with not-for-profit marketing, small firms marketing is a loose, generic circumstance where marketing can occur in a diverse range of circumstances. For example, a small firm in an industrial sector will perform significantly different marketing from small firms in consumer or services sectors. The skills of the entrepreneur will also determine the sophistication or simplicity of the marketing practised, therefore competencies in marketing will be highly influential on marketing activity. Similarly, the entrepreneur's network of personal contacts will have considerable influence on an entrepreneur's marketing thought and behaviour. These aspects of marketing development are areas which will occupy marketers' thinking for some time to come.

Industry-specific marketing

As marketing evolves as a discipline so it becomes more situationally specific. One manifestation of this is how marketing can differ according to the industry in which it is situated. Thus marketing in an engineering industry may be distinctly different from marketing in the clothing and textiles industry. Of course, the basic and underlying principles and theories of marketing will be the same, but the underlying characteristics pertaining to a specific industry will influence, indeed determine, the character of the marketing which is performed in that industry.

Long-established industries have strong and established marketing customs and practices. These marketing norms have evolved and have been refined over many years in line with environmental changes and influences. However, as the domain of marketing has widened and as new industries grow, so new aspects of marketing are added. Such marketing uses the established concepts and theories but they are applied differently in the new circumstance. Like any new circumstance, there is rapid change and development and this is equally so in terms of the marketing activity in the new circumstance. Good examples of marketing development in new industries or sectors are represented by the following. *Travel* and *tourism and leisure* may be deemed to be long-established industries, but only in the context of being available to the privileged few. The travel and tourism and leisure industries in the modern sense are only about thirty years old and are still very much in their infancy. Their rapid growth will continue for the foreseeable future and this growth will stimulate new methods of marketing and subsequently, greater sophistication. Similar reasoning applies to *professional services* in a whole range of industries, such as the *medical professions, financial services* and *architecture* and *legal professions*, etc. These and others are all industries which are learning marketing and, equally, the marketing profession must learn to adapt to the requirements of these industries.

New marketing is also being developed for new and developing economic and geographical areas. For example, marketers have long been aware of the potential of the Pacific Rim as a cohesive market area. Marketing approaches here originate from a multiplicity of different cultural backgrounds but it must cohere into acceptable norms of behaviour and understanding. Similarly, emerging markets in the Far East and the Third World countries and Central and Eastern Europe will all require new and innovative marketing. Current marketing approaches may be unsuitable for many aspects of these markets. Many of the developing areas of marketing mentioned above will be crucial to the development of these new emerging markets. As marketing learns more about strategy and planning, global dimensions, relationships, small business, etc., so these new concepts can be applied to all market sectors.

Conclusion

All the aspects of marketing described in this chapter are important to the text. Because we are concerned with SMEs, the small business context of marketing is of prime importance. Also, because SMEs, more often than not, must conform to the marketing norm dictated by the industry in which they exist, the industry-specific aspects referred to earlier will have a significant influence. These aspects will be explored later in the text when we consider them in the context of SMEs and of entrepreneurship.

Summary

Marketing as a discipline can trace its roots back to the nineteenth century. Rapid evolution of the discipline has occurred since the 1950s. The cornerstone of modern marketing lies in a customer-focused managerial approach. Since the 1970s marketing researchers have increasingly been concerned with the customer orientation of marketing activity. This orientation has led to concentration on aspects of servicing the customer through intimate relationship building and understanding. In this period also, there has been a growing awareness of the need to understand markets in all their guises, both locally and globally. This has led to new approaches to marketing, both in a global market sense and in the situation specific of individual local markets and specific industries. These new approaches are situated primarily in new approaches to customer orientation.

Learning questions

After reading this chapter the reader will be able to answer the following questions:

1. In general, how has marketing evolved?
2. What are the leading developments in marketing?
3. What is meant by marketing in context?
4. How has global marketing evolved?
5. How has services marketing evolved?
6. What are the likely trends in marketing in the future?

Notes and references

1. Gummesson, E. (1993) 'Marketing according to textbooks: Six objections', *Proceedings – Rethinking Marketing: New perspectives on the discipline and profession*, Warwick Business School, University of Warwick, pp. 248–58.
2. Kotler, P. (1972) 'Defining the limits of marketing', in B. W. Becker and H. Becker (eds.), *Marketing Education in the Real World*, Fall Conference Proceedings, Chicago: American Marketing Association, pp. 48–56.

3. Hunt, S. D. (1983) *Marketing Theory: The philosophy of marketing science*, Chicago, IL: Richard Irwin, pp. 10–11.
4. Meinert, D. B., Vitell, S. J. and Reich, R. V. (1993) The domain of marketing: How are the boundaries of the marketing discipline established?', *Journal of Marketing Theory and Practice* 2 (1), pp. 1–13.
5. Semenik, R. J. and Bamossy, G. J. (1993) *Principles of Marketing: A global perspective*, Ohio: South-Western Publishing Co., p. 521.

Further reading

Gronroos, C. (1990) *Services Management and Marketing*, Lexington, MA: Lexington Books.
Gundlach, G. T. and Murphy, P. E. (1993) Ethical and legal foundations of relational marketing exchanges, *Journal of Marketing* 57 (4), October, pp. 35–46.
Kashani, K. (1992) *Managing Global Marketing: Cases and Text*, Boston, MA: PWS-Kent.
Shostack, G. L. (1977) 'Breaking free from product marketing', *Journal of Marketing* 41 (2), pp. 73–80.

Chapter 4

The concept of entrepreneurship

Objectives

After reading this chapter, the reader will be familiar with a number of approaches to understanding the concept of entrepreneurship, and will have an appreciation of the significance of entrepreneurship in determining a context for management. The reader will also have an insight into the appropriate management response to the challenge of managing an entrepreneurial SME.

An overview

Entrepreneurship is about change and the roles people play to bring it about. It is about innovation and doing new things to improve the circumstances of the enterprise. It is best understood as a process, the constituents of which are entrepreneurs, their persistent search for opportunities and their efforts to marshall the resources needed to exploit them. It can occur in either a new venture start-up or within an established enterprise. Developments in the social, technological and economic circumstances in which the entrepreneurial enterprise operates have an impact on it. The lead entrepreneur is prompted as a consequence to instigate and carry through such changes in the enterprise as are necessary in response. We need to consider and understand what type of person might make that response and how.

The entrepreneur is central to the entrepreneurial process, s/he is the driving force behind it. Without the entrepreneur's commitment, energy and ambition it would not happen. However, given the central role the entrepreneur plays in it, there is a notable lack of any agreed definition or clear understanding in the literature of who the entrepreneur is or what s/he does. It depends, it seems, on the individual researchers personal perspective and approach as to how the entrepreneur and entrepreneurship are ultimately interpreted and defined.

One approach, taken from psychology, is to develop an understanding of who the entrepreneur is by focusing on a set of personality traits and characteristics. Another approach is to consider the social context in which the entrepreneur is embedded and which will have an influence on her/his potential for success in venture creation and development. Entrepreneurship is not an activity conducted in isolation but is practised in the midst of an often dynamic environment which impacts on the entrepreneurial effort. The behavioural approach provides us with yet another way of understanding the entrepreneur and entrepreneurship. This approach views the entrepreneur in terms of a set of activities associated with venture creation and development. In this instance the focus is more on what entrepreneurial managers do than how well they do it.

The debate on the supremacy of the different approaches continues and each approach has its champions. The position in this chapter is that all three approaches contribute significantly, in their own way, to enhancing our understanding of who the entrepreneur is and what s/he does. No one approach has the definitive answer, but together they bring us close to some greater degree of clarity. In the following sections we shall consider contributions from each approach to a definition of entrepreneurship. We shall conclude with a definition of entrepreneurial management.

Trait approaches to understanding entrepreneurship

Who is the entrepreneur?

The approaches offered by trait theorists to understanding entrepreneurship focus on the personality or psychological makeup of the individual entrepreneur. The presumption is that s/he projects a particular personality type.[1] Researchers in the area have therefore sought to identify and extract those personality traits which might be considered to be uniquely entrepreneurial. They then seek to categorize and organize them like pieces of a jigsaw puzzle that comes together over a period and in a way that ultimately reveals a person who at first glance seems a larger-than-life character, a superhero, a 'do anything, go anywhere' type. They emerge as people who see what others cannot and do what others would not dare. Successive research projects, by applying personality theory, have sought to identify and measure the personality traits of entrepreneurs and have highlighted a number of factors as typically entrepreneurial. Factors such as a high need for achievement, beliefs about locus of control, a propensity to take calculated risks, a high tolerance of uncertainty and ambiguity in addition to other personal values such as honesty, integrity, duty and responsibility.[2]

Table 4.1 lists some of the key characteristics of successful entrepreneurs taken from the growing literature in this area.

Table 4.1 Key characteristics of successful entrepreneurs

Personality traits

Calculated risk-taking and risk sharing propensity
Need for achievement
Locus of control
Personal values, integrity
Need for power
Need for affiliation
Commitment, determination and perseverance
Assuming personal responsibility
A grip on reality
Sense of humour
Tolerance of ambiguity, stress and uncertainty
Decisive, urgent
Tolerance of failure.

Limitations of trait approaches

A good deal of criticism has been levelled against trait approaches for a number of reasons. One problem is their apparent inability to differentiate clearly between entrepreneurial small business owners and equally successful professional executives in more established organizations. This latter group has demonstrated comparable levels of achievement motivation or risk-taking propensity, two apparently distinctive entrepreneurial traits. This raises questions about the value of trait approaches in identifying what is particularly entrepreneurial.

A further criticism against trait theorists relates to the emphasis they have placed on identifying the supposed key trait that is most characteristic of the entrepreneur. The single trait approach seeks to identify and prioritize the aspects of a person's personality that are deemed to be particularly entrepreneurial.

Third, it is suggested that trait theories need to recognize that entrepreneurship is a dynamic, constantly changing process. As the venture develops and grows over its lifecycle new challenges with attendant levels of instability and lack of predictability emerge. These have implications for the entrepreneurial personality. The entrepreneur will be required to adapt continuously and change his/her psychological frame of mind and outlook as the enterprise itself grows and changes. There is clearly a need to define and redefine entrepreneurial characteristics according to the stage of development the entrepreneur and the enterprise have reached.

A further problem with the trait theorists' approach is the apparent implication that one either already has entrepreneurial traits or one has not, as a result of one's upbringing and a lifetime's influence from education, religion, socialization and culture. The argument appears to be that the fundamental building blocks of one's personality are formed during the early, more formative years of one's life. These values and attitudes remain constant during later life, even in the face of subsequent changes in circumstances. Having been inculcated in the individual over a lifetime it is unlikely that they can or will be developed at some later stage in any effective way.

Part of the problem with trait approaches arises from how the entrepreneur and entrepreneurship are defined. In the first instance a focus only on the individual who establishes a new venture is arguably too narrow. It fails to recognize sufficiently the entrepreneurial potential of people who work to develop and grow established enterprises. In addition, there is the difficulty raised by the fact that entrepreneurs are not an easily identifiable, homogeneous group. Entrepreneurs, it appears, come in all shapes and sizes, from different backgrounds, with varying motivations and aspirations. They are variously represented and addressed in the literature as opportunists or craftworkers, technical entrepreneurs or so-called intrapreneurs.

However, recognizing that entrepreneurs are a fundamentally heterogeneous population, coming from various backgrounds and circumstances, frees the researcher from the restrictions imposed in trying to define 'the entrepreneurial personality'.[3] The view is emerging that psychological variables might be more usefully studied in clusters or constellations of traits. This does much to defuse some of the criticism-levelled at trait approaches and allows more people to be seen as potential entrepreneurs. Timmons[4] offers an example of such clustering of what he calls 'desirable and acquirable attitudes and behaviours' for entrepreneurs. They include commitment and determination, an opportunity focus, a tolerance of risk, ambiguity and uncertainty, creativity, self-reliance and adaptability, motivation to excel and leadership.

A point of importance to note is that aspects of the entrepreneurial personality can be developed in order to improve the prospects of greater entrepreneurial success. One view is that personalities do continue to change and develop as a consequence of personal experiences and the changing nature of social relationships. It is recognized that basic traits may well be formed in early life, but it is also acknowledged that experiences in later life can play a role in shaping the personality and influencing a person's ideas and ambitions for an entrepreneurial career.

The value of trait approaches, while the subject of continuing debate, must be recognized. It is clear that the psychological perspective of entrepreneurship research, in emphasizing the intrinsic personality characteristics of entrepreneurs, has made and continues to make valuable contributions to our current understanding of entrepreneurs and their distinct role in new venture creation.

The social psychological approach

The origins of the entrepreneur

The social psychological perspective defines those external factors that act as potential stimulants to entrepreneurial activity. This approach places entrepreneurship within the wider social environment. It acknowledges the influence of numerous social factors on the propensity of an individual to behave entrepreneurially and to do so continuously. Examples of such factors are family and social background, education, religion, culture, work and general life experiences. As a widening of the psychological perspective this approach sees the entrepreneur as being embedded in a complex set of social networks. These will either facilitate or hinder the potential of the individual to launch new ventures or further develop an existing one.

They will do this in a number of ways. In the first instance the social background in which the individual is embedded will be a key determining factor of her/his personality as discussed earlier. In addition the social context of the entrepreneur provides the link between the entrepreneur, the opportunity identified and the resources needed to exploit it. This development of skills and use of social networking allows the entrepreneur to build an appropriate profile within society for the entrepreneurial role s/he wishes to play.

Social marginality theory suggests that when inconsistency exists between an individual's personality and the role s/he plays in society, s/he may be prompted to act to resolve that inconsistency. The pull of assuming a more attractive role in society and the push to do something about the inconsistency acts like a catalyst. Such effort to acquire a desired profile or role in society, however, may well act ultimately as a brake on continued entrepreneurial effort. The possibility of compromising one's hard-earned standing in society may prompt the individual to adopt a style of entrepreneurship that is less growth-focused, with all the risk and uncertainty that attends it.

An example in the literature which sees entrepreneurs very much as a product of their upbringing is offered by Kets de Vries.[5] His entrepreneurial individual emerges as a deviant personality − rebellious, insecure, a person of low self-esteem, one who could not work in a structured environment, who resents authority and almost as an act of defiance establishes, by extraordinary effort and fear of failure, a commercial enterprise. As a product of her/his upbringing, s/he then runs this venture with great energy and determination and high self-reliance and thus low dependence on others. This approach can have a number of outcomes. Either the enterprise will continue to grow until it becomes too large to be managed effectively by one person, when it will ultimately collapse or be forcefully taken over by others. Or the entrepreneur will undergo what is in effect a difficult personality change and learn to trust and share.

Behavioural approaches

What the entrepreneur does

The third pillar to our understanding of the entrepreneur and entrepreneurship is outlined by the behaviourial approaches. In addition to having some idea of who the entrepreneur is and the factors in her/his background that influence her/his personal development and decisions, we need to ask: What do entrepreneurs do? We need some insight into how they think, what actions they take and how they go about creating and developing a new venture. The focus is on understanding how attitudes, behaviours, management skills and know-how, past experience, and so on, all combine in determining entrepreneurial success.

Timmons suggests that successful entrepreneurs share a number of common behaviours and attitudes: they work extremely hard, apparently with unlimited energy; they work with commitment and determination; and they work with a competitive zeal and an ambition to excel and win. They thrive in situations of constant change, the more radical the better. It is after all in change that opportunities for new ideas are hidden for those with the vision to see their potential. They work to succeed, and in every setback there are lessons to be learned for the future. They move with the certainty of people who know that they are making the difference in the ultimate outcome of their ventures and the lives of those involved in it with them.

So, successful entrepreneurs are individuals who have a flair for creativity and innovation and are primarily driven by opportunity and its attendant change. The ability to exploit opportunities and cope with change will depend on the entrepreneurs' ability to take decisions and to judge the value of these decisions. Consequently, entrepreneurs require a broad portfolio of general management competencies and access to a wide network of personal contacts. (Competencies and networking will be the subject of later chapters.)

Entrepreneurship as a process

The entrepreneurial process is an action-oriented way of thinking and behaving which determines the way in which individuals approach their jobs and responsibilities, how they acquire resources, manage people, market their enterprise or produce products. It reflects the efforts and activities of the lead entrepreneur in any given venture somehow to make and manage a fit between an opportunity identified in the marketplace and the resources needed to exploit it.

The background to this effort will be one of environmental turbulence and uncertainty, and this highlights the need for a particularly entrepreneurial type of management response.

Entrepreneurial managers

What managers do to become and remain successful as entrepreneurs is that they are consistently innovative and committed to change; they are opportunity-focused, constantly on the lookout for new ideas, they take well thought out, calculated risks; they give leadership, energizing people who work with them, building them into cohesive, motivated entrepreneurial teams; they negotiate and persuade those with the necessary resources (financial, capital and human) to support the opportunity that they have identified. However subconsciously, they are forever networking, gathering information, confirming decisions made.

The entrepreneurial manager as an innovator and change agent

The classical school of entrepreneurship is the essence of this approach. The focus is on creativity, innovation and the constant search for new product or process ideas. The focus is essentially on opportunities and their successful development and management through to implementation. As change is the ultimate outcome of such activity to do new things, the entrepreneur must be seen as one who deals in change and change episodes. This approach to understanding entrepreneurship highlights the entrepreneurs' role in bringing about change in what might be called 'the established order of things'. Whether establishing a new enterprise or renewing an existing one, they are challenging the status quo.

The entrepreneur as an opportunity-focused manager

A major constituent of the entrepreneurial process is the opportunity. An entrepreneurial manager will be steeped in and committed to the search for new ideas which have real potential for future development. In the dynamics of an entrepreneurial marketplace an opportunity might be a new market opened up or a new product identified. It might be a new production process developed or a more efficient source of supply of raw materials identified. It might even be the introduction of new structures into the enterprise as it grows and develops. What the entrepreneurial manager seeks is that one idea on which the window of opportunity is opening and which offers the prospects of a worth while return on effort and resources invested, for some time to come.

We have considered entrepreneurial managers to be agents for change. The current entrepreneurial environment in which they operate may also be described as one of constant dynamic change. It is characterized by chaos, ambiguity, inconsistencies and substantial knowledge and information gaps. Entrepreneurial managers, though, will be steeped in the market for their chosen industry's goods and services. They will know (or make it their business to find out) what their customers want and what challenges the marketplace is likely to present to their ambitions. Entrepreneurs will combine their skill for creative thinking with their relatively keen vision for an opportunity which has its origins in what customers and the marketplace want. Successful entrepreneurial managers understand the marketplace as a source of opportunities and never forget it.

The entrepreneurial manager as a calculated risk-taker

Rapid changes in technology, in social and cultural norms, in economic circumstances, in people's lifestyles and the rapid emergence and decline of different markets and products create not only opportunity, but increasing levels of uncertainty in the environment. In the wake of such uncertainty comes what is for most of us unacceptable and debilitating levels of ambiguity and risk. For the action-oriented entrepreneurial manager, however, in such dynamic change lies opportunity. But the potential of those possibilities must be worked out or calculated, in a bid to keep that risk at a level that is acceptable to the entrepreneurial manager. Entrepreneurs demonstrate time and again a combination of a strong positive outlook with a higher tolerance of uncertainty, risk and ambiguity than most.

Entrepreneurial managers rarely own the financial resources they invest in their enterprises. What they risk, primarily, is their personal standing and reputation – not only in their own eyes but in the eyes of their social peers. Entrepreneurial managers are drawn from and work in a social context that strongly influences, if not actually determines, the roles they play, their outlook and career. Building and maintaining a reputation demands a level of caution and a calculation of the risk element involved in entrepreneurial decision-making.

The entrepreneurial manager as an entrepreneurial team builder

Successful entrepreneurial managers compete with themselves, setting personal standards to achieve and excel. They drive themselves, managing the stresses and strains that appear to be endemic in entrepreneurial life, in pursuit of their own self-imposed standards and goals. They are energetic self-starters who, uncomfortably for some, seek as much energy and effort from those who work with them as they do of themselves.

They know that they do not have all the knowledge and skills needed to run an entrepreneurial enterprise successfully. They appreciate their own strengths and weaknesses when it comes to managing the business and understand that its future prospects depend on their addressing the existing skills and knowledge deficit. Developing an entrepreneurial team as a means of doing so means finding and recruiting people into the enterprise, either on a full-time or part-time basis. In addition, they need to establish contacts with those outside the enterprise who can contribute, by their knowledge and skills, to the development of the venture. They recognize that if they are to build a successful entrepreneurial firm, they cannot do so alone. Building and developing the internal team requires leadership and vision.

The entrepreneurial manager as an entrepreneurial leader

The leadership style of the entrepreneurial SME will reflect the personality of the lead entrepreneur. Conventionally, it is seen as highly personalized, centralized, essentially autocratic. However, successful entrepreneurs know that if their small, potentially entrepreneurial firms are to develop and grow, they ultimately need to be able to recruit and retain people with the necessary skills and knowledge to help them to do it; people who, not unlike themselves, enjoy the prospect of and are competent in new ideas generation and change.

Owner managers who would be successful as entrepreneurs will seek to adapt their style of leadership to encourage the creation of an environment within their enterprise that is and will remain broadly attractive to such people. Without surrendering ultimate authority (there must always be a lead entrepreneur), the emphasis will be on a greater degree of participation. The lead entrepreneur will seek to exercise influence rather than formal control or direction, on motivating and empowering people within the enterprise to excel, on selling a vision of how the firm might develop and grow, on conflict resolution through persuasion, mediation and negotiation, on making heroes out of people, on sharing credit for achievement. The facts are that any dictatorial and adversarial management style which seeks to dominate people in the enterprise will lead ultimately to difficulties which will rob it of access to people of high calibre who will make the difference between being truly entrepreneurial or not.

The entrepreneurial manager as a negotiator

Acquiring the necessary resources to exploit a potential opportunity is a key part of the entrepreneurial process. The successful exploitation of any opportunity, however, requires sufficient funding, materials, equipment and labour. Since entrepreneurs rarely own resources in adequate quantities, they need to build effective relationships with investors, creditors and suppliers. They also need to create a large network of direct and indirect contacts who will keep them informed of possible supplies of necessary resources. Persuading those who own those resources to make them available, though, requires that entrepreneurs be particularly skilful in negotiating. They may be selling an idea for an opportunity which may have no tangible characteristics beyond that of a business plan.

The entrepreneurial manager as a networker

The management of personal contact networks is developed in Chapter 14. However, its importance as a particularly entrepreneurial activity and competency deserves recognition here. The entrepreneurial small firm is characterized by its need continually to identify opportunities and its limited access to the necessary resources to exploit them. In circumstances of constant, often radical, change, characterized by great risk and uncertainty, entrepreneurs must make decisions and take action, the consequences of which can have extremely lucrative or disastrous results for the enterprise. The importance of being able to gain access to rich supplies of focused, concise and current intelligence and be able, through good contacts, to confirm the validity of decisions made, preferably before implementation goes too far, could hardly be overstated. Such information and confirmation is possible through the peculiarly entrepreneurial activity of using personal contact networks.

Summary

Entrepreneurship is best understood as a process, an action-oriented way of thinking and behaving, the focus of which is innovation and change. Key constituents of the process are the entrepreneur, the opportunity and the acquisition and management of resources. The entrepreneur plays the central role in managing a good fit between the opportunity and the resources needed to exploit it.

Understanding entrepreneurship is made difficult by the apparent lack of clarity about how the entrepreneur should be defined. Trait theorists, social psychologists and behaviourialists all have contributions to make. An effective understanding of the entrepreneur can be distilled from the contributions of all three.

Managing the entrepreneurial process is the ultimate challenge confronting the entrepreneur. A consideration of this challenge gives us a brief insight into the profile of the entrepreneurial manager. The central core of entrepreneurial management is *change* and *growth*, and *continuous commitment to it*.

Learning questions

1. How might entrepreneurship be best understood?
2. What is your understanding of the entrepreneurial process? What are its key constituents?
3. What role does the entrepreneur play in the entrepreneurial process?
4. Comment on the contributions of trait theorists, social psychologists and behaviouralists to our understanding of the entrepreneur.
5. What is a useful and workable definition of the entrepreneur?
6. Discuss the implications for the entrepreneur of managing the entrepreneurial process.

Notes and references

1. Gartner, W. B. (1989) '"Who is the entrepreneur?" is the wrong question', *Journal of Entrepreneurship Theory and Practice* 13, (4), Summer, pp. 47–68.
2. Chell, E. and Haworth, J. M. (1992) 'The development of a research paradigm for the investigation of entrepreneurship: Some methodological issues', *Proceedings of the UIC/*

AMA Research Symposium on Marketing and Entrepreneurship, INSEAD, France, June, pp. 1–15.
3. Chell, E., Haworth, J. M. and Brearley, S. A, (1991) *The Entrepreneurial Personality: Concepts, Cases and Categories*, London: Routledge.
4. Timmons, J. A. (1990) *New Venture Creation*, 3rd edition, Chicago: Richard Irwin.
5. Kets de Vries, M. F. R. (1977) 'The entrepreneurial personality: A person at the crossroads', *Journal of Management Studies* 14, pp. 34–57.

Further reading

Adam, E. and Chell, E. (1993) 'The successful international entrepreneur: A profile', *The Proceedings of the European Foundation for Management Development's 23rd European Small Business Seminar*, Northern Ireland, pp. 147–65.
Brockhaus, R. H. (1982) 'The psychology of the entrepreneur', in C. A. Kent, D. L. Sexton and K. H. Vesper (eds.), *Encyclopaedia of Entrepreneurship*, Englewood Cliffs, NJ: Prentice Hall, pp. 39–57.
Carsrud, A. L. and Johnson, R. N. (1989) 'Entrepreneurship: A social psychological perspective', *Journal of Entrepreneurship and Regional Development*, 1, pp. 21–31.
Chell, E. (1985) 'The entrepreneurial personality: A few ghosts laid to rest?' *International Small Business Journal* 3 (3), pp. 43–54.
Cromie, S. and Johns, S. (1983) 'Irish entrepreneurs: some personal characteristics', *Journal of Occupational Behaviour*, 4, pp. 317–24.
Cunningham, J. B. and Lischeron, J. (1991) 'Defining entrepreneurship', *Journal of Small Business Management* 29 (1), pp. 45–61.
Gibb, A. and Ritchie, J. (1981) 'Influences on entrepreneurship: A study over time', in *Bolton Ten Years On – Proceedings of the UK Small Business Research Conference*, 20–21 Polytechnic of Central London.
Hornaday, J. A. (1970) 'The nature of the entrepreneur', *Personnel Psychology* 23, pp. 47–54.
Hornaday, J. A. and Aboud, J. (1971) 'Characteristics of successful entrepreneurs', *Personnel Psychology* 24, pp. 141–53.
Lynn, R. (1969) 'Personality characteristics of a group of entrepreneurs', *Occupational Psychology* 43, pp. 151–2.
McClelland, D. C. (1961) *The Achieving Society*, Princeton, NJ: Van Nostrand.
Stanworth, J. and Curran, J. (1973) 'Growth and the small firm – an alternative view', in *Management Motivation in the Smaller Business*, Aldershot: Gower Press, pp. 171–6.

Chapter 5

Management in SMEs

Objectives

After reading this chapter readers will be able to:

- Understand the importance of SMEs in most economies.
- Describe the ideal environment for SME success.
- Make the connection between the business and personal goals of entrepreneurs.
- Recognize the competitive advantage of SMEs.
- Appreciate the difficulties small firms have in gathering resources.
- Understand that SME owners use resources carried by others.
- Understand that SME managers lack power over outsiders.
- Appreciate the importance of political skill for owner managers.
- Describe the main structural features of SMEs.
- Understand why SME structures are informal and flexible.

- Recognize the craft nature of many small firms.
- Recognize the limits to growth of small firms.
- Recognize the power of owner/managers within their firms.
- Appreciate how the owner/manager achieves control and coordination.
- Depict the key skills and competencies of SME managers.

Introduction

If new business opportunities are to be uncovered, the resources needed assembled and marketable goods and services produced, then these activities must be managed if productivity is to increase in market economies. Distinct managerial functions must be carried out in all organizations but it has to be recognized that the managerial process differs from situation to situation. Factors such as the nature of the organizational environment, the technology it uses to transform inputs into outputs and the size of the venture will impact on the managerial process. Small firms are important in Britain. Organizations employing fewer than 200 people accounted for 44.1 per cent of all employment in manufacturing establishments in the United Kingdom in 1924, 36.9 per cent in 1948, 29.9 per cent in 1968 and 39.2 per cent in 1988[1] and it has been claimed that they were the major providers of net new jobs in the United Kingdom and United States in the 1970s and 1980s.[2] Consequently, we intend to focus on business size as a major influence on a range of managerial and organizational matters.

Organizational size, however, is a contentious issue for management researchers and our first task is to define what we mean by large and small organizations. It has been suggested that the small organization is characterized by the limited scale of its operations.[3] Restricted activity in terms of market share and limited turnover are indicative of a small scale of operation but the most frequently used indicator of size is the number of employees. Small organizations will normally employ fewer people than larger ones, although opinions differ about the number of people employed in them. Nowadays government statistics in the United Kingdom concentrate on those firms that employ fewer than 200 people but the definitions vary from country to country.

Small firms are important, but we must point out that they are not mini-versions of large corporations; they do have features in common with all organizations but they also have unique characteristics and attributes which are reflected in the manner in which they are organized and managed. In our discussion on management in Chapter 2, we noted that the basic managerial functions include planning and decision-making, allocating, motivating, controlling and coordinating, and that the issue of power and influence was crucial. We shall not deviate substantially from these topics in this chapter and shall restrict our investigations to:

1. The lack of environmental control by small firms and its impact on planning and decision-making.

2. Their limited resources and the implications for the assembly of essential inputs.
3. Their particular organizational arrangements.
4. The unique ways by which they are managed.

Small firms and their environments

The small scale of their operations means that small ventures have little impact on their surroundings and have limited power to modify environmental forces to their advantage. Classic economics would suggest that they accept their industry's price and that their output has no impact on the overall market for their goods or services. In addition, they will seldom be able to exert a strong influence on suppliers, the legal fraternity, politicians or the local community. However, their weaknesses in these areas can be counterbalanced by the ability of smaller ventures to react quickly to environmental changes. Large, bureaucratic ventures require stability, indeed it has been suggested that stability encourages bureaucratic organizations, which in turn have a vested interest in reinforcing environmental stability.[4] However, try as they will, large organizations have a limited capacity to control environments and very stable environments are rather uncommon nowadays. Fundamental changes in social values, consumer tastes, technological developments, managerial techniques, financial markets, and so on offer the smaller, flexible, responsive organization an advantage over giant organizations. Their non-bureaucratic structural arrangements, together with the concentration of decision-making power in the hands of the owner, allows growth-oriented small ventures to capitalize on the opportunities which emerge from environmental changes.

Small organizations usually thrive in a changing environment, but several authors have pointed out that the environment must not be unduly complex.[5] By this they mean that the tasks completed by the organization are relatively easy to comprehend. If the organization is required to solve a complex problem for its customers – the design and manufacture of electronic surveillance equipment, for example – the owner is unlikely to understand the fine detail and rapid developments of the technology. To operate successfully in this kind of business it is necessary to employ experts and delegate a significant amount of decision-making authority to them. Since most owners of small firms are reluctant to delegate important decisions to their employees it is unlikely that small owners and owner-managers will feel comfortable in this kind of environment. The larger small firm, with a fully fledged group of non-owners in managerial roles, might cope in a more complex environment, but it has been pointed out that even in these organizations owners simultaneously grant their managers decision-making freedom and retain the authority of ownership.[6]

Senior managers in small organizations are vitally involved in formulating strategy, but since entrepreneurs own the enterprise, its strategy will closely reflect their personal goals. While entrepreneurs may consult managers and employees, it is likely that they will develop a vision for the venture which reflects their personal aspirations and values. Strategy formulation is essentially a top-down process, by which owners develop a strategic stance and ensure that their managers and workers understand the strategy and behave in a manner commensurate with that strategy.[7] A large number of proprietorial prerogatives exist in organizations and non-owning managers, acting as the owners' agents, are charged with representing the interests of the owners. This occurs in all organizations but in large ones, especially where control is separated from ownership, managers often act in ways that serve their own purposes. This, however, is unlikely to occur in the small firm: omnipresent owners will ensure, in face-to-face contact, that their wishes prevail.

In formulating personal and organizational strategy, owners use their contacts to develop an image of the environment and pursue opportunities which offer potential and which accord with their values. They are personally involved in seeking opportunities, and the changes that occur in the turbulent small firms environment present openings which many owner/managers will grasp. Given the limits imposed by a small scale of operations evidence suggests that growth-oriented owners of small firms pursue opportunities flexibly and innovatively. Unlike their counterparts in large organizations, entrepreneurial owners pursue a number of opportunities, but they refuse to be constrained in their search by the assets currently under their control. They make many tentative investigations of promising projects and they frequently assume that techniques and technologies which are not currently available will be developed in the near future. In this sense they pursue riskier opportunities but they are ready to meet these risks. Not having sufficient resources to underwrite their opportunities, they develop creative and innovative ways of acquiring the requisite resources. The owners are centrally involved in the process of pursuing, evaluating and resourcing new opportunities and they normally have full confidence in their ability to make things happen.[8]

Turning now to market matters, one can see that small firms are not in a position to manipulate their markets and they do not have the volume to compete with large ventures on the basis of price. As a result, it has been suggested that their best option is to seek market niches and avoid market penetration or diversification as a developmental strategy.[9] Through appropriate market or product development strategies suitable niche markets and products can allow a small firm to grow. The inability of the small firm to dominate a market suggests that they will need to spend considerable time in the pursuit of orders and recent research evidence reveals that owners are closely involved in seeking new orders and in developing new markets. The head of the consulting firm or the small engineering business is often to be found on the road.[10]

Overall, we can see that in assessing entrepreneurial and market opportunities SMEs, through the centralization of strategic decision-making power and their flexible structures, respond rapidly to openings and use their creative skills to acquire the resources they need. Strategic planning and implementation are flexible, though dominated by the lead entrepreneur's vision.

Acquiring resources

Let us explore the matter of marshalling resources in more detail. The senior managers in John Kotter's study used their network of contacts to overcome any difficulties in getting sufficient resources to allow them to produce their goods or services. However, as mentioned above, small firms face special difficulties in doing so. Suppliers are keen to reduce their administrative and transport costs by processing large orders and they are sometimes reluctant to supply small quantities of their materials. In addition, the price discounts that are available to large buyers are rarely offered to small ventures. In large organizations expert procurement officers who fully understand the buying process and command significant buying power can ensure that appropriately priced materials arrive at their warehouses just in time, but this managerial function will be handled by generalists in very small and small firms. Lack of specialized expertise and leverage can place the small firm at a disadvantage.

The acquisition of adequate finance is no less troublesome. Financiers require access to detailed financial information if they are to offer large sums of relatively cheap money to businesses. However, many small firms are not quoted on the securities market and they are understandably reluctant to divulge sensitive financial data to outsiders. They are therefore at a serious disadvantage, and this, coupled with their problems in managing cash flow and getting paid, can lead to under-capitalization problems.

Matters are no easier when it comes to hiring labour. Research reveals that small firms, which cannot compete on salaries offered by giant corporations, have difficulties in recruiting enough skilled workers.[11] Many owner/managers complain about the attitudes of their employees. Most owner/managers are deeply committed to their ventures, but work is merely an instrumental activity for many people. When owner/manager expectations are not realized, labour–management conflict can come to the fore in small firms. Considerable problems arise also in hiring and developing managerial personnel. It has been shown that many small firms are started by individuals with some experience of production or general management. Few firms have financial expertise at their disposal and only growth-oriented ventures have access to marketing talent. As firms grow, they invariably need additional managerial expertise in finance and this gap is usually filled by hiring accountants from the labour market. Marketing and personnel activity are more likely to be carried out by the owners themselves or by promoted employees. However, difficulties arise because of the scarcity of well-qualified people who will work in small firms and by the reluctance of owners to develop their managers. They fear that skilled managers will leave and set up in competition.[12]

This brief review reveals that small firms do experience problems in acquiring resources and that their lack of specialist expertise coupled with the small scale of their operations affords them little purchasing power. An additional problem arises from the intermittent nature of their demand for resources. We noted that small firms thrive in changeable conditions but, unless they are prepared to hold large stocks, the variation in the demand for final products will be reflected in an irregular demand for resources. In general, the difficulties in procuring resources emanate from two sources: (1) changeable demand, and (2) lack of leverage.

Coping with turbulence

In coping with the first of these difficulties the owner must avoid permanent or binding links with suppliers, financiers and other contacts. To maximize the advantages of operating in a turbulent environment, entrepreneurs must 'travel light'. They must not be burdened with a large labour force, long-term loan arrangements or extended purchasing contracts. It is much better to employ staff on short-term contracts, to commission consultants for special jobs, to hire equipment and to subcontract aspects of their work. Owner/managers are often innovative people and the best of them become fully aware of the novel and creative arrangements that emerge in capital and other markets. In a sense the owner/manager utilizes resources carried by others.[13]

This line of reasoning was advocated by Orvis Collins and David Moore in their classic study of entrepreneurship. In their view entrepreneurs should develop a transactional mode of personal relationships; that is, relationships which are useful to the entrepreneur. These authors argue that relationships should be strictly functional and devoid of emotional content. They suggest that the entrepreneur quickly learns to end abruptly all relationships which 'hamper his present action and restrict his future'.[14] Collins and Moore argue that entrepreneurs are terrified of permanent relationships because of their inability to relate to others – something they have experienced since childhood; but in view of what we said above, this psychological explanation may be exaggerated. They break relationships because permanent associations greatly inhibit their desire to pursue, evaluate and reject immediately projects that do not look promising.

Increasing leverage

The situation we have described places entrepreneurs in something of a dilemma. In seeking new opportunities they need instrumental relationships; in managing their current business they need strong relationships. Unfortunately, the two are mutually exclusive; if entrepreneurs gain a reputation for using others, suppliers and customers will treat them as outcasts. One solution is to separate the development of a new firm from the management of an existing one. There is some suggestion that true entrepreneurs quickly tire of managing the ventures they create and sell them off before seeking a new business opportunity, but those entrepreneurs who develop and manage firms will need to weigh up their relationships carefully.

Small firms are generally in a weak position *vis-à-vis* large associates, and a subtle approach to building relationships is needed. In seeking new deals and in sustaining ones with large firms small business proprietors must be aware that several people in the target organization will either reject new developments or be reluctant to proceed with them. New arrangements involve change and this can upset many people and their interests. It is incumbent, therefore, on the weaker partner, the small firm, to assess precisely (1) what the large organization really wants, and (2) what the small firm can do to make it easy for the large business to get what it wants. In many instances owners of small firms will have to exercise political skill and use their creative skills to generate solutions for their clients' problems. In some cases it may be necessary initially to render a new arrangement risk-free for their partner or to demonstrate the superiority of the proposed new arrangement over the old.

In others, an indirect approach to the key personnel in the large organization is advisable. In some cases it may be possible to gain access to the key contact's superior, in others alliances may be formed with people inside or outside the target organization. In yet others small business proprietors will gather crucial information about the problems faced by the target organization, and the best way to solve them by using personal contacts who also have links with the targeted venture. If direct contact is made, then small business owners will need to use relationship skills to get along with their associates. Easy conversation, personal disclosure and general agreement on a range of topics can help develop a relationship which can be sustained by asking for advice or volunteering to find solutions for the target organization's problems.[15]

The structure of SMEs

In our discussion we have concentrated principally on the external environment of the small business and its impact on strategic planning and decisions about acquiring resources.

However, we need to look inside and observe how the major management functions are carried out. Owner/managers need to think of suitable structural arrangements for the production of goods or the provision of services. We noted in Chapter 2 that organizations often break down tasks into their component parts and assign specialist staff to complete their part of the overall task. However, specialization is only economically feasible if a venture has a large output. There is no merit in dividing work into specialized components and hiring experts to complete it unless the experts are to be fully employed. If the volume of work does not warrant the recruitment of a specialist, then this work will have to be done by someone else – by a consultant, a non-specialist or the owner in person. Since it is highly unlikely that the non-specialists will be as proficient as the specialists, some of the cost advantages of specialization will be lost to the small firm.

Specialization requires volume but it also needs stability. Specialist employees perform the same task over and over again and perfect their skills. However, if a business is constantly seeking new opportunities or being forced to produce new products because of changing market demand, the nature of the work will change rapidly. Old skills will have to be applied in new situations and new skills will be required. In these conditions generalists, not specialists, are needed.

Once we understand that small firms thrive in changeable environments and that, by definition, the volume of their output is small, we can see that they are generalist organizations which tend to produce custom-built products or small batches of standardized goods. Because they respond to changing customer needs one batch of products may not be like the other, and consequently they need flexible, multi-skilled personnel and general-purpose machines, which can produce a range of products.

The organizational consequences of these realities are clear. Small firms have non-sophisticated, flexible and organic organizational structures, which exhibit few of the structural characteristics of the bureaucratic organizations described briefly in Chapter 2. The flexible production requirements mean that the workers have to be given considerable discretion when completing jobs. They will assess jobs, decide how to do them, organize the materials and machinery to facilitate production and employ their craft skills to complete customer orders. Two points immediately spring to mind. In these organizations the separation of work, into the more mundane aspects completed by workers, from the management process carried out by managers, is much less pronounced than in bureaucratic organizations. The flexible, skilled workers plan, manage and perform work activities; they both manage and complete their work. In the second instance these organizations have far fewer rules and regulations than large businesses. The flexible working practices and interchangeable roles render the rules redundant.

The working arrangements in a small firm are those of a problem-solving team. We can imagine the owner coming to a work-group with an order received from a customer. For example, the customer may want a unique batch of fully leaded glass crystal giftware for a special client. On being presented with this job the glassblowing craftworkers will hold discussions with their colleagues in the cutting and polishing departments about the special problems this batch might incur. Work will be planned and executed, but reworking will almost certainly be necessary. The problems that arise will be discussed in face-to-face meetings between the owner, the managers of the blowing and cutting departments and the craftworkers, who will have to use their skill and knowledge to develop new approaches for this job. These informal discussions, with two-way lateral and vertical communications, participative decision-making, the control and coordination of the work process by adjustment between the members of the work team, and the direct supervision of the owner and his managers, are important structural features in small firms. In reality, the informality and flexibility is the antithesis of structure.[16]

In addition to the issues examined above, small firms do not normally exhibit the complicated, sophisticated structure, the managerial hierarchies or the formalized behaviours which are found in large organizations. We can best illustrate these matters by pointing out the administrative arrangements which are instigated as firms grow.

As organizations get bigger and sell more goods and services they tend to increase the division of labour. For example, the owner/manager will gradually tend to cease being involved in the production and selling processes and will hire specialists to make products, inspect them, purchase raw materials, recruit staff, etc. If the firm grows even larger, the additional volume of production will suffice to keep even more specialists fully occupied. Instead of simply having a salesforce to sell the product, specialists, market researchers, advertising experts, etc. will be employed to support the sales effort. This increase in specialization will create a significant horizontal division of work.

These special departments perform different tasks but there is evidence to show that the departments develop different managerial styles, time-horizons and structural arrangements, and this increases the problems of integrating the activities of these separate departments. As a consequence, a selection of structural devices, such as management information systems to effect planning, liaison personnel to bring the parties together and rules and procedures to regulate interdepartmental interaction are introduced. An additional managerial level is often introduced to help coordinate the efforts of the managers of the different departments. Finally, since there are now numerous second-level managers and because the managerial span of control is quite small, a third level of management will be required to coordinate the input of second-level managers.

While small enterprises usually employ staff who perform a range of tasks, large organizations tend to use specialists who perform the same activity time and time again. This means that procedures, rules and general instructions can be formulated for the latter's work, which can then be written down in manuals, etc. In other words, the tasks in large organizations become formalized. We can see, therefore, that many of the structural features of small ventures arise because they are small.[17]

Production processes, organizational matters and motivation

While size has an important impact on structural arrangements it is worth reflecting on the classic study carried out by Joan Woodward on the impact of the production methods on organizational arrangements.[18] She showed that firms with different production technologies tended to have different structural arrangements and managerial practices. She compared these in firms employing small-batch, mass and process production technologies. In general, firms employing small-batch production technology tend to have a smaller scale of operations than the other two. In line with our discussion on structural complexity, Woodward found that small-batch firms were less specialized than the other types, had fewer levels of managerial authority and the first-line supervisors had relatively small numbers of workers in their charge. The need to conduct a flexible team approach to production meant that supervisors were unable to manage large numbers of personnel, that the workers took on a range of roles and that there was no large gap in status and authority between those doing the work and those managing it. The span of control of the chief executives was also small; much of their time is taken up with marketing and chief executives are unable to handle a large managerial span of control.

These organizations are essentially craft businesses whose functioning revolves around the skills and expertise of the operators. Managers are thin on the ground. The unit production businesses also had the most harmonious labour relations, a considerable amount of verbal communication took place and they had the most flexible organizational structures. The arrangements were most appropriate because, unlike the mass production firms, much less of the 'brainwork of production' was separated out and delegated to staff experts.[19] In unit and small-batch firms the operators used their brains to devise appropriate mechanisms to get the operational work done.

Woodward's study was based in manufacturing firms, but similar arguments apply to service organizations. Consider two consulting firms. One develops a range of solutions and training packages for the common problems which organizations face and, by repetition, perfects the delivery of these programmes. This is a bureaucratic response, and administrative arrangements will have much in common with bureaucracy; indeed, it has been given the name 'professional bureaucracy'.[20] The other firm, when asked by a client to assist, diagnoses the difficulties that are faced and then sets about solving their unique problems. In the latter instance managerial and administrative approaches will be *ad hoc* and akin to the production process in a craft firm.

If we recall our discussion on motivation in Chapter 2 we will see that the work carried out by individuals and teams in these organizations is not precisely prescribed, that considerable thinking is needed, that individuals will use a range of skills, that they will make complete units of work and they will receive regular feedback from the owner and the working team in the small, closely knit work environment. These are the conditions that allow individuals to experience motivation not from extrinsic rewards such as money, but intrinsic rewards from the work itself. It is not surprising, then, to note that craft ventures had harmonious labour relations.

Additional management matters in small organizations

Before we look in some detail at the managerial activities that are carried out in small ventures, let us remind ourselves of the ground we have covered. We have argued that the owner is closely involved in seeking opportunities, formulating strategy, acquiring resources and building and breaking relationships. We have also noted that the limited scale of operations prevents extensive specialization with a consequent need for organic, flexible non-sophisticated organizational structures. In essence, the environments they inhabit, the opportunity seeking of their owners, their need for flexible, creative means of acquiring resources, the organic organizational structures and the craft nature of much of their operational activity means that fluidity, innovation and change are the order of the day for owners. In this situation the proprietor and many of the staff will be generalists and the brevity, fragmentation and varied aspects of all managerial work will be amplified in these organizations.

Organizational goals

However, whether these forces lead to change, innovation and growth will depend to a considerable extent on the aspiration, ability and managerial approach of the proprietor. The owner/manager is the crucial actor in determining whether the business is to grow. Therefore, the goals of the organization will reflect, in considerable measure, the aspirations of the owner. Let us consider the motivation of business owners. It is well documented that proprietors have a strong interest in autonomy, a sense of achievement and job satisfaction. It is also recognized that after a certain stage of development a comfort factor becomes important to business owners and many run 'lifestyle' firms. This conservatism can be even more marked in the numerous family firms which dominate the small firm sector. Owners feel responsible for a complete family and therefore take few risks. In addition, there is evidence to show that the conflicts that arise between owners and their successors inhibit the former from planning for succession and the continued development of the enterprise.[21]

The wishes of owners are very important in small firms but, in spite of their dominant position, they will also have to consider the opinions of their managers and workers. In small firms in general, and family firms in particular, there are limited possibilities for promotion. If the inducement of promotion is rarely available it may be sensible for the owner to consult and involve the managers in planning the firm's future to retain their motivation.

In addition, we have shown that employees and managers in small firms carry out much more 'brainwork' than their counterparts in large organizations. The expertise, opinions and knowledge of employees is a crucial resource for the small firm and the owner is foolish to ignore them.

Managerial power and influence

The owner experiences tension between exercising the right to dictate organizational policy and goals and at the same time react and respond to the knowledge and wishes of the personnel in the firm. Some of these tensions are shown in the top half of Table 5.1. *Ad hoc*, flexible approaches are required in small firms and a closely knit cooperative team approach is needed. It is clear also that the owner occupies a dominant position and it would seem that a potential for tension exists between the desire of the owner to exert a strong influence on events and the need to empower personnel.

Owner/managers are powerful people, but it is important to recognize the sources of their power. We argued in Chapter 2 that managers have various sources of power, including coercive power, the control of economic resources, the release of technical and administrative information and normative power. We noted also that on many occasions employees resist or reject attempts by managers to influence them; consequently they often resort to justifying or legitimizing their actions. For example, they may argue that given the state of the economy, they have no choice other than to behave in a prescribed manner. They also use the organization structure to 'manage through organization'. They use impersonal organizational procedures and rules, control mechanisms, job descriptions, and the like to get things done without personally confronting an employee. This is how things are in bureaucratic organizations, but how will they look in an organically structured small firm?

In an organic organization there are few structural imperatives and therefore the owner/manager is denied the possibility of 'managing through organization'. As a result the managerial style will be much more personalized: s/he will be in face-to-face contact with the managers and employees and will tend to issue directions, cajole laggards, persuade skilled craftworkers and use personal contacts inside and outside the organization to smooth the ground for her/his favourite projects. But what power bases will owners in small firms utilize? Colin Hales suggests that coercion and moral appeals are not appropriate in large organizations. Instead, managers normally resort to the exchange of monetary resources, or information, in return for the calculative involvement of personnel.[22] Owners of small firms will also offer monetary and knowledge inducements to secure compliance but they may well be able to make more use of coercive and normative power.

Employees in small firms are normally in a weaker position than their counterparts in large firms. They are seldom members of trade unions, extensive statutory rights do not extend to very small firms, entrepreneurs use more part-time workers and offer short-term employment contracts more often than big firms, many small firms fail and the demand for their products often fluctuates. Under these conditions employees are rather vulnerable and are more easily coerced. On the other hand, entrepreneurs, inspired by missionary zeal, are sometimes able to gather around them a group of individuals who are totally committed to the goals of the organization and in these instances staff have an emotional commitment to the organization. They do what the owner asks because they have faith in the owner, the organization and its goals.

Whichever power base is used owner/managers are closely involved personally in the management process. The result is often a strong, directive, leadership role (see the lower section of the left-hand side of Table 5.1). They coordinate the activities within their organization by the direct, face-to-face supervision of others; they use one-way communication; and the decision-making process is centralized in the person of the owner/manager.

The picture we have painted above is that of an owner/manager with incontestable power. This concentration is extremely useful in presenting a clear, recognized and understood vision for the venture and in ensuring effective coordination and prompt decision-making, but unbridled power also corrupts.

It has been suggested that the power owners exercise can impair organizational effectiveness by undermining the processes that lead to change and growth. Some entrepreneurs begin to think that they are always right and that their employees are untrustworthy. When this happens they do not share information, engage in one-way communication and resent any negative feedback from managers or employees.[23]

Table 5.1 Managing the small firm: tension between controlling and empowerment forces

Pressures for Control		Pressures to Unshackle
		Owner is close to employees and consults them
Owners use entrepreneurial flair to determine their and the organization's goals		Owner needs cooperation of staff
Owner is independent		
		Employees carry out management functions
No divorce of ownership from control		
		Career prospects for managers must not be ignored
Family control is strong		
....	The owner must monitor activities, become aware of the	....
Little management through organization, therefore personalized management style	tensions and resolve the conflicts which arise between these opposing forces	Organic structures, employee discretion call for a team approach
All-powerful owner adopts a directive leadership style		Small size encourages participative approaches
Coordination by direct supervision		Coordination by mutual adjustment
Centralized decision-making		Autonomy and discretion afforded to employees
Top-down communication from the owner		Two-way communication for problem-solving
Owner uses transactional approach to relationships		Owner and others seek collaborative relationships.

This behaviour is dysfunctional in most organizations, but especially so in small firms. Change and innovation require an open, challenging, problem-solving approach wherein status, personal power and political gamesmanship are minimized and individuals are valued according to the quality of their ideas and the effectiveness of their behaviour. In other words, in the volatile environment of the small firm it is incumbent on the owner to harness all the talent within the organization to produce requisite goods and services, solve today's problems and develop tomorrow's products. As we have shown on the right-hand side of Table 5.1, this requires consultation, participation and teamwork; the delegation of discretion and decision-making authority to many people; the coordination of activities by mutual adjustments between members of the workforce; two-way communication and a collaborative approach to work.

Empirical evidence shows that these participative practices do take place in small firms. Communication is predominantly verbal and two-way, owners do involve their employees in planning and keep them informed, their management style is employee- as opposed to task-oriented and the owners performed the roles of leader, monitor, resource allocator and entrepreneur more often than the other managerial roles described by Mintzberg.[24] The managerial processes described above are in keeping with the flexible, participative approach which small firms need, but the fact that the dominant managerial role is that of leader and that decision-making is highly centralized gives credence to a major paradox in the management of small firms. Owners want to retain a substantial element of decision-making power while also seeking to promote flexibility, innovation and problem-solving among their employees.

Managerial control

This paradox is addressed directly in a fascinating study of family firms in the general building and personal services sector by Robert Goffee and Richard Scase.[25] Goffee and Scase found that the structural arrangements in their sample were flexible and organic and that the owners did delegate a degree of decision-making autonomy to their non-owning managers. However, as we shall show in our chapter on managerial relationships, delegation involves trust, and undue trust in another can be very dangerous. Drawing on the work of others, Goffee and Scase show that informal, organic structures and centralized decision-making can coexist. In the case of the owners in their study, Goffee and Scase indicate that the managers managed flexible, organic, informal departments and were delegated decision-making autonomy in some instances while the owner retained control over other decisions. In addition, if the occasion warranted it, owners would override their managers even in those areas where decision-making authority had been delegated to them.

The retention of authority in key areas by owners and the occasional intrusion into the managers' territory will cause a little tension, but if the owners intercede on a regular basis the tension may become unbearable. For this reason the owners in this study, rather like the chief executives in John Kotter's study, influenced their managers by indirect methods to ensure that they made the 'right' decision.

Goffee and Scase show that the owners took advantage of the flexibility, ambiguity and lack of rules in their organizations to bring their influence to bear upon many decisions. Owners and managers revealed that they were in constant discussion with one another and consequently a degree of 'telepathy' developed between them. However, the managers reported that it was more important for them to understand how owners thought than vice versa. They understood that if regular differences of opinion arose between owners and managers the latter would have to leave. Having the 'right' personality and being able to get along with the owners was of paramount importance. Managers also reported that they were fully aware that while they had invested their time in the business the owners had invested much more. For this reason, managers recognized the legitimacy of intrusions by the owner/manager into their territory.

In addition to these methods of influence some owners reported that in their attempts to achieve control and autonomy they created separate cost centres or subsidiary organizations and placed managers in charge. They then agreed with their managers the financial and other targets for the centres, left the managers fairly free to get on with managing, and regularly reviewed managerial performance.

Overall, the need to retain control and to offer managers and operatives extensive autonomy creates tension in the small firm. Owner/managers have to be adept at recognizing potential sources of conflict and dealing with it as it arises.

Managerial skills

Having discussed various aspects of the management of small firms we now propose to speculate on those skills which managers in small ventures might be well advised to develop. As we review the material in this chapter, the words creativity, adaption, change, ambiguity, flexibility, problem-solving, collaboration and organic structures occur at regular intervals. This is because small firms exist in a changeable environment where firm orders are hard to come by, and this makes predictions, planning and formalization difficult. As a consequence, in the formulation of strategy, the acquisition of resources and the organization of production, temporary, *ad hoc* project and production teams are put together to meet the demands of an ever-changing environment. These organizations require extremely flexible, non-specialized resources which are organized in novel ways to meet the challenges clients present. People are the most flexible resource, so these organizations require adequate supplies of adaptable personnel who can perform many of the tasks that managers perform in other organizations. In parallel, the owners of small firms exercise firm direction and control, and this acts as a counterbalance to the more anarchic aspects of small firms.

Owners have an idea of what they want and set about identifying moderately risky opportunities which allow the organization to move towards these objectives. In doing this they must be comfortable with change and be prepared to create new markets, build new alliances and design sound organization structures. Since many of these market and project investigations are exploratory owners must be proficient at decision-making and problem-solving in uncertain conditions. Because of the temporary nature of their explorations and commitments, owners must have a varied and dense network of individuals and organizations, which can supply them with information, exchange resources or act conjointly with them. In general, entrepreneurs need to excel in the areas shown in Table 5.2, when seeking new opportunities.

When arranging for an adequate supply of resources and contracts to supply their clients, entrepreneurs also need to retain as much flexibility as possible. If promising projects suddenly fail, or take off into sustained growth, the owner wants the freedom to cut associations or extract the greatest benefit from them. Many of the skills mentioned above are important, but most important of all are those of networking, negotiating and political skill. Owners need to know whom to turn to for information,

Table 5.2 Opportunity-seeking skills of SME managers

Visioning	Assessing risks	Managing change
Creation	Adaption	Managing ambiguity
Decision-making	Problem-solving	Networking
Forming relations	Political skill	Negotiation

advice, necessities and market opportunities, and they need to be skilled at influencing and doing deals with primary or secondary contacts.

In producing goods or services small firms rely on semi-permanent or temporary work constellations. Within these fluid arrangements owners and managers must exercise leadership and let people know what they are supposed to be doing, promote team working and use their considerable influence to make sure that employees do the 'right' things. Since things are rarely clear-cut in small, fluid firms numerous disagreements will arise and the managers will have to be adept at resolving disputes. In general owners will need to master the skills depicted in Table 5.3.

In large organizations many of the managerial duties are accomplished by indirect means but in small firms the owner often becomes directly responsible for these tasks. The opportunity seeking, resource marshalling and production skills of the managers in an SME, along with their essential knowledge and personal characteristics, will have some correspondence with those of managers in general. However, there will be differences. Since planning is strongly identified with the owner/manager, the implementation of the strategic plan may not require the development of an extensive network of reliable associates, and the fluid, craft nature of small organizations will obviate the need for skills associated with the control and coordination of activities. The latter will take place by means of the direct supervision of the manager, mutual adjustment, specialist coordinating individuals and peer group control.

So far we have described a number of managerial skills which are based on a review of the issues raised within the body of the chapter, but we are fortunate in having access to a recent research study on the competencies of senior managers in successful, growth-oriented firms in Northern Ireland.[26]

Philip Lindsay and his associates distinguish between competence domains, competencies and elements of competencies. They argue that it is important to distinguish between competencies – 'integrated sets of behaviours' – and those areas of the business in which successful managerial behaviour is essential for organizational effectiveness. They describe the latter as competence domains and their research indicates that the vital domains are marketing, strategy and an overall concern for profitability and sound commercial acumen. Next in order of importance

Table 5.3 Production-oriented skills of SME managers

Assign tasks	Delegate authority	Lead
Persuade and influence	Manage groups	Coordinate activities
Resolve conflicts	Motivate	Exercise control

are issues of control and organization, followed by innovation, human resource management and the acquisition of resources. While marketing is regarded as more important in absolute terms than any other feature of the businesses, it ranks second to the overarching areas of profitability and strategy because the latter grouping has a higher mean ranking score in terms of its importance to the organization. In general, successful SMEs need to focus attention on markets, opportunities and profitability; on organization and control; on adaption and change; and on the acquisition of resources, including human resources.

Next we turn to specific competencies. Table 5.4 is an adaptation of the work of Philip Lindsay and his colleagues and we find that the descriptions of their twenty key competencies have quite a lot in common with the skills we mentioned above. Developing a vision, remaining flexible and building effective relationships are seen to be important but this research emphasizes sets of behaviours which our discussion did not allude to directly. These behaviours include drive, determination and single-mindedness, financial skills and the ability to be honest with oneself.

In the final part of their analysis these researchers divided the competencies into constituent elements of competencies but they found that respondents in their study could not easily distinguish between these items. Therefore, they conducted a cluster analysis on the elements of competencies and this resulted in a set of eight competency clusters. These are: (1) winning business in the market; (2) leadership integrity; (3) profitability; (4) operational relationships; (5) building relationships; (6) strategic guidance; (7) entrepreneurial flair; and (8) technical innovation. There is

Table 5.4 Core competencies

Foresight and strategic planning
Flexibility – Ability to change
Having a focused mind
Fearless, tenacious, drive and dedication
Communication skills
Initiative/flair
Being able to create good profit margin
Global awareness
Ability to motivate
Financial assessment skills
Advertising skills
Assessing people and their fit in the organization
Ability to socialize easily
Understanding outside forces
Ability to identify customer needs
Teaching/training skills
Problem-solving capability
Being adventurous financially
Honesty with yourself
Ability to sell ideas

Source: P. R. Lindsay, R. Stuart and J. Thompson (1993), 'Development of the top team: The definition of competence framework to small and medium sized firms', Proceedings of the 23rd EFMD European Small Business Seminar, Belfast, pp. 167–206. Reproduced with permission.

therefore a strong correspondence between these clusters and the competencies presented above on the basis of the material in this chapter. The importance of opportunity-seeking, adaption, innovation and entrepreneurship, relationship-building alongside a focus on profit and overall leadership and control is in keeping with the topics which were discussed in this chapter. Competence is crucial for effective managerial performance and we shall develop this matter when we examine entrepreneurial and marketing competencies in Chapter 13.

Summary

Small firms are a potent force in very many economies but it is important to recognize that they are quite different from their larger counterparts. The small scale of their operations reduces their power in relation to their environment but their centralized decision-making, flexibility and closeness to the customer afford a competitive advantage. Many of their markets are niche markets and the congruence between the personal goals of the owner and the organization's goals will ensure that all employees are aware of the mission of the firm. As a result, the inversion of means and ends, which is common in large ventures, is unlikely to be prevalent in small ventures.

Lack of leverage may present problems for SME managers in acquiring resources and it is incumbent on them to fine tune their political and relationship skills to allow them to marshall their inputs.

Organizational structures in SMEs are much less rigid, sophisticated and complex than in bureaucracies and their fluid arrangements will not inhibit the creativity and flexibility which is necessary for continued entrepreneurial success. Working arrangements tend to be *ad hoc* and individual and other resources are general purpose, not specialized. These working arrangements tend to be more interesting and rewarding than those in bureaucracies but coordination can cause problems. The small number of managers will be kept busy maintaining an overview of activities and a good deal of trust is needed since self and peer control are quite common. Managers must adopt a personalized approach to coordination, control and motivation since the impersonal means of influence available in large concerns are absent. Managers in SMEs cannot deflect the frustration of employees onto impersonal procedures, rules and systems; they must confront their staff personally with the realities of business life and use all their interpersonal skills to evoke full commitment from their people.

Owner managers in SMEs have to achieve a skilful balance between offering staff the freedom which is necessary to sustain entrepreneurial opportunity seeking and innovation, while ensuring that current activities are fully directed towards attaining present day goals. Delegation of authority is practiced but indirect influence and effective socialization of others ensures that 'appropriate' decisions are made.

The effective management of SMEs will occur when the owners and their managers are competent to do the job. Some of the necessary knowledge, personal attributes and skills are similar to those deemed necessary for all managers but unique competencies, such as the ability to initiate action, being able to sell ideas and retain an adventurous spirit, differentiate the effective SME manager from others.

Learning questions

1. Examine the environment in which the SME functions. What are (a) the advantages to the small firm, and (b) the drawbacks of operating in such an environment?
2. 'The small firm is an organization and it needs to be managed just like any other organization.' Do you agree?
3. 'Entrepreneurs are all-powerful inside their organizations but rather powerless outside it.' What are the implications of this state of affairs for the management style of owners/managers?
4. Comment on the usefulness of the classical theories of organization for those who have to design organizational structures for small firms.
5. In the light of your understanding of small businesses, in what way might their requisite competencies differ from those needed for competent performance in larger organizations.?

Notes and references

1. Stanworth, J. and Gray, C. (1991) *Boltom Twenty Years On*, London: Paul Chapman, Table 1.1.
2. *Ibid.*, see pp. 9–10.
3. Price, J. L. (1972) *Handbook of Organizational Measurement*, Lexington, MA: D. C. Heath.
4. Robbins, S. P. (1992) *Organization Theory*, Englewood Cliffs, NJ: Prentice Hall.
5. See Mintzberg, H. (1979) *The Structuring of Organizations*, Englewood Cliffs, NJ: Prentice Hall, pp. 267–87.
6. Goffee, R. and Scase, R. (1985) 'Proprietorial control in family firms: Some functions of quasi-organic management', *Journal of Management Studies* 22, pp. 53–68.
7. Mintzberg, H. (1982) 'Tracking strategy in the entrepreneurial firm', *Academy of Management Journal* 7 pp. 465–99.
8. Stevenson, H. H. and Gumpert, D. E. (1991) 'The heart of entrepreneurship', in Sahlman, W. A. and Stevenson, H. H. (eds.), *The Entrepreneurial Venture*, Boston, MA: Harvard Business School, pp. 9–25.
9. Perry, C. (1987) 'Growth strategies: principles and case studies', *International Small Business Journal* 5, pp. 17–25.
10. Lindsay, P., Stuart, R. and Thompson, J. (1993) 'Development of the top team: The definition of a competence framework to small and medium sized firms'. Proceedings of the EFMD European Small Business Seminar, Belfast.
11. Storey, D. J. (1985) 'The problems facing new firms', *Journal of Management Studies* 22, pp. 237–45; and Stanworth and Gray (1991) *op. cit.*, chapter 10 for problems in hiring managers.
12. Cromie, S. (1991) 'The problems experienced by young firms', *International Small Business Journal* 9, pp. 43–61; and Watkins, D. (1982), 'Management development and the owner manager', in Webb, T., Quince, R. and Watkins, D. (eds.), *Small Business Research*, Aldershot: Gower.
13. Stevenson and Gumpert (1991) *op. cit.*
14. Collins, O. F. and Moore, D. G. (1970) *The Organization Makers*, New York: Appleton-Century-Crofts, p.89.

15. Macmillan, I. C. (1991) 'The politics of new venture management', in Sahlman and Stevenson (1991), *op. cit.*, pp. 160–8; Fisher, R., Ury, W. and Patton, B. (1991) *Getting to Yes*, New York: Penguin Books.
16. See Gibb, A. A. (1984) 'The small business challenge to management', *Journal of European Industrial Training*, 7, pp. 3–41; Mintzberg (1979), *op. cit.*, pp. 305–13.
17. See Robbins (1992) *op. cit.*, pp. 149–74.
18. Woodward, J. (1958) *Management and Technology*, London: HMSO.
19. The phrase is attributed to Taylor, F. W. (1947) *Scientific Management*, New York: Harper & Row.
20. See Mintzberg (1979) *op. cit.*, pp. 348–79.
21. Sexton, D. L. (1989) 'Growth decisions and growth patterns of women-owned businesses'. in Hagan, O., Rivchun, C. and Sexton, D. (eds.), *Women Owned Business*, New York: Praeger.
22. Hales, C. (1993) *Managing Through Organisation*, London: Routledge.
23. Osborne, R. L. (1991) 'The dark side of entrepreneurship', *Long Range Planning* 24, pp. 26–31.
24. Cromie, S. and Ayling, S. (1991) 'Work activities and organisational structures of business proprietors', *Journal of Irish Business and Administrative Research* 12, pp. 52–66.
25. Goffee and Scase (1985) *op. cit.*
26. Lindsay, Stuart and Thompson (1993) *op. cit.*, on the management of information.

Marketing in the context of SMEs

Objectives

This chapter addresses the role of marketing in the context of the small to medium-sized enterprise (SME). It examines those factors that influence and impact on marketing activity in such enterprises. The chapter also highlights the marketing advantages of SMEs and examines how SMEs and their owner/managers actually go about practising and implementing marketing.

Introduction

Marketing is a business philosophy, based on the principle of putting the customer first. It is an attitude of mind, an approach to doing business, which should be accepted by the whole organization. One of the main problems in looking at the role of marketing in any enterprise, however, is people's inability to see how the philosophy and principle of marketing combine with marketing practice. The principle of marketing theory is one of a sound sequence of activities, properly ordered and meticulously adhered to. A perfect example of this order is provided by the marketing planning process, which is a series of progressive and interlinked sequential steps which, if followed correctly, will produce a sound marketing strategy and plan. The convention of a model(s) to illustrate this type of planning process has found wide acceptance in the marketing literature over the years. The progression dimension of these models leads to some inherent characteristics of formal marketing planning which can broadly be described as structured, sequential, disciplined and systems-oriented.

If these characteristics are representative or indeed symptomatic of formal marketing in the conventional organization, then what shape does marketing take in the context of SMEs? There are several factors that clearly impact on the marketing management decision-making activities of SMEs which must be taken into account. These are the inherent characteristics of SMEs and how these impact on formal marketing approaches. Similarly, we must take account of entrepreneurial characteristics and how these impact on SME marketing decision-making activity. Other issues too, such as marketing management style and the organization of marketing, will also be addressed in more detail in an effort to gain a better and more reasoned insight into how all these factors impact on an SME's marketing strategy.

Characteristics of SMEs

The concept of an SME has been amply defined and described in previous chapters. We shall take a moment however to summarize briefly the main characteristics of SMEs from the perspective of their management and decision-making activities.

SMEs by definition are small in size. This obvious observation has a major significance on the management and decision-making capability of such organizations. It means the existence of certain significant deficiencies. Internally, SMEs are shackled by a general lack of financial resources which suppresses their growth potential. Similarly, they do not have the benefit of a team of specialist experts in functional aspects of business but instead must rely on generalist Jack-of-all-trades individuals, usually the owner/manager. Externally, the SME's small size means that it does not have any control over its environment and certainly has little influence or impact on this environment. One manifestation of this is its vulnerability to adverse environmental change and competitive threats.

An SME is also characterized by its entrepreneur, as we shall see. The entrepreneur is likely to dominate all decision-making throughout the enterprise. The style of this decision-making will be heavily influenced by entrepreneurs' culture and background and will be dominated by their personality and desire for power and influence.

As a consequence of size limitations and entrepreneurial influence, such decision-making is also likely to be lacking in structure and processes, and therefore is likely to be non-sophisticated, even simplistic, in nature. It will, however, be opportunistic and flexible, changeable and innovative in a competitive and customer-oriented way.

Clearly, these characteristics will have an impact on the marketing activity of

SMEs. Before we examine this impact more carefully let us consider some dimensions of formal or mainstream marketing, which are normally described in the marketing literature as being essential to sound marketing practice. Consider a few of the mainstream strategic aspects of marketing management, for example, market positioning and targeting and market share. Market positioning entails a firm positioning itself in its market by taking account of a range of factors, primarily in relation to the competition it thinks it can outperform and the market opportunities that appear to be most attractive. Targeting entails developing a highly focused strategy aimed at a specific grouping of potential customers who have been identified as being most receptive to a firm's offerings. Market share is another tool of marketing which companies use as a strategic objective and as a means of measuring competitive performance comparison.

Similarly, if we consider some of the standard marketing activities and decision-making within the firm we would expect to take decisions in relation to the product range, such as a balanced mix of products ranging from new introductions, growing stars, mature cash cows and declining old products. This range might also transcend aspects of quality differentiations, different purpose in use, and so on. Pricing decisions may be taken strategically in relation to expanding market share or consolidating or changing a market position. Promotion decisions will seek to achieve a balanced mix between advertising media and direct customer communications. Distribution decisions may incorporate a balanced choice of distribution channels ranging from directly to the end-user to connections with many intermediaries, who might also be involved in physical handling of the products.

To the experienced marketer, the outline examples above are entirely common-sense dimensions of normal marketing practice. Of course these, and many others are the standard frameworks of marketing management decision-making. But if we consider these same examples in the context of SMEs and their characteristics we find some serious shortcomings in standard approaches to marketing. For example:

Since SMEs have little control of or influence on the environment in which they operate they find it difficult to position themselves against a competitor. Indeed, there is likely to be no one competitor deemed to be major; instead, there will be a number of competitors. How these impact specifically on an SME will require sophisticated evaluation and analysis procedures which are likely to be beyond an SME's capability. Similarly, targeting requires substantial resource sophistication in order to know precisely which target market to aim for and exploit with precision. In any case SMEs are likely to take orders from any source, and so much time will be taken in servicing these orders that there will be few resources remaining for concentrated targeting. In relation to market share, the benefits of performance assessment and comparison that this concept offers are lost to an SME because its size and range of activities mean that it will have an insignificant and often immeasurable share of the market. The resource energy required to determine an insignificant and meaningless market share would be far in excess of any marginal benefit accruing.

In relation to internal dimensions of marketing activity, SMEs cannot aspire to the comparative sophistication demanded by standard or formal marketing. For example:

Most SMEs will not have broad, all-encompassing and carefully planned and balanced product ranges. Instead, they are likely to have narrow product bases, in some cases single products or a core product with a few minor variations. Quality and purpose are likely to be one-dimensional. Pricing decisions are unlikely to be taken with any sophisticated strategy in mind. More often than not a price will be set on the basis of cost plus a percentage for overheads and profit, or discounted because of competitive pressure or at best set at the same or near a competitor's price. SME limitations will restrict meaningful and therefore substantial expenditure on promotional activity, thus it is unlikely that an SME will employ a balanced mix of media and direct communication but will instead do what it can afford and probably spend such resources inefficiently. Similarly, distribution and delivery will be limited to servicing individual customers' requirements and will not conform to a coordinated pattern.

We are making a clear statement here that the characteristics of SMEs are such that it is unlikely that they can accept and engage in standard and formal marketing activity. Such a conviction is reinforced when we examine further the inherent characteristics of entrepreneurs. Let us consider how entrepreneurs will influence and impact upon normal marketing activity.

The entrepreneurial influence on marketing in SMEs

It is fair to assert that since many SMEs are owner-managed, their marketing activities must be shaped and influenced to a large degree by the lead entrepreneur. The entrepreneurial/marketing interface is dealt with in more detail in Chapters 4 and 10, but let us turn our attention here to the way in which entrepreneurial characteristics impact on and help to shape the marketing activities of the SME.

Change-focused: Entrepreneurs do not conform to the boundaries of a structured situation but instead tend to be change-focused individuals. SME entrepreneurs indeed are noted for their propensity to seek new opportunities. In the context of SME marketing such dimensions manifest themselves in terms of an entrepreneur thinking creatively about marketing issues. The entrepreneur who is constantly innovating and seeking out new opportunities or ways in which to develop the enterprise is engaging in proactive marketing activity.

The natural propensity for change inherent in entrepreneurs leads to considerable movement in the enterprise's growth direction. Because of the entrepreneurial change focus, this growth is not planned or coordinated but is characterized by sporadic and spasmodic decisions, which impact on the overall direction in which the enterprise is going. The constant search for new opportunities and the generation of new ideas are often likely to lead the enterprise into new and unplanned directions, even to a change of emphasis of the entire business. The much vaunted notion of niche marketing whereby enterprises identify specific target markets and set out to exploit them can be undermined by this change focus. Indeed, the entrepreneurial change focus can often lead to an enterprise falling into a new niche and subsequently exploiting this to the full. This new niche may require a different marketing emphasis which may also entail the entrepreneur experimenting with new approaches to marketing.

Risk-takers: Risk-taking in the entrepreneurial context generally refers to someone who specializes in taking risks in relation to the coordination of scarce company resources. There are, of course, degrees of risk. Risk-taking may be derived from circumstances of diversity whereby, for example, the existence or very survival of the enterprise may be under threat, or a major competitor initiative may undermine the activities of the enterprise. In other circumstances risk may be taken in ignorance because the entrepreneur has not researched the circumstance rigorously or has not gleaned all relevant information because information has been gathered entrepreneurially, that is, informally. Equally, risk may be taken in a circumstance of over-confidence when the entrepreneur has been convinced that the circumstance will lead to success and for this reason any perceived risks have been rationalized to a minimum. There are, of course, some circumstances where an entrepreneur will be risk-averse. This can often occur when an enterprise has been damaged by previous risk-taking and the entrepreneur is subsequently reluctant to take any kind of risk until confidence returns.

In relation to marketing, the entrepreneur's degree of propensity for risk will influence substantially the kind of marketing undertaken. In a circumstance of low risk-taking, it is likely that marketing activity will be kept to a minimum and as a consequence opportunities may not be exploited fully, and such marketing activity that is undertaken will be inefficient and even ineffectual. In such a circumstance, marketing activity is likely to be confined to personal selling and simple literature. On the other hand, in a circumstance of high risk-taking, marketing activity is likely to be expansive and perhaps disproportionately expensive and no less inefficient. Such marketing is likely to include potentially expensive activities such as advertising, sponsorship and exhibitions or over-packaging or over-delivery. There is no guarantee that such marketing will be efficiently coordinated and integrated over time.

Motivation: It has been suggested that entrepreneurs tend to be highly motivated individuals. Such motivation stems from the entrepreneurs' powerful drive and enthusiasm for their enterprises and a desire to see them succeed. Such drive and enthusiasm will be far in excess of that of their employees regardless of their motivation. Coupled with such drive is a tenacity and determination to overcome problems and barriers to success. In relation to marketing such motivation can assist marketing activity, particularly in developing new products or markets and acquiring new customers. Indeed, new customers are often stimulated by what is perceived as the entrepreneur's enthusiasm and dedication and will often benefit from the resulting high level of personal service. This perception will create a high degree of customer satisfaction.

Power and Influence: These characteristics, often associated with ambition and a domineering personality, are closely linked to the entrepreneur. Entrepreneurial power impacts significantly on the SME's marketing activities. Power influences marketing activities both internally and externally.

Internally, power within the SME remains largely in the hands of one individual, that is, the owner-manager/entrepreneur. The typical SME entrepreneur is happy to interact with a wide circle of people, including staff and customers, but on occasions uses such interactions only to help make better marketing decisions. There is a general reluctance to entrust responsibility for key marketing activity to others. Also, it may be that the unwillingness to delegate decision-making or to empower subordinates is more deeply rooted in a desire to hold on to and increase personal power and influence throughout the enterprise. The impact of this characteristic on marketing is most pronounced at the entrepreneur/customer interface. The entrepreneur will derive satisfaction from maintaining and developing relationships with key customers. In doing so, the entrepreneur may interfere in aspects such as distribution and delivery which may result in giving greater service to a favoured customer to the detriment of others. Similarly, in relation to pricing, the entrepreneur may strike a special price which is different from that offered to others. More generally, the entrepreneur will exert power and influence over marketing expenditure by deciding to do promotions or advertising based on a whim rather than on sound, logical decision-making. As the enterprise grows it is increasingly difficult to exert internal power and to influence company marketing activity in this way. The entrepreneur finds that some power must be relinquished if the company is to grow and develop successfully.

In relation to the external dimensions of power the entrepreneur seeks to influence circumstances for the benefit of the enterprise. Subversive or manipulative power will be manifest in the way in which entrepreneurs use personal contact networks to develop dimensions of marketing activity. Perhaps power in this sense may help entrepreneurs make better marketing decisions. They might try, for instance, to influence key people or to cultivate relationships with key players in the marketplace in an effort to secure business contracts or to gain vital market information. Networking will be discussed in greater detail later in this text.

Task Orientation: Entrepreneurs tend to be task-oriented and this impacts considerably on how they perform their marketing activities. This characteristic will be evident in the concentration of marketing effort on operational or tactical issues and short-term objectives as opposed to longer-term strategic activities. Entrepreneurial marketing, therefore, is often characterized by firefighting where the owner/manager is dealing with and getting caught up in problems associated with the day-to-day running and maintenance of the enterprise. Examples of such marketing activities would be frequent renegotiation or haggling on price issues, dealing with queries on deliveries, concentrating on making one particular sale, answering telephone inquiries, dealing with problems and complaints and unfulfilled promises.

Generalists: Since SME entrepreneurs wish to be involved in all aspects of the company's marketing activity they tend to be generalists rather than experts or specialists in any particular area. This dimension, however, is equally attributable to

Important!

the fact that SMEs are also characterized by limited expertise. This limitation often applies to marketing. Limited expertise and the lack of resources to enable the acquisition of staff with particular marketing skills means that entrepreneurs/owner-managers will dabble in all areas of marketing activity. It is not unusual, therefore, to find owners closely involved in sales, distribution matters, price-setting and product development.

SME entrepreneurs may sometimes be charismatic individuals, who by their very presence, can inspire a total organization. The charisma exuded by entrepreneurial owner-managers creates a positive marketing aspect for the company. In such circumstances the entrepreneurial personality becomes a sort of embodiment of the marketing concept.

Culture and Background: As we discussed in Chapter 4, there is a solid body of literature to support the notion that the culture or background of entrepreneurs will form the bedrock of their personality and this will have a significant influence on the SME culture. Naturally, this culture and background impacts on the type of marketing undertaken in an enterprise. Depending on the personality traits, marketing activity may be cavalier, cautious, haphazard, structured, introvert, extrovert, aggressive, docile, and so on. Indeed, such is the power of this dimension that, once established as a particular enterprise's image or style it is most unlikely to change, since any change is extremely difficult.

The culture and background dimension is not confined to that of the individual entrepreneur. It will naturally influence the profile of the personal contact network and since much of the marketing decision-making in an SME is influenced by this network, this will also impact significantly on the enterprise's image.

In summarizing the entrepreneurial influence on marketing in SMEs it is clear that whatever the mix of entrepreneurial characteristics the outcome will be a marketing style that is unique to the SME. Let us explore this style and how it can impact on actual SME marketing activity.

SME marketing management style

What is the importance of marketing to SMEs? Marketing after all is about being customer-focused, opportunity-focused and forward-looking and is inextricably linked with company growth and survival. All firms must grow to survive; therefore, it should follow that all firms will view marketing as important.

The use of marketing, however, is often considered peripheral to many of the small firms' business activities. The key reason for this is because marketing does not appear to 'fit' with or have any significant or immediate impact on company performance. It could be argued that marketing in many ways has been reduced to a dangerously oversimplified state. For many SME owner/managers or entrepreneurs marketing is represented by dubious interpretations of a customer-focused marketing concept or the four Ps of marketing: product, price, promotion and place. These aspects are in spite of their highly interactive dimensions, being adopted to varying degrees by small firm entrepreneurs. The reason for this is that such individuals have a tendency to focus on general concepts rather than wrestle with the specifics, which are the real value of such concepts. This, however, is arguably wholly inappropriate if effective marketing practice is to be established. The entrepreneurial SME owner/manager needs to embrace a form of marketing that extends beyond a nodding acquaintance with the general concepts. This suggests that formal and structured marketing techniques must be adopted. However, the strong entrepreneur will most probably pick and choose those preferred aspects in a haphazard fashion. This is entirely in line with the entrepreneurial nature and personality and at odds with formal marketing requirements. What emerges is a unique style of marketing, which does not conform to formal marketing approaches but which is most often effective and appropriate for the SME. This unique style will have certain advantages which can enhance the marketing performance of the SME. Let us briefly summarize what these marketing advantages are.

Marketing advantages of SMEs

Loyalty. It has been suggested that the work environment within a small firm is likely to be more harmonious than that within larger companies as the employees are usually closer to the lead entrepreneur, and because of the latter's influence these employees must conform to the entrepreneur's personality and style characteristics if they are to remain as employees. Indeed, it is true that in many instances the owner/manager does have an increased opportunity to be acquainted with most employees on an informal basis. When this is the case it is important to note that increased worker loyalty, pride and commitment are likely to ensue. This then translates into a marketing advantage for the SME.

SME/customer interface. Another marketing advantage of SMEs is closeness to the customer. It has been noted that SMEs quite often have a narrow customer base and customers are usually concentrated in a local market. This in turn means shorter lines of communication between the enterprise and its customers. Owner/managers consequently often know their customers personally and the resultant interactions of such relationships lead to benefits, including customer loyalty and higher levels of customer satisfaction.

Flexibility. Because of its size the SME is usually more flexible in responding to customer inquiries. If, for example, a customer of a small engineering firm requires a customized piece of plant, this can be accommodated fairly quickly and without the major retooling effort that would be required in a larger enterprise. SME flexibility also implies speed of response to customers' inquiries.

Speed of response. This reaction to market changes is also a marketing advantage of the SME. Because of their closeness to the market they can identify changes in marketing trends, consumer demand and a host of other areas more easily than large firms, and therefore are usually quick to react. Because of their size they are less cumbersome and usually less hidebound, and because of their nature they are seldom committed to long-term courses of action. Any change of marketing direction is therefore more easily attained. In large companies changes, however small, are often discussed for far too long and the lead-time between identification of a market opportunity and doing something about it can be too long.

The speed with which marketing decisions are made in the entrepreneurial firm is also a significant advantage. As a consequence of owner-management and of the resultant predominant influence of the lead entrepreneur, marketing decisions are usually the responsibility of one or at the most a few individuals. SME owner/managers do not have to attend interminable meetings to reach a decision. Quite often marketing decisions are made without reference to anyone else. This means that important marketing decisions are made quickly, without undue delay, and this places the SME in a position of potential superiority over larger firms competing in the same markets.

Opportunity-focused. As a result of their entrepreneurial nature SMEs tend to be more opportunity-focused than larger enterprises. Closeness to the market and the customer feeds this propensity to seek out and exploit opportunities. Once identified opportunities are analyzed and decisions made quickly. This facility and willingness to embrace opportunities readily is another advantage over the larger enterprise. Allied to this opportunity focus is the ability of the SME to concentrate in lucrative market niches. Such market segments are often too insignificant for larger firms to target but are substantial, actionable and viable in respect to the SME. Consider a small fruit importer who decides to concentrate on citrus fruit only, specializing in large-sized fruit and offering these to a selected niche of the market at premium prices – a prestige chain of specialist greengrocers, for example. Larger fruit importers will require more extensive product portfolios for their customers and need to concentrate resources and effort in this direction. Thus large fruit firms find it difficult to compete in these niche areas.

Easy access to market information. Allied to all of the above is access to and use of market information. SME marketing decision-makers are close to their customers and markets, close to their staff and generally operate shorter lines of market communication. The entrepreneur usually gathers information in an informal manner and prefers face-to-face communications in doing so. As a consequence, the small firm owner/manager is constantly accessing vital and inexpensive market information. As a result of their entrepreneurial nature and their own industry knowledge and experience, small firm owner/managers are able to synthesize this information and use it to make better marketing decisions. Experience of working with small firms shows that although many small firm entrepreneurs do this, they do it unconsciously. None the less, the ability to gather and use information in this manner is an advantage over larger firms which do not exhibit the same informality and which quite often are forced to rely on commissioned market reports as their source of vital marketing information.

Such marketing advantages allow the SME to be insulated against direct competition from larger organizations by focusing on:

- Exploiting market niches, perhaps targeting a specific sector of the market.
- Reducing the cost gap between themselves and larger competition.
- Persuading customers that only they can produce real quality and that cost differentials remaining are worth it to obtain the right product.

Let us now consider how these advantages translate to marketing management practice.

Marketing management practice in the context of SMEs

Cannon[1] suggests that the notion of the universality of marketing has much to commend it, especially when the concept is stripped down to its essential core of customer and need orientation. Difficulties, however, begin to emerge when issues of implementation and marketing management are raised in the SME. Such difficulties are rooted in two key dimensions. First, the behaviour of the SME entrepreneur or owner/manager must be considered in respect of the demands of marketing management. Such entrepreneurs are usually generalists with no specialist expertise in any one area. Further, entrepreneurial characteristics will mean that they usually operate on short-term planning horizons. Conventional planning processes are, therefore, usually unsuited to their nature and personality.

Second, marketing management in the conventional sense demands something different although it is essentially about marketing decision-making. In particular, the conventional approach is concerned with analyzing opportunities, planning, implementation and evaluation and control of marketing activities. The role of marketing management in SMEs and larger firms, therefore, differs as a consequence of a range of influencing factors. These differences are highlighted and manifest in relation to the form of strategy or tactics in a small enterprise as opposed to a larger corporation. These issues will be addressed in respect of the SME.

Marketing decision making in SMEs

In the SME the critical success factors relevant to marketing decision-making will generally be those related to the success or failure of the entire company. This differs markedly from the decision-making behaviour of other staff in larger firms who are generally only concerned with decisions in their own areas of operations or responsibility within their organizations.

More important, however, is the potential impact of the nature and characteristics of an entrepreneurial owner/manager on the entire decision-making process in the SME context. The typical owner/manager engages in interaction with everyone in the organization whatever their level of responsibility. Marketing decision-making in such organizations is therefore characteristically flexible, with a highly centralized power system, usually the owner/manager, allowing for rapid response. In the SME the creation of a marketing strategy, such as it is, is likely to be devised by the entrepreneur. Thus the approach tends to be highly intuitive and often oriented to the aggressive search for opportunities. It is not surprising, therefore, that the resulting strategies employed in the context of SME marketing tend to reflect the owner/managers' or entrepreneurs' implicit vision of the world, and are often an expression of their personality.

Marketing decision-making in the context of SMEs, therefore, is different in some way from decision-making in larger, more structured and highly developed enterprises. Let us consider some aspects of marketing decision-making as an illustration of this point.

Analyzing marketing opportunities

In the formal marketing context this involves a careful and integrated analysis of the market incorporating considerations of a broad nature such as the influence of political, social, economic and technological events in a market. It also involves more specific market influences such as competitor activity and market trends and more specifically still, evaluation of actual marketing activity within a market. Formal marketing would summarize such an analysis by determining the *strengths, weaknesses* and *threats* in the market and focusing on the *opportunities* that might exist.

How does this process occur in an entrepreneurially led SME? An inherently similar process is followed but without structure and clear purpose. Indeed, it is likely to be an unconscious process. Evaluations are based on intuition, supposition and often guesswork. Information is almost always incomplete and fragmented. The whole process is dominated by the desire and sometimes the need to find a circumstance which is ripe for *exploitation*. It is easy to see here why entrepreneurial risk is a characteristic of entrepreneurship.

Planning

Formal marketing planning involves a series of sequential steps leading from a foundation of market analysis to determining clear objectives and strategies for marketing activities. It will be characterized by careful coordination and integration and short-, medium- and long-term time-scales.

In an entrepreneurial SME marketing planning or decision-making is again intuitive, loose and unstructured. It is simple in comparison to formal approaches and it is almost always short-term focused. It is characterized by frequent change and flexibility. It is often unconsciously or subconsciously performed and is merged with the intuitive decision making practices of the entrepreneur. It certainly does not conform to the diktats of conventional planning models.

Implementation

In the entrepreneurial SME issues of implementation are usually characterized by informality. Marketing plan implementation is usually more akin to the stringing together of a series of marketing tactics rather than a logical process. Implementation of marketing activities is undoubtedly characterized by being haphazard, inefficient, reactive to market events, situation-specific to an issue or problem, and lacking in integration and coordination.

Organization of marketing activity

SMEs tend to concentrate their efforts on those aspects of the marketing mix that are associated with short-term/operational benefits. The question then is: How does this manifest itself in marketing activity? The one relative constant is the product. An entrepreneur will only change this as a last resort. It may be refined or adapted from time to time but is generally viewed as the bedrock of the enterprise. In relation to other marketing variables such as pricing decisions, promotional activity and distribution and delivery there is unlikely to be any clear and coordinated strategy.

The level of marketing activity may be influenced by the age of the firm, the nature of the market in which it operates and the marketing resources and abilities it possesses. It is possible to categorize the level of marketing activity in three broad ways: where a firm does little or no marketing; implicit or simple marketing; or explicit and sophisticated marketing.[2]

1. *Little or no marketing.* This occurs when SMEs do just this. It is usually manifest when firms are largely reactive to customer enquiry. In these circumstances they have little or no knowledge of who their customers are or where they come from. Any knowledge that such enterprises possess is usually patchy and fragmented. Similarly, any marketing activity in which they indulge is fragmented, haphazard and disjointed. Indeed, it could be contended that such marketing is carried out without any clear purpose in mind.
2. *Implicit and simple marketing.* This type of marketing is prevalent in many SMEs, usually occurring as an instinctive activity. These firms engage in marketing as a natural part of business activity but their marketing remains fragmented, owing to a lack of resources, lack of knowledge of marketing activities in general and of the necessity for this type of knowledge at all.
3. *Explicit and sophisticated marketing.* This occurs in those SMEs that do any marketing activity as part of a coordinated and integrated programme with clear objectives and purpose. Quite often this will not be explicitly stated, but none the less will reveal itself and often be obvious from the way a firm analyzes a particular marketing situation and in the breadth of marketing activities utilized.

Having described how marketing occurs in SMEs and the degrees to which SMEs actually engage in marketing let us now consider the question of whether SMEs actually organize for marketing activities.

Traditionally, it has been argued that organizing for marketing is imperative if companies are to display a commitment to and belief in marketing to their customers. Organizations must indicate that they want marketing to happen and in doing this they need to remove at least some of the most blatant organizational barriers to serving customers that seem to exist everywhere.

Small enterprises lack structure, systems and formal organization. This relates to the total organization and all its functional areas but experience indicates that in practice it seems that such enterprises are particularly weak when it comes to implementing marketing. Most SMEs do not organize for marketing. When the overall nature of management in SMEs is considered it is clear that it is not a straightforward exercise to set up an organization system for marketing.

In addition, there is the implicit assumption that organizations are very able entities. There is also the underlying assumption that structure follows strategy. In practice this is not the case, as most small firms are operationally focused and consequently marketing activity is usually an unstructured stringing together of marketing tactics. If systems in this context were to be actually developed around the stringing together of marketing tactics instead of a coherent strategy as suggested, then surely a haphazard system would result. This would merely serve to accentuate the difficulties that SMEs experience as they attempt to organize for marketing.

In small to medium-sized firms the form the marketing activity will take depends largely on the stage of the development of the individual firm. One might expect that the more developed the firm the more likely it is to organize marketing along traditional, formal lines. The reality, though, is that the state of marketing in the SME will depend quite often on the background of the owner/manager. An entrepreneur with a background in sales and marketing is more likely to be customer- and market-driven than, say, someone from a background in production. In addition, the predominance of the culture of the owner/manager throughout all areas of most SMEs means that marketing decisions usually remain within their domain rather than being assigned to someone performing a different role.

Summary

Marketing in small firms is not properly structured and does not follow classical approaches. This does not mean that SMEs do not engage in marketing. Most SMEs are doing marketing, but marketing according to their own terms and requirements and not according to a theoretical framework. Whether such marketing can lead to rapid income-generation is more problematic, but it is their style and it may well serve them or suffice until SME owner/managers or entrepreneurs decide that they want to expand and perhaps move from the entrepreneurial stage of development of their business to a managerial phase.

Furthermore, taking account of the inherent characteristics of small firms and their owners, some general conclusions about marketing in SMEs can be made. It is believed that SMEs have a distinctive marketing style, which has a number of unique characteristics. These can be described as follows:

- *Inherent informality in structure, evolution and implementation.* Small firms' marketing activity is inherently informal in structure, evolution and implementation. SMEs exhibit little or no adherence to formal structures and frameworks; instead, marketing is practised according to the SMEs' capabilities and circumstances.
- *Restricted in scope and activity.* Because of their limited resources, the marketing activity of small firms is inevitably restricted in its scope and intensity. In addition, SMEs have neither the need nor the will for large, expensive strategies and plans.
- *Simple and haphazard.* The limitations of resources manifest themselves in marketing which is simple, haphazard, often responsive and reactive to competitor activity.
- *Product- and price-oriented.* Small firms, particularly those in the early stages of development,

are inherently product-oriented, so it is not surprising that much of their marketing is also product-oriented. Similarly, small firms' marketing is oriented around price, which may well result from the fact that they feel vulnerable on price, particularly in relation to large competitors.

● *Owner/manager involvement*. Perhaps the most significant factor contributing to SME marketing style is the omnipresence of the owner/manager. The business proprietor is involved in all aspects of the business and this is no less true in marketing. Consequently the marketing style can be described as involved and reliant on intuitive ideas, decisions and, probably most importantly, common sense.

Learning questions

1. What do you understand to be the key factors influencing and impacting on SMEs' marketing activities?
2. Discuss the key marketing advantages of SMEs. How could an entrepreneurial SME owner/manager use such advantages to exploit product development opportunities?
3. Select an SME with which you are familiar. What approaches to marketing organization would you recommend for this enterprise?
4. It has been suggested that the conventional marketing management process is unsuited in the context of SMEs. Do you agree?

Notes and references

1. Cannon, T. (1987) 'Marketing for small firms', in M. J. Baker (ed.), *The Marketing Book*, London: Heinemann, pp. 386–403.
2. Carson, D. J. (1990) 'Some exploratory models for assessing small firms' marketing performance (a qualitative approach)', *The European Journal of Marketing* 24 (11), pp. 5–49.

Further reading

Carson, D. J. (1985) 'The evolution of marketing in small firms', in Marketing and Small Business (Special Issue), *European Journal of Marketing* 19 (5), pp. 7–16.
Carson, D. J. and Cromie, S. (1989) 'Marketing planning in small enterprises: A model and some empirical evidence', *Journal of Marketing Management* 5 (1), Summer, pp. 33–50.
Hill, J. (1992) 'Entrepreneurial influences on marketing planning activity: An industry-specific study in a regional economy' in G. E. Hills, W. R. LaForge and D. Muzyka (eds.), *Research at the Marketing/Entrepreneurship Interface*, Proceedings of The University of Illinois at Chicago Symposium on Marketing and Entrepreneurship, 1992, pp. 29–50.
Leppard, J. and McDonald, M. H. B. (1987) 'A reappraisal of the role of marketing and planning', *Journal of Marketing Management*, 3 (2), pp. 159–71.

Part Two

Chapter 7

Management and marketing competencies

Objectives

After reading this chapter the reader should be able to distinguish between management skills and management competencies, outline the key management competencies and define what is meant by marketing competency. The reader should also be able to outline the key marketing management decision-making competencies and entrepreneurial marketing management decision-making competencies.

Introduction

The focus of this chapter is on the identification of management and marketing competencies. There is a varying degree of overlap in relation to the competencies required for the effective performance of both management and marketing tasks. The extent of this overlap will depend on a range of factors, including the background of the person performing the task, the task itself and the organizational environment – issues we shall explore in this chapter.

It has been said that a manager is someone responsible for the work of other people. This implies that managing is a specific kind of work which can be analyzed, studied and improved systematically.

This view of management does not take account of the fact that in many organizations there are people who manage important aspects of the business but are not defined as managers as they are not directly responsible for the work of other people. Such people in organizations are key players and are deemed to be individual contributors rather than managers. Nevertheless, such people are frequently members of top management.

It is important, therefore, that we consider what really defines a manager. Every manager does many things, which are not literally managing, and widespread evidence among management writers indicates that managers may indeed spend much time on them. This is not to suggest that such activities are unimportant. On the contrary they usually pertain to a particular management function, are very necessary and need to be performed well.

General management functions

There are five basic approaches to management which are generally accepted as the work of the manager. A manager sets objectives, plans, organizes, communicates and controls people.

Undoubtedly, every manager engages in these activities to some degree, even if sometimes unconsciously. But ultimately the effective manager needs to be able to set and achieve objectives and emphasize inter-personal and human dimensions through sound communication.

By even asking what managers do and by trying to understand the job of management there is the underlying belief that there actually is a management job. It also suggests that there are common elements in any management task. This implies that there may be common elements in the work of a general manager in a small firm, a marketing manager in a medium-sized firm, a director of a large multinational, a chief executive, an administrator, and so on.

Various authors have suggested what these common elements might be. The major problem, however, has been that it is difficult to define something that is constantly changing and difficult to grasp. Achieving results through other people is probably as good a common denominator of prevailing definitions as any.

In essence the manager's job can be defined in two ways. (1) Those definitions that suggest concisely that management is largely about making decisions and getting things done through people. Or (2) definitions that expand on these two dimensions and define management in a sequential manner, beginning with setting objectives, planning, motivating, controlling, communicating and measuring.

It is contended, therefore, that effective managers are individuals capable of determining what to do despite uncertainty, great diversity and an enormous amount of potentially relevant information. Opting for the concise definition, effective management is about getting things done through a large and diverse set of people despite having little direct control over most of them. Management is about the creation and maintenance of a system which is capable of transforming human and material resources into productive services.

Without doubt management tasks and skills have a distinctive nature which arises from their role in establishing, maintaining and changing organizations and using their resources effectively. Consequently management tasks tend to be relatively unstandardized and of necessity are changeable. In addition, management skills are inherently susceptible to change and difficult to standardize since they are specific to situations rather than to specific problems.

The belief that all organizations need to be managed implies the need for competent managers to realize organizational objectives effectively and efficiently. It is widely accepted that general management covers all aspects of an organization, including production, marketing, finance and personnel. Within these functional areas the role of management is usually referred to as planning, organizing, controlling, coordinating and motivating. It is reasonable to conclude that all managers, in managing their businesses, perform these roles to varying degrees, but what is important is that in their specific roles (for example, marketing), a particular concentration of skills and competencies is required in order to carry out any specific tasks effectively.

Management skills vs management competencies

It is important to clarify the use of language employed when talking about skills and competencies. To this end it is suggested that a competent manager is an effective manager and competencies are the relevant qualities and management skills that lead to effective job performance. We adopt Klemp's[1] definition of management competency as 'an underlying characteristic of a person which results in effective and/or superior performance in a job'.

It is important none the less to state that a skill *per se* differs in essence from personality traits (e.g. being aggressive), motives (e.g. the need for self-esteem), roles (e.g. leader) and functions (e.g. controlling) in that it involves a sequential pattern of behaviour performed in order to achieve a desired outcome. A management skill implies an ability that can be developed, and which is not necessarily inborn, usually manifested in performance, not merely in potential.

It is not uncommon to use the terms skills and competency interchangeably when addressing effective managerial performance. Middleton,[2] for example, defines a skill as a capacity for voluntary, intentional and objective-related behaviour, which can be observed at a level of effectiveness that could not be expected to be found in an untrained individual, and a competency as a combination of knowledge, skills and attitudes which are given reference in the task environment. Generally, it is the skill dimension that is recognized, suggesting that competency and skills are discrete dimensions of behaviour a person must display in order to perform the tasks and functions of a job competently. Taking this skill/competency debate a stage further, it can be said that the term *skill* suggests that a certain level of *proficiency* can be attained and maintained with constant practice or training.

In essence, management competence can be recognized to the extent that others will call the manager's behaviour competent, even allowing for a high degree of interpretive variation. As Pye[3] suggests, 'It is a particularly difficult subject to tackle because it seems our language fails to reflect adequately the multidimensional matrix of qualities which are perceived of "good" or "effective" managers.'

In this text the term competency refers to observable behaviour. That is, a sequence of observable activities where none of these separate actions constitutes a competency but the entire sequence of behaviour does. Take, for example, someone with planning ability. This might manifest itself in a manager being able to take appropriate steps to attain a specific objective. Such a manager can envisage potential problems and find or prepare solutions in advance or as they arise. Such a manager can gather, synthesize and use appropriate information and use other sources effectively in attaining company goals.

Levels of competency

It is necessary when addressing management competency to go further than mere definition. So far little mention has been made of the various levels at which skills and competency exist. In addressing this issue Boyatzis makes a clear distinction between a threshold competency and a competency. It is suggested that a threshold competency is essential if a management task is to be performed. A threshold competency differs from a competency in that the latter incorporates those characteristics that differentiate superior performance from average and poor performance. This is really addressing the issue of adequacy and poses the question of whether competency development (or indeed, specific skill development) should be concentrating on developing adequacy in the performance of managerial performance as opposed to inadequacy or whether the goal should always be superior performance. (These issues will be explored further in Chapter 13.) None the less, there is a fairly wide acceptance among management theorists and writers that different levels of competency can and do exist. Indeed, it has been argued that traits and skills themselves are actually different levels of competency.

It is important also to draw a clear distinction between *levels* of competency and *types* of competency, where the latter pertains to a different domain or arena of human function. The argument, therefore, is that to understand fully the capability an individual brings to a particular task, it is important to be able to understand fully the distinction between types and levels of competency.

In summary, competencies may exist within the individual at various levels, with motives at the unconscious level, self-image at the conscious level and skills at the behaviourial level. It is worth restating, however, that this text is concerned with competency at the behaviourial level/skill level.

Awareness of competencies

A major issue when discussing management competencies is the 'competency awareness' perspective. Advocates of this awareness approach identify a number of conscious competent perspectives. These are as follows.

Conscious/competent

This perspective points to a typical situation where someone possesses key management skills and can use them effectively and efficiently. This type of manager is not only competent when confronted with challenging management tasks but is conscious of being competent and is aware of her/his abilities, capabilities and talent.

Unconscious/competent

Alternatively, the unconscious/competent label suggests that it is possible for someone to be competent or to possess the necessary skills to perform a key function of management activity and to be totally unaware of possessing such abilities. This is arguably of prime importance in understanding competency because this unconscious/competent state may hold the key to competency development for managers. This issue is vital and will be discussed in detail in Chapter 13.

Conscious/incompetent

Allied to the previous dimension is the concept of a manager who feels inadequately qualified or insufficiently experienced to handle a particular task or function of management. This awareness of an inability to perform certain managerial functions might also help to address the problem of developing managerial competencies/skills. An example from the managerial context might be a manager who knows that s/he is incompetent at interpreting company financial statements.

Unconscious/incompetent

The most serious dysfunctional dimension of this view of management skills and ability lies in the unconscious/incompetent domain. In this circumstance a manager is incapable of performing certain key managerial functions/tasks. Not only is such a manager unable to perform effectively but also lacks any awareness of this inability. Here we have within the organization a manager who, through a combination of ignorance and inability, may be mismanaging the business. This poses the question of whether management education can develop an individual such as this to become an effective manager.

The scope of management competencies

Having considered these issues, what are the competencies required for effective management? Historical and indeed much contemporary work has resulted in the production of lists of competency and skills frameworks (see e.g. Table 7.1). What all these have in common, however, is that a competent manager is an effective manager and competencies, therefore, are the relevant qualities of management that lead to effective job performance.

It is also worth noting that the wide range of competency frameworks merely serves not so much to confirm as to augment the argument that management is not an exact science. It suggests also that there may be tasks and techniques common to all managers, but these need to be applied to specific individual circumstances and situations.

Table 7.1 A synthesis of management competency

Vision
Innovative capability
Lateral thinking
Creative talents
Coordination skills
Intelligence
Leadership skills
Communication skills
Motivation skills
Positive attitude
Self-confidence
Intellectual ability
Foresight
Intuition
Analytical thinking
Judgement

Management style and the organizational environment

Management competencies must be considered in the context of management style and organizational environment. Management style is arguably closely related to the management function. Indeed, it is widely accepted that there is no one correct management style. It has even been suggested that management styles are a combination of factors and are largely dependent on an individual's competencies, the competencies required to perform a particular job and the organizational environment. It can be argued, for example, that there is no single, typical accountant, production or marketing manager. Basically, they carry out similar functions but their roles vary according to their position within the organization and their management style.

In discussing management competencies it is also necessary to consider the organizational environment in terms of cultures and climates. These dimensions become relevant when considering the impact of an organization's structure, policies and procedures on its members. The organizational environment impacts on the goals of managers. Equally, the goals set by management are affected by the organizational environment.

Similarly, some managers may possess key skills and competencies, (e.g. the ability to plan), which might be inappropriate for an organization in that they might operate in an environment that does not encourage forward planning. If managers use management competencies wrongly, their behaviour might be deemed inappropriate or dysfunctional.

Organizational considerations are, therefore, highly relevant when examining, analyzing or attempting to develop managerial skills.

Marketing management decision-making

So far we have examined definitions of management and of management competencies and examined speculatively some of the areas of interface and commonality via a closer examination of specific skills and component activities of effective *marketing management*. What remains to be done is to bring these together within the context of the objectives of this text. This will be done under the umbrella activity which characterizes management decision-making in a general and functional-specific sense. Our objective is to identify management competencies which are particularly appropriate for marketing decision-making.

Essentially, managers face two types of decisions: tactical decisions, which are largely internally focused, and strategic decisions, which are largely externally focused. It has been argued that both strategic and tactical decisions should be made interfunctionally and interdivisionally, and that a large part of being market-driven is the way that different jurisdictions deal with one another.

What management abilities and skills characterize a clear and effective decision-maker? A clear decision-maker is characterized by the ability to think analytically. The analytical thinker is able to evaluate data, analyze business and market trends and develop a marketing strategy and consequent marketing plans.

It is important to note that the analytical marketing manager must also be an effective problem-solver. More importantly, while problem-solving and decision-making are key to the interface between marketing and management, an overemphasis on these skills tends to distort managerial growth because it leads to the overdevelopment of analytical ability to the detriment of the ability to take action and get things done.

The inherent decision-making abilities required for effective management are also those required for marketing management and as such highlight, possibly more than any other aspect, the interface between the functions of management and marketing. Any differences lie in the kind of management skills required for the effective performance of a particular marketing management activity.

There is no doubt that given our understanding of the broad components of marketing management, some management skills and abilities may seem more appropriate than others. The consequence is that those management abilities and skills that are most applicable to marketing management are changing and variable, and dependent on the following conditions:

1. The dynamics of the wider environmental forces.
2. The organizational environment.
3. The specific task being performed.
4. The characteristics, traits and personality variables of the manager responsible for performing the task.

This touches on a serious and most important issue because it calls into question the personal characteristics and traits of the manager which undoubtedly influence the presence of particular skills/competencies within an individual's spectrum. This issue is best considered under the auspices of 'awareness of competencies' outlined above.

Marketing management, like general management, is a process involving analysis, planning, implementation and control. Direct reference to marketing management competencies are few and those that do exist offer nothing of significance in the area of marketing skills. An analysis of the literature, however, suggests the following marketing management competencies with respect to marketing attributes: communication, creativity, imagination and initiative; with respect to management attributes: analytical, organizational and planning skills; with respect to personality attributes: motivation, resilience and entrepreneurship.

There are numerous commentaries on the role of the marketing manager which have a bearing on the issues of competency and from which a more focused view of what the key marketing management competencies might be. Recent work by the authors of this book emphasizes the importance of such key competencies as vision, leadership, creativity, intuition, motivation, initiative, communication, adaptability and analytical and judgement skills, for effectiveness in marketing decision-making.

Table 7.2 Management and marketing management competency spectrum

Management Competency Spectrum		Marketing Management Competency Spectrum
Vision		
Innovative capability		
Lateral thinking		Vision
Creative talents	→	Creativity
Coordination skills		Leadership
Intelligence		Communication
Leadership skills	→	Motivation
Motivation skills		Initiative
Positive attitude		Intuition
Self-confidence	→	Adaptability
Intellectual ability		Analytical
Foresight		Judgement
Intuition		
Analytical thinking		
Judgement		

Table 7.2 combines the management competencies of Table 7.1 with the marketing management competencies outlined above.

The interface between marketing and general managerial competencies

We can conclude from Table 7.2 that many of the core general managerial competencies are equally if not more applicable in the context of marketing. This is a fluid situation, however, and the interchangeability and emphasis on particular skills will vary and depend on the situation in which a particular task is being performed.

Let us examine both sets of competencies from the aspect of management functions. Setting objectives, for instance, requires certain abilities which require judgement between a manager's view of business results and what an individual manager believes in. Setting objectives requires analytical and synthesizing ability.

Similarly, organizing requires analytical ability. It requires judgement on the use of company resources. More importantly, it is largely concerned with dealing with people and touches on dimensions of personal integrity. Analytical ability and integrity similarly are required for the development of people. Since marketing management often involves developing staff, the desirability of a competency in motivation and communication is obvious.

Measuring and controlling management activities requires judgement and people-related skills. First and foremost, however, it requires analytical ability. An important dimension here lies in the manager's self-control. The inability of managers to show self-control and instead abuse their ability to control others is an observable weakness in management behaviour today. This is no different in marketing management.

Setting objectives, organizing, motivating and communicating, measuring and developing people are formal categories of management behaviour, but only a manager's experience can breathe life into them and turn them into something observable and meaningful. It is contended that despite their formality they apply to what every manager does. They can, therefore, be deemed to be common ground between general management and the marketing functions.

Entrepreneurial competencies

Allied with this it has been widely observed that characteristics such as innovation, risk-taking, creativity, adaptability and task orientation are the hallmarks of the entrepreneurial personality. This suggests: (1) That such obviously important attributes are often ignored by the organization. (2) Having such characteristics may mean that the entrepreneurial manager who creates and develops the new product might not possess the skills and abilities to manage that product into maturity. (3) The forte of entrepreneurial managers is risk-taking and innovation. The important dimension, however, is that such abilities are crucial to the marketing manager in enabling the identification of new markets and in the development of new products.

Many organizations and management theorists are now convinced that risk-taking and other entrepreneurial skills are vital in today's changing environment. Indeed, this realization has had an effect on many organizations where managers are expected to develop their businesses. In other words, managers are expected to be entrepreneurs as well as efficient operators.

Vision, adaptability and innovation

These competencies are closely interlinked and readily associated with entrepreneurship. Peter Drucker has suggested that entrepreneurial innovation will be as important to management in the future as the managerial function itself is today. These competencies also include lateral thinking and forward thinking, which means building up something new rather than analyzing something old. Innovation and creativity thus encompass forward thinking.

Entrepreneurial marketing management competencies

The entrepreneurial personality impacts on any marketing management competency spectrum. For the entrepreneurial firm this also introduces other key and important dimensions, such as the characteristics of SMEs and their marketing performance. It is important, therefore, to identify the optimal marketing management competencies best suited to the SME sector with specific relevance to entrepreneurial marketing decision-making.

It is suggested here that experience, knowledge, communication and judgement are the key entrepreneurial competencies. More importantly, however, it is suggested that a wider spectrum of entrepreneurial marketing management competencies exists. Thus it is appropriate not only to discuss these competencies but also to comment on other predominant competencies. First, however, it is necessary to address the four key competencies.

Experience

Experience is evident in a variety of ways but indicative via the following criteria:

- The number of years doing a particular job.
- Learning from others' actions.
- Learning from mistakes.
- Purposeful observation of competitor and industry activity.
- Gathering and using information well.
- Industry knowledgeable.

Not only is experience a key entrepreneurial competency but it is seen to be based on a range of other sub-factors which extend beyond these criteria. More importantly, entrepreneurs are accutely aware of the importance of learning from their own actions and acknowledge that the competency of experience is enriched as more lessons are learnt from on the job. This, it is contended, leads to higher levels of confidence which, when combined with past knowledge, results in improved, experiential decision-making.

Knowledge

It can be contended that knowledge is an essential dimension of the entrepreneurial decision-making process. Studies of entrepreneurial small firms have demonstrated evidence of knowledge based on information from both internal and external sources, sound relationships with established, new and incidental contacts, knowledge yielded from varying degrees of experience and *finally* knowledge yielded from and dependent on an individual's level of interest in specific jobs or tasks.

Knowledge undoubtedly is a key entrepreneurial marketing management competency. The competency is particularly evident when entrepreneurs engage in discussions of product and service ranges, customers and markets. Characteristically, entrepreneurs indicate a willingness to acquire new knowledge continually, whether from formal or informal sources, planned or unplanned. In certain companies, (e.g. precision engineering or computer-related industries) significance would probably be attached to technical knowledge.

Communication

Elton Mayo was the first writer on management to identify communication as the most vital competency required to direct an organization. Communication is an all-pervasive dimension of good management performance, which transcends all functional boundaries. It involves selecting staff as well as recruiting, training, developing, leading and motivating. This encompasses judgement of character, training skills, selling skill and the ability to inspire and enthuse people.

Agris highlights the interpersonal dimensions of communication and suggests that interpersonal competencies consist of being aware of human problems and solving them in such a way that they remain solved, without undermining the problem-solving process. If marketing managers are working in a challenging and changing environment, and are being innovative and creative, then interpersonal skills are an integral part of the process of marketing.

It is also contended that the competency of communication based on the internal and external perspectives of the SME is essential to the entrepreneur. Internally, the emphasis tends to be on staff and levels of staff awareness, staff confidence and entrepreneurial confidence. Externally, the key indicators centre on customers, markets, suppliers, competitors and the formal actors of the entrepreneur's personal contact network.

Every entrepreneur attaches a high degree of emphasis to the need for good communications both internally and externally. This varies from individual to individual. An example might be a sales person who states that communication with customers is the vital ingredient to doing successful business.

In other circumstances internal communications may be more important. In this case one would expect to find an entrepreneurial manager who is committed to improving business performance through better staff relations, gathering vital internal information on key activities and decisions, and through the stimulation of innovation.

Communication is also deemed to be vital in relation to the whole process of entrepreneurial marketing decision-making, but it too depends on a range of component skills, e.g. knowledge, confidence, the ability to listen and to use simple and uncomplicated language, and the ability to use experience and judgement.

Judgement

If control of the organization demands concern with strategic focus, profitability and efficiency this will involve setting standards for performance. The competence required here is judgement.

A manager who possesses competencies such as powers of perception, awareness, assertiveness, intuition and the ability to accept risks has judgement, and can therefore be deemed to have effective control. In the case of a marketing manager, such effective judgemental thinking means making sound assessments of marketing plans through accurate monitoring and evaluation of marketing performance on an ongoing basis.

The judgement competency is key in the entrepreneurial decision-making processes. Judgement results from combinations of various other component factors. For example, the ability systematically to gather and use information discriminately, the objective analysis of such information, the ability to analyze the results of prescribed courses of action or the impact of certain decisions and to learn from this experience. Additionally, inherent in this competency is the ability to identify opportunities and to be able to assess such opportunities in the light of alternatives. Linked closely to judgement are the abilities to make a decision and to follow this decision through.

It is not being suggested, however, that entrepreneurial marketing management competencies are confined to those addressed above. A wide range of other competencies could effectively be argued for.

Summary

In summary the areas of management and marketing have much in common. In essence, management is about planning, organizing, controlling, coordinating and motivating. Marketing management activity is no different as the marketing manager is engaged in making and implementing decisions, planning, organizing, controlling and coordinating company marketing activity. Only the management style and organizational environment differentiates the specific management skills required, and this depends on the actual situation. A competent manager is an effective manager, and competencies are the qualities and management skills that lead to effective job performance. A management skill implies an ability that can be developed (it is not necessarily inherent) and that is manifested in performance, not merely in potential. Management competence can be seen and has to be seen in order that others might see the behaviour as competent. A threshold competency is essential if a management task is to be performed, whereas a competency is about superior performance.

When discussing management skills and competencies it is important to consider management style and the organizational environment. A management competency spectrum suggests that there are certain tasks and techniques common to all managers and that there are certain competencies that should be common to all managers. The same applies to the marketing management competency spectrum.

The most important marketing management competencies are communication, judgement, vision, adaptability and innovation. Entrepreneurial competencies can also be identified. These are crucial to entrepreneurial decision-making. Key entrepreneurial competencies are experience, knowledge, communication and judgement.

Learning questions

1. The literature abounds with generalizable frameworks of management competency. Do you feel that these are appropriate categorizations of effective managerial performance?

2. Select an organization with which you are familiar. What is the impact of the organizational environment on effective managerial performance?
3. What are the key dimensions of management activity that impact on the development of competencies?
4. It has been suggested that certain management competencies are more appropriate for marketing management decision-making. Is this reasonable given the varying nature of the decisions the practising marketing manager has to make?
5. In relation to the gathering of information for marketing decisions, do you feel that certain competencies are more appropriate? If so, what are these competencies? Do you feel that a marketing manager can be successful without these skills?
6. Select several key activities that a marketing manager might engage in. What are the competency constellations or clusters required for effective performance?

Notes and references

1. Klemp, O. G. in R. E. Boyatzis (1982) *The Competent Manager: A model for effective performance*, New York: John Wiley.
2. Middleton, B. and Long, G. (1990) 'Marketing skills: Critical issues in marketing education and training', *Journal of Marketing Management* 5 (3), pp. 325–43.
3. Pye, A. (1991) 'Management competency', in M. Silver (ed.), *Competent to Manage*, London: Routledge.

Further reading

Agor, W. H. (1986) 'The logic of intuition: How top executives use their intuition to make important decisions'. *Business Horizons*, Jan.–Feb., pp. 49–53.
Albanese, R. (1986) 'Competency based management education', *Journal of Management Development* 8 (2), pp. 66–70.
Benfari, R. C. and Wilkinson, H. E. (1988) 'Intelligence and management'. *Business Horizons*, May–June, pp. 22–8.
Burgoyne, B. (1989), 'Creating the management portfolio: Building on competency approaches to management development'. *Management Education and Development* 20 (1), pp. 56–61.
Carson, D. J. (1993) 'A philosophy of marketing education in small firms', *Journal of Marketing Management* 9 (2), pp. 189–205.
Collins, A. (1989) 'Managers' competence: Rhetoric, reality and research', *Personnel Review* 18 (6), pp. 20–5.
Constable, C. J. (1988) 'Developing the competent manager in a UK context', *Report for the Manpower Services Commission*, Sheffield: Manpower Services Commission.
Cunningham, B. J. and Licheron, J. (1991) 'Defining entrepreneurship', *Journal of Small Business Management* 29 (1), pp. 45–61.
De Bono, E. (1967) *The Use Of Lateral Thinking*, London: Jonathan Cape.
Drucker, P. (1973) *Management Tasks, Responsibilities and Practices*, New York: Harper & Row.
Fayol, H. (1949) *General and Industrial Management*, London: Pitman.
Foster, S. (1991) 'Hemery's way', *Management Week*, September, pp. 48–50.
Glaze, T. (1988) 'Perfect teams for imperfect people', *Personnel Management*, November.

Glaze, T. (1989) 'Cadbury's dictionary of competence', *Personnel Management*, July–August, pp. 44–8.

Klemp, G. O. Jr. (ed.) (1980) 'The assessment of occupational competence', *Report to the National Institute of Education*, Washington, DC.

Kotter, J. P. (1990) 'What leaders really do', *Harvard Business Review*, May–June, pp. 103–11.

Lessem, R. (1986) *Enterprise Development*, Aldershot: Gower.

Mayo, E. (1933) *The Human Problems of an Industrial Civilization*, New York: Macmillan.

Pearson, A. F. (1989) 'Six basics for general managers', *Harvard Business Review*, July–August, pp. 94–9.

Powers, E. A. (1987) 'Enhancing managerial competence: The American Management Association competency programme', *Journal of Management Development* 6 (4), pp. 7–18.

Rothwell, S. (1990) 'Managerial competences', *Manager Update*, 3, Spring, pp. 18–27.

Schroder, H. (1986) 'Managerial competence and style, University of South Florida, Mimeograph.

Short, E. C. (ed.) (1984) *Competence: Inquiries into its meaning and acquisition in educational settings*, Lanham: University Press of America.

Whetten, D. A. and Cameron, K. S. (1984) *Developing Management Skills*, Glenview, IL: Scott Foreman.

Chapter 8

Marketing management decision-making

Objectives

After reading this chapter, the reader should be able to understand what a decision is and define marketing decision-making; outline a model of the decision-making process; understand the nature and scope of marketing management decisions; understand the factors influencing decision-making; and finally, outline what is meant by entrepreneurial decision-making.

Introduction

People make decisions every day of their lives. Most decisions are small and inconsequential and are taken without thinking much about them. Of course, the amount of time spent on making a decision will depend on the level of complexity attached to it. Routine purchases, like petrol or a daily newspaper, are made frequently, account for little expenditure and consequently do not demand much thought. Other purchases, however – the selection of a new computer system for the enterprise, for example – will be much more complex, requiring a greater commitment of time and thought before a decision is made and implemented.

The study of decision-making in general has given rise to a great deal of research. The reason why decision-making is of such interest and importance is because of the impact that decisions can have on individuals, organizations, governments and society at large. Decisions are a key determinant of people's behaviour in that people respond to a decision and try, through their actions, to deal with the demands and implications that arise. Studies of decision-making generally have focused on how people make decisions, which factors have an impact on their decision-making behaviour and how individuals might become more effective and efficient in the decisions that they make. Decision-making, it has been widely argued, is the basis of all the functions of management. Nowhere is the importance of decision-making highlighted more forcefully than in the words of Drucker:[1]

> Whatever a manager does, he does through making decisions. These decisions may be made as a matter of routine. Indeed he may not even realise that he is making them. Or they may effect the future existence of the enterprise and require years of systematic analysis. But management is always a decision making process.

In this chapter we shall concentrate on marketing management decision making. In addition, we shall consider a whole range of factors which impact on and strongly influence the marketing decision-making process and those decisions ultimately made. The chapter concludes with a model of entrepreneurial marketing management decision-making.

What is a decision?

There are many ways to define the word 'decision'. It has been described simply as an act of making up one's mind about a particular issue. It is a choice made by a decision-maker about a course of action from among available alternatives. A decision is the outcome of a process in which a problem or challenge is analyzed, evaluated and ultimately judged on in favour of one course of action over another.

The importance of decision-making to every facet of a manager's job cannot be overstated. As Table 8.1 illustrates, decision-making permeates all managerial functions. This, to some degree, explains why marketing managers, when they plan, organize, implement and control, are frequently referred to as decision-makers. In such circumstances it is reasonable to assert that decision-making is synonymous with managing.

Table 8.1 Examples of decisions in the marketing management function

---

Planning
What are the organization's long-term marketing objectives?
What marketing strategies will best achieve these objectives?
What should the organization's short-term objectives be?

Organizing
How should the marketing function be organized (a) to ensure efficient operations within the function; and (b) to ensure that marketing is represented appropriately throughout the wider organization in order to reduce dysfunctional behaviour?

Implementing
What actions need to be taken to ensure the implementation of marketing strategies and tactics both outside and inside the organization?
What steps should the marketing decision-maker take to encourage employees to adopt an appropriate marketing orientation?

Controlling
What marketing activities need to be controlled?
How should these activities be controlled?
What type of marketing information systems should the organization have?
How should company profitability be monitored?

Source: Adapted from Stephen P. Robbins (1994), *Decision-Making; The essence of the manager's job*, Hemel Hempstead: Prentice Hall.

The decision-making process

All decision-making as a process is a series of steps through which a decision-maker goes before finally making a choice about courses of action to take to solve problems or address a challenge. One thing that needs to be made clear though is that the decision-making process is a complex activity. All decisions are related to other decisions, and the contexts in which decisions are made are usually far from ideal. Because managers at all levels must make decisions pertaining to planning, organizing, implementing and controlling on a daily basis and because the eventual success of the enterprise depends on the effectiveness of these decisions, efforts have been made by management theorists to systematize and improve the decision-making process. Consequently, many normative models of the decision-making process have been developed. An example of such a normative model is given in Table 8.2. These models can be widely applied to marketing management decision-making.

Normative models present a systematic approach to resolving problems or responding to challenges. By going through a series of sequential steps or stages, the marketing manager is provided with a structured approach for reaching a decision on any given issue. It is important to note, however, that following these steps does not automatically guarantee a good decision. Ultimately, managers are responsible for effectively applying their intuition, experience and common sense to the process. These factors are developed later. The activity starts by defining what the problem or challenge is.

Table 8.2 A normative model of decision-making

Problem definition
Information gathering
Identification of possible solutions
Evaluation of possible solutions
Choice of an ideal solution
Implementation of chosen solution
Review of effectiveness of decision(s) made

A problem is invariably seen as the difference between a desired state and an actual condition. The characteristics and dimensions of the problem – where it starts and finishes and where the next problem begins – need to be defined and understood. Time spent on this part of the model is well spent because an accurate analysis of the problem's specifics suggests a corresponding level of accuracy in outlining the response. The subsequent parts of the decision-making process address what to do about the problem or challenge. There will be an extensive gathering and processing of data, the identification of possible solutions, their evaluation and, finally, the selection from the many of the one to be adopted. Then there is the implementation and review of the effectiveness of the decision and where necessary revisions will be made.

The following example of a family-owned retail fashion outlet illustrates the applicability of such a model in a marketing circumstance.

A retail fashion outlet

Problem definition

A sudden loss of sales.

Information gathering

The decision-maker, usually the lead entrepreneur, seeks to gather as much relevant information as possible given resource constraints, in order to gain a fuller understanding of the specific causes and nature of the problem. In doing this s/he will talk first to employees in the business and subsequently to customers, suppliers and even neighbouring traders and others whose opinion is regarded as valuable. In addition, s/he will reassess the competition as well as endeavouring to establish if there are any other factors which may be precipitating the problem.

Identification and evaluation of possible solutions

Having gained a better understanding of the precise nature of the problem, the entrepreneur identifies options for its resolution. S/he then evaluates these options in an effort to determine the optimum course of action. The sort of decisions made will be determined by the degree to which the factors affecting the enterprise might be considered fundamental to its future prospects. It might be sufficient when faced with a drop in sales to have a sale or to increase promotional activity in some other way, for example, increase advertising in the local newspaper. However, if sales have fallen because of some structural change in the market then the entrepreneur may be faced with the prospect of having to relocate the business. In certain circumstances it might even have to be shut down.

The evaluation process will be influenced by such factors as company resources (human and financial) and where the entrepreneur sees the enterprise's future direction.

Choice of solution

Before opting for one particular solution the entrepreneur will evaluate each against a set of criteria, for example, the need for a speedy return to profitability, the ambition to maintain costs within acceptable levels, or how others in the company might react to the decision. Assuming a non-structural problem the entrepreneur may opt for a low-risk, easily implemented solution of an in-store sale.

Implementation and review

The entrepreneur now decides which products to reduce in price and by how much. Stock supplies are assessed before embarking on a sale. In addition, suitable support materials will be prepared, perhaps even enhancing these with special bargain purchases. During the sale the movement of stock must be closely monitored, and the entrepreneur will ensure that sales are reaching expected levels and that past, existing and potential customers are attracted to the store.

Factors influencing decision-making

The normative model outlined in Table 8.2 and illustrated by the case study above is too simple, however, in that it fails to take cognizance of the specific circumstances in which the individuals involved in the process are making choices. There are many factors that influence or impact on the individual decision-maker and these create all manner of pressures for one decision over another. In order to understand the decision-making process fully we need to consider what those factors are and try to understand the influence that they can exercise.

Table 8.3 lists the key factors that influence the decision-making process. They have been analyzed with respect to the marketing management making the decisions, the resources available, the nature of the decision and the decision process itself.

Table 8.3 Factors influencing the decision-making process

With respect to management:
Experience
Skill
Style
Intuition
Judgement
Motives

With respect to resources:
Availability of information
Availability of time

With respect to the nature of the decision and the decision-making process:
Level of risk
Degree of uncertainty
Potential impact
Degree of structure
Degree of complexity
Degree of formality
Level of urgency
Degree of routine

Marketing management decision-making

Different types of decision, the time to acquire and process information to make a decision and the level of urgency, complexity and uncertainty attached to the decision are the key determinants of managerial decision-making styles of individuals in firms.

Types of decisions

The types of decision taken by the lead entrepreneur can be represented as a continuum, ranging from routine and low in terms of complexity and urgency, on the one hand, and strategic decisions at the other extreme, suggesting higher levels of complexity and urgency. The implications are that the higher levels of complexity and urgency attached to the decision to be made, the greater the need for substantial amounts of accurate information pertinent to the decision and the time to process it. More routine decisions demand less attention of the lead decision-maker in terms of effort; previous experience may be enough. Such decisions may be so simple that they can confidently be left to trusted subordinates to get on with.

Time availability for decision-making

When it comes to marketing decisions which are perceived to be highly urgent and complex, the availability of current information, in sufficient quality and quantity, is critical. Enough time to gather information, process and evaluate it and distil from it appropriate intelligence is also vital. The more quality intelligence available and the time to gather and process it, the greater the prospects of making a good decision.

The process may be highly formal and conscious, as in a large and bureaucratic organization, or informal and unconscious, as in a growing entrepreneurial SME. In these two examples the context in which decisions are made is significant and we need to give some consideration to this.

Conventionally, the entrepreneurial SME owner is represented as an individual for whom there are never enough hours in the day. Decision-making characteristically is *ad hoc* and unplanned. The context within which the owner is making often critical decisions which affect the future potential of the firm is one of narrow margins for absorbing error, but limited access to quality information. The entrepreneur depends on intuition and experience to come up with speedy solutions to often complex and fundamental challenges and opportunities. It is questionable whether quality decisions can be made in these circumstances.

Urgency in decision-making

The level of urgency attending a decision reflects how fundamental to the future of the company a correct decision will be. Two key issues are the level of importance of the outcome to the enterprise and its ability to absorb the impact of an incorrect decision. For example, the level of urgency attached to a decision may be reflected in the amount of resources required to implement it. A hundred pounds' expenditure would be relatively less urgent in terms of expected impact than one requiring an expenditure of one hundred thousand pounds. Such a commitment of resources becomes more critical when, as is so common in the context of the SME, those resources are not owned by the entrepreneur but are acquired from others through activity in the marketplace. Any decision to pursue an entrepreneurial marketing strategy, therefore, requires an assessment of the likelihood of success if those resources are not to be squandered and the future of the enterprise compromised. The more urgent the decision to be made, as reflected in the amount of resources committed to it, the more considered and planned the approach to making that decision needs to be. Given the conventional view of the entrepreneurial SME owner as a highly independent, self-sustained and opportunistic individual, one might question the owner's commitment to such an approach.

Complexity in decision-making

An increasing level of complexity in decisions to be made is reflected in the increasing number and significance of the variables that need to be considered at any one time. As the small firm grows into a medium-sized enterprise, the individual entrepreneur's natural management style may well come under increasing pressure as s/he strives to comprehend and assimilate the increasing number of changes that are occurring both outside and within the enterprise. For example, take the pursuit of a market extension strategy by an SME. Key issues are the acquisition and processing of accurate and current intelligence on customers' needs in the new target market and the firm's ability to deliver an appreciation of the likely competition in the targeted market, and/or the availability of the necessary resources to be committed to the market development campaign. Issues like these must be identified and harmonized if a quality decision is to be made. The ability of the individual entrepreneur to manage the complex dynamics of these variables alone as the enterprise develops and grows and still make quality decisions is questionable.

In summary, we can state that the entrepreneurial approach to decision-making is normally made against a background of limited margins for absorbing error but with equally limited time to access quality information to help in decisions made, thus raising questions about the quality of those decisions. Furthermore, given the conventional view of the entrepreneurial SME owner as one who is largely independent, self-sustained and opportunistic, one might question the owner's commitment to a more thoughtful, planned approach to decision-making. Finally, an increase in the complexity of the type of decisions made will raise questions about the individual entrepreneur's ability to retain a highly centralized, personalized decision-making style and still make quality decisions.

A model for entrepreneurial marketing management decision-making

As we are concerned with decisions about marketing in the context of entre-preneurship, we must take account of the inherent characteristics of both. Thus marketing management decision-makers will desire some semblance of formality while entrepreneurial-type decisions will invariably reflect the opportunistic nature of the entrepreneur himself.

In this entrepreneurial context there are two broad bands of decision-making. First, there are those decisions that are made in the context of the formal marketing management, ranging on a continuum between highly structured and planned at the one extreme and less formal and unplanned at the other, reflecting the availability of time for decision-making and the skills required to take decisions. The directional thrust of marketing decisions is towards increased commitment to planning marketing decisions so as to minimize risk and increase control of marketing activity and resources.

The second band of decision-making reflects at the one extreme the entrepreneurial character of the SME owner-manager manifested in a haphazard and uncoordinated approach which is largely reactive and where the level of risk is low. The other extreme reflects a grandly opportunistic approach which may be seen as largely proactive, where the level of risk is substantially higher and the degree of complexity attached to the decisions made is greatly increased. The consequence of increased risk and complexity of decision-making, coupled with greater urgency but less time to take decisions leads to ever-increasing chaos surrounding the entrepreneur's decision-making activity. This is in sharp contrast to the relatively simple decision-making at the other end of the continuum.

At first sight it would appear that these two continuums are mutually exclusive and destined to lead to conflict and dichotomy whenever they are brought together. However, by merging the two bands we can create a matrix as presented in Figure 8.1.

When we consider this matrix it is possible to identify four categories of entrepreneurial decision-making which allow us to redraw the matrix as presented in Figure 8.2.

The four possible scenarios range from *laissez-faire* through shared decision-making, to consultative and entrepreneurial decision-making. In these four scenarios the decision-making approaches characteristic of the entrepreneurial manager in the early pioneering days of small firms venturing can be compared with the more formal marketing management approaches of the firm as it becomes increasingly sophisticated in its decision-making activity. In the former case, particularly in relation to strategically important decisions, with critical implications for the future of the SME, the pioneering and entrepreneurial manager's decision-making approach will tend to be *ad hoc*, unstructured and independent. This approach will reflect the owner's sense of self-sufficiency and belief in her/his judgement. So decisions that are highly complex and fraught with risk and uncertainty will be made quickly and with determination based on experience and belief in the owner's intuition or gut feeling that the decision is right.

With successful growth comes an increase in the apparent magnitude of the decisions made and the implications of failure. The pressure to adopt a more planned approach to decision-making increases, particularly when making the correct decision is fundamental to the future of the firm. A continuum of decision-making styles suggests a range from continued autocracy, so typical of the pioneering entrepreneur, through to *laissez faire*, where management effectively abdicates their responsibility for making decisions to others. The type of decision made will influence the approach adopted.

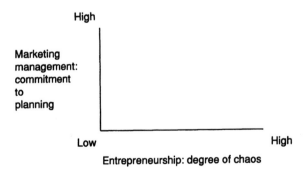

Figure 8.1 Two continuums of marketing management and entrepreneurial decision-making.

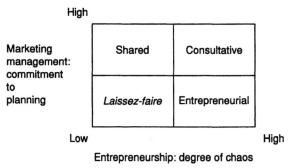

Figure 8.2 Matrix of entrepreneurial management decision-making styles.

Figure 8.2 presents these marketing management decision-making styles. We consider some of the characteristics of each in more detail below.

Laissez-faire Decisions

There are always very simple, routine jobs in every enterprise which require little skill and the minimum of direction and supervision. It might be that a new and very junior member of staff is given responsibility to chase up progress in the production of a publicity brochure or to pack and dispatch sales promotion materials to valued customers. Such jobs, in addition to being extremely simple and often highly routine, are non urgent, low-risk areas of decision-making, requiring little in the way of time or effort to ensure progress. Failure on the part of the employee to perform, while irritating, will not be critical to the future prospects of the enterprise. The lead entrepreneur in such circumstances would have to think again, however, about the choice of person to whom to leave such decisions.

Shared decisions

Decisions are also made in an enterprise which might be described as being essentially routine, with a strong operational focus. Such decisions might deal with the timing for the recommencement of a regular promotions campaign, for example, or how some small improvements might be introduced to a tried and tested method of distribution. These scenarios are low in terms of urgency, complexity and risk. There is already a workable practice in place even if suggested improvements do not work out. Such decisions are likely to have critical implications for the future of the enterprise. In addition, the amount of time to gather information and for discussions on the implications of the proposed improvements is high. One might speculate, therefore, that the lead decision-maker might be persuaded to share decision-making with subordinates.

Consultative decisions

When a decision has the potential to impact fundamentally on the future prospects of an enterprise, then it is one of considerable importance. Such decisions are characteristically more complex in that they are essentially strategic and therefore non-routine. The levels of risk and uncertainty attending these decisions will be relatively high. The availability of good quality, up-to-date information, in sufficient but appropriate volumes, is clearly critical. So too, however, is the need for sufficient time to gather available information, to process and evaluate it and to distil from it appropriate intelligence pertinent to the decision, the argument being that the more quality intelligence available and the time to gather and process it, the greater the prospects of making a good decision. In such circumstances the lead decision-maker at least has the opportunity to consult with colleagues and peers both inside and outside the enterprise before making a choice – a choice that the entrepreneur will ultimately make personally.

In such a scenario all sorts of modelling possibilities can be considered and reflected on until the most feasible is identified. An example of a highly complex and risky marketing strategy for any enterprise is to diversify its activities into new products for new markets. With no track record in either, the lead entrepreneur will need to make substantial efforts to fill in the inevitable knowledge and experience gaps in relation to the proposed strategy, before committing resources to its execution. Intuition might be just too tenuous a basis for deciding to pursue the option or not. As a longer-term strategic decision, consultation with peers within the enterprise, members of a leading entrepreneurial team perhaps and with associates outside the enterprise through personal contacts becomes critical.

Entrepreneurial decisions

Typical entrepreneurial decision-making is best reflected in the bottom right-hand quadrant of Figure 8.2. It is represented as a highly personalized, largely autocratic style of management decision-making. Consequently, the entrepreneurial owner-manager is represented as someone who operates in circumstances characterized by limited information, limited margins for absorbing error and often rapidly changing environments. Yet in such circumstances he must make critical, often strategic decisions, which will have a bearing on the future development of the enterprise into the immediate and longer term.

Equally typical of the entrepreneurial scenario is the apparent lack of time available to the entrepreneur to acquire and process what information is available from the dynamic environment in which the firm operates. The prospects for a quality decision must necessarily be considered limited, because decision-makers have little or no time to consult with anyone, even if they had the inclination to do so. They must make the decision alone and face the consequences arising from their choice. A large number of crises and a degree of chaos tend to be the constant characteristics of the scenario. Decisions made by the lead entrepreneur are likely to be *ad hoc*, essentially highly informal in character and largely focused on more operational issues. The approach to making decisions will tend to be unstructured, though highly flexible, essentially reactive and often 'on the hoof' as events unfold. Such an approach to decision-making will be largely unskilled and reliant on personal experience and intuition. Strategic choices made against such a background of significant self-reliance will increase the level of risk of making a poor choice. With limited margins for absorbing error, entrepreneurial small firm owners need to minimize the number of occasions they get it wrong. One possible consequence arising from this situation may be the build-up of pressure on entrepreneurial decision-makers to consider moderating their approach to one that is at least marginally consultative in character.

Additional factors influencing decision-making

Another factor, which introduces additional complications to our model, is the level of commitment in terms of time and resources already made to a particular line of action. The argument is that the more time and resources that have already been committed, the more difficult it becomes to abandon the decision. The level of formal training, knowledge and experience that the decision-maker has had in making marketing decisions in the different situations or scenarios represented in Figure 8.2 will be important. The decision-maker's inherent good judgement and intuition, as the situation becomes more complex and risky and information remains incomplete, are further examples of factors influencing the decision-maker. Allied to all of these are the personality traits of the decision-maker − tolerance for risk, attitude to ambiguity, need for achievement, and so forth.

Summary

It is clear that normative models of the decision-making process, while offering a framework for understanding how decisions are made, are inappropriate for understanding decision-making in the context of the entrepreneurial firm. What makes entrepreneurial decision-making different is that it is essentially influenced by the special circumstances in which the entrepreneur is likely to operate. In addition, due consideration must be given to the characteristics and personality of the entrepreneur and how such factors influence what s/he does.

Most decisions made by the entrepreneur are opportunity-focused and must, therefore, be viewed as marketing in nature. The implication, certainly tacit if not explicit, is that when addressing entrepreneurial decision-making, it should be recognized that what is in question is most probably marketing decision-making.

Learning questions

1. What are the key differences between decision-making in the context of the entrepreneurial SME and the larger enterprise?
2. It is suggested that logic and intuition influence management decision-making. What is the appropriateness of this assertion in the context of the entrepreneurial SME?
3. Discuss the importance of information to the marketing management decision-making process?

Notes and references

1. Drucker, P. (1967) *The Effective Executive*, London: Pan, chapter 6, pp. 115–45.

Further reading

Agor, W. H. (1986) 'The logic of intuition: How top executives make important decisions', *Organisational Dynamics*, Winter, pp. 157–70.

Barnard, J. (1992) 'Successful CEOs talk about decision making', *Business Horizons*, September–October, pp. 70–4.

Cohen, M. D., March, J. G. and Olsen, J. P. (1989) 'A garbage can model of organisational choice', *The Administrative Science Quarterly* 4, Winter, pp. 1–17.

Cray, D. *et al.* (1991) 'Explaining decision processes', *Journal of Management Studies* 28 (3), May, pp. 227–51.

Eisenhardt, K. M. (1990) 'Speed and strategic choice: How managers accelerate decision making', *California Management Review*, Spring, pp. 39–54.

Harper, S. C. (1988) 'Intuition: What separates executives from managers?', *Business Horizons*, September–October, pp. 13–19.

Harrison, F. L. (1977) 'Decision-making in conditions of extreme uncertainty', *Journal of Management Studies* 14, pp. 169–78.

Harvey, H. F. (1982) *Business Policy and Strategic Management*, Columbus, Ohio: Charles E. Merrill.

March, J. J. and Simon, H. (1958) 'Decision making theory', in *Organisations*, New York: Wiley, pp. 137–50.

McDonald, M. H. B. (1992) 'Strategic marketing planning: A state of the art review', *Marketing Intelligence and Planning* 10 (4), pp. 4–22.

Miles, R. E. and Snow, C. C. (1992) 'Causes of failure in network organisations', *California Management Review*, Summer, pp. 53–72.

Mintzberg, H. (1975) 'The manager's job: Folklore and fact', *Harvard Business Review*, July–August, pp. 49–61.

Perkins, S. W. and Rao, R. C. (1990) 'The role of experience in information use and decision making by marketing managers', *Journal of Marketing Research* 27, February, pp. 1–10.

Rice, G. H. (1983) 'Strategic decision making in small business', *Journal of General Management* 9 (1), pp. 58–65.

Robbins, S. P. (1994) Decision-making: The essence of the manager's job, Hemel Hempstead: Prentice Hall.

Schoemaker, P. J. H. (1993) 'Strategic decisions in organisations: Rational and behavioural views', *Journal of Management Studies* 30 (1), pp. 107–29.

Chapter 9

Managerial relationships

Objectives

After reading this chapter readers will appreciate the vital importance of relationship formation and maintenance for the effective performance of the entrepreneurial, marketing or managerial job. They will appreciate the importance of: persuasion in ensuring that strategic thrusts are initiated; maintaining strong contacts with suppliers; and developing enduring associations with customers. They will appreciate the contribution that rewarding relationships can make in achieving these objectives by non-directive means. They will also understand that internal cooperation is necessary for superior organizational performance and recognize the part played by good working relationships in attaining this state of affairs.

Readers will also be aware that effective working relationships emerge: (1) when interacting parties communicate openly and regularly; (2) when a degree of trust develops between individuals and groups; (3) when the parties understand the viewpoint of their counterparts; (4) when non-coercive methods of influence are utilized; (5) when those who interact accept that their adversaries have a legitimate right to express their point of view; and (6) when joint decision-making is neither unduly emotional nor hard-headed. Finally, readers will have an opportunity to synthesize the material in the chapter when it is applied to a model of relationship marketing.

Introduction

In discussing management, marketing and entrepreneurship in this text it has been recognized that there is a significant interpersonal aspect to this work. Managers accomplish much of their work through people and it has been increasingly recognized that their power over others is less pervasive than it used to be. Indeed, Colin Hales argues that 'the future basis for managerial authority must lie in the recognition of the interdependent and cooperative character of work'.[1] This is especially true in modern organizations where rapid increases in knowledge, ideas and market opportunities require the active cooperation of all staff to develop the new products and markets which are necessary for organizational survival.

In the marketing domain it is essential for managers and others to keep in close touch with customers to assess their needs and aspirations. It is also beneficial to maintain a long-term relationship with customers. Loyal customers who continue to purchase particular goods or services over time are very attractive to businesses. The costs of acquiring new customers is considerable and the latter are likely to be more fickle and responsive to marginal additional benefits provided by competitors. Long-term relationships generate a self-sustaining dynamic which allows each party to weather the storms that arise between interdependent people.

Entrepreneurs tend to generate and develop business ideas without undue regard to the resources at their disposal. They assume that if the business concept is good enough, resources will become available. Consequently, they are inclined to enter into non-restrictive associations with their suppliers to allow them some flexibility if ideas do not reach their projected potential. Under these conditions entrepreneurs are asking individuals to support them and their speculative business proposals; a good working relationship with backers is of inestimable value in this delicate situation. In addition, if entrepreneurs want the freedom to form short-term associations with resource suppliers, they will need to be fully aware of the sources that are available. They need to know who has what on offer and they can best acquire this information by developing a large number of personal contacts.

These interpersonal aspects of business and management have been recognized for many years by behavioural scientists, management theorists and those who are interested in developing managerial competencies, but little has been written on the development and maintenance of relations between managers, entrepreneurs and their contacts.[2]

Developing and maintaining relationships

Externally oriented individuals in organizations make contact with a large variety of individuals and groups such as government representatives, suppliers, customers and competitors in the course of their work, but the relationship between the parties is rarely the principal reason for their interaction. In each case there will be a substantive issue for discussion, such as the role of government in regulating the environment, delivery times from suppliers or the preferences of customers. However, individuals rarely jump straight in and discuss substantive issues when they meet. Meetings generally open with an exchange of pleasantries, jokes, enquiries about mutual friends and general chit-chat. It is important to establish rapport, and general discussion can accomplish this. If sufficient affinity is established between contacts, a personal friendship may emerge which can facilitate the conduct of substantive business between the parties. Friendship is useful when doing business as friends may do unsolicitated favours for their associate, transmit useful information or generally represent the interests of their companions.

Friendship has an impact on the conduct of business, but so does animosity. If a regular contact is difficult to deal with, managers can come away from a meeting with a good deal, but may feel drained by the interaction. They may feel so annoyed that, in spite of the potential for mutual benefit, they are disinclined to meet the contact again. The feelings, emotions and attitudes of the parties to a discussion have an impact on the discourse and outcomes, and the latter depend on the manner in which people decide to conduct themselves when dealing with others. People must be aware that their behaviour will elicit a reaction.[3]

The links mentioned above were with outsiders and because managers have no formal authority in this situation they will be left in little doubt about the impact their behaviour has on the bond between their associates and them. However, managers have numerous links with people inside their organizations. In these situations the power of managers is an important intervening factor. Our review of the literature on developments in management indicate that managers use a range of sources of power in their dealings with others, but regardless of the derivation Etzioni argues that in a relationship parties will respond in quite predictable ways to attempts to sway them. He suggests that coercion begets alienative involvement, moral persuasion evokes moral involvement, while the release of tangible resources and information will bring about calculative involvement.[4]

What implication does the association between the method of influence and the reaction of the party being induced have for the type of relationship an individual develops with contacts? It is useful to draw an analogy between this situation and the model of leadership effectiveness presented by Frederick Fiedler.[5] He argues that leaders adopt two broad behavioural orientations: a concern for people and a concern for the task, and that, in conditions which are very unfavourable or very favourable for the leader, effective leaders will be task-oriented. In intermediate situations the leader will adopt a people or relations orientation. Fiedler's rationale is as follows. If the situation is unfavourable, no amount of relationship building will secure superior job performance from subordinates, therefore the leader spells out what is needed, draws up schedules and adopts a directive, task-oriented approach. If the situation is highly favourable, relationships between leaders and their subordinates will be good and managers do not need to devote time and energy to building relationships. They simply issue instructions and their subordinates will willingly comply. In the latter case, however, leaders must be sure that they do not destroy good relationships.

In the intermediate position Fiedler argues that the effort devoted to improving the relationship will receive a pay-off. Since the relationship is moderately good, moving it to good should get more willing compliance, while letting it deteriorate will lead to alienative compliance.

In discussions between managers and their intra-organizational associates coercion will bring about deep resentment, but if managers have sufficient power they can enforce compliance. If moral persuasion is used it will, in all probability, bring about commitment and perhaps identification with the persuading manager. In the intermediate situation, and in most dealings with external contacts, the response of the people being influenced depends on their assessment of the value of any inducements on offer compared with the extra energy they will need to expend to obtain any reward. In this situation the quality of the relationship between the parties could be crucial in gaining compliance, and consequently managers are more likely to focus some of their attention on relationship building as well as negotiating concrete, substantive agreements between the parties. A word of warning is in order though. There is sometimes a temptation to trade off a substantive decision to preserve a relationship, but that is unwise; it can lead to demands for many concessions in the supposed interest of preserving a relationship. It has been suggested that relationship issues and substantive matters, even though there is an interplay between the two, should be addressed separately.[6]

The length of the association between two parties will also influence their approach to relationships. If one party makes contact with another in the realization that it will be a single encounter, in all probability they will conduct the exchange in a competitive, business-like manner. Since relationships take time to develop, and since the association will not be continued, there is little incentive to build a strong relationship. If, however, the parties will meet again and again, they are more likely to adopt a collaborative stance and invest in building a good relationship.[7] With this in mind, let us proceed to examine some of the recurring associations managers have with others and the type of relationships that might emerge.

Recurring relationships

Strategic contacts

Managers are responsible for the strategic thrust of their organizations and senior managers are constantly in touch with associates from inside and outside their organizations when formulating their strategic plans or agendas. They also use them in creating a network of associates when implementing their plans. John Kotter showed that, in their interaction with others, chief executives were adept at asking questions to glean the substantive information they needed but they also spent considerable time in seemingly inconsequential conversation.[8] The latter was done to develop and maintain relationships to allow them to gather up-to-date and relevant information. Good relations were even more important when implementing their agendas. They did this by securing the active cooperation of individuals in many walks of life and Kotter's chief executives made sure that they had cooperative contacts in key positions inside and outside their business.

At another level senior managers are keen to influence rather than react to events and it has been shown that it is more effective to ensure that key decisions are in accord with one's wishes rather than modify decisions once they have been taken. Consequently, senior managers are often keen to bring politicians, community activists or customers around to their way of thinking. They often achieve this by promoting a project and then actively seeking support for it. For example, a manager may be keen to export to a given country and will, therefore, have an interest in getting that country's tariff barriers reduced. In this situation a manager will not be in a position to exercise coercive methods of influence; rather, s/he will use interpersonal and relationship skills to bring others around, usually by pointing out the benefits to be gained by the various interest groups. Research indicates that the most successful managers are prepared to modify their proposals to accommodate the needs of those whose support they seek. Referring to work carried out by Mary Parker Follett in the 1940s, Mintzberg notes that it is not a matter of abandoning part of the project to secure support for a compromise proposal, but of conducting a creative discussion, with all the parties involved, to produce an amended proposal which meets the needs of all.[9] In these endeavours managers utilize all their relationship building skills, as they are in no position to coerce and unlikely to be able to offer moral or remunerative inducements to their allies.

Links with suppliers

Let us address some regular relationships within the industrial arena. One of the principal ones is the association between manufacturers and their suppliers. Many writers have noted that these relationships are often adversarial and that this arises because of the functioning of the free enterprise system. The supreme advocate of *laissez-faire* economics was Adam Smith, who wrote: 'It is not from the benevolence of the butcher, the brewer or the baker that we expect our dinner, but from their regard to their own interest. We address ourselves, not to their humanity, but to their self love, and never talk to them of our own necessities, but of their advantage.'[10] In other words, buyers and sellers look to their own self-interest and this results in the most efficient distribution of resources imaginable.

However, this is not always how events work out. John Carlisle and Robert Parker point out that British and US motor manufacturers in the 1960s and 1970s demanded rock bottom prices from their suppliers of raw materials and sub-assemblies.[11] In response to these demands from powerful buyers suppliers did indeed reduce their prices but to make any profit something had to be sacrificed. This was quality and as a result numerous poor quality parts were incorporated into motor cars with predictable consequences. Any readers who bought a British car in the 1970s will remember its regular breakdowns. Little wonder then that when Japanese cars arrived in these two markets in the late 1960s there was a pent-up demand for them.

Carlisle and Parker suggest that it was not until UK and US manufacturers realized how interdependent buyers and sellers really are that they began to compete effectively in international markets. Rather than driving such a hard bargain, buyers began to realize that they had to attend to their own needs and those of their suppliers. Manufacturers have to attend to the needs of the final customer and it is important, therefore, that every link in the supply chain is also attending to those needs. This will only occur if manufacturers enter into collaborative associations with their various suppliers with a view to sustaining their relationship over a period of time. This is especially true when manufacturers enter into just-in-time arrangements with suppliers. In return for reducing the stock levels that are carried by the manufacturers, suppliers must have their needs attended to. A cooperative, problem-solving relationship can 'utilize the experience, innovation and efficiencies which are available within the collective talents of all buying and selling firms in a given production chain'.[12] It is important to remove the coercive bullying of the buyer and the calculative involvement of the supplier in favour of long-term cooperative arrangements.

Acquiring finance

Supplies of finance come from a variety of sources and it has been argued that the system works best when an effective capital market is in operation. Firms seeking finance publish their accounts, investors evaluate performance and offer to lend funds at an appropriate rate of return. If the market is efficient, buyers and sellers will accept the market price and there is no need to build a good relationship with a counterpart. If one or other party fails to honour their part of the bargain, legal remedies are available. The market mechanism renders good personal relationships between buyers and sellers of capital redundant: indeed, they will normally conduct their business through impersonal intermediaries such as stock brokers.

However, it has been pointed out that there are numerous imperfections in capital markets. Myron Slovin and John Young suggest that these are especially prevalent when one party has greater access to and control over information than others.[13] This condition obtains quite often in the case of family firms and with small companies not quoted on the stock exchange. The family member or principal entrepreneur will often have a detailed understanding of the management of the venture, but may well be reluctant to disclose information to others. Under these conditions, suppliers of capital can be placed in an unenviable position. Slovin and Young point out that they face the possibility of deception; and since the subsequent success of the business depends, to a significant extent, on the abilities of the owner, they need to be sure that the individual in question is worth supporting. Consequently, these authors argue that it is important to build a relationship between financiers and proprietors in an attempt to overcome some of these concerns.

Slovin and Young suggest that, over time, both parties provide one another with information and this normally alters the degree of risk both assign to the transaction. This two-way exchange of data depends on and, if it is successful, enhances the trust between the two sides. Trust is an essential ingredient for an effective relationship and it will only develop if both parties are convinced that the other will not use privileged information for financial ends. As trust develops, a personal bond develops between lender and proprietor, which cements the relationship and compensates, to some extent, for the absence of a financial market.

Customer relations

Let us turn our attention to links with customers. Since entrepreneurs and managers are not in a position to coerce or morally involve buyers, it is sensible for them to conduct themselves in a manner that encourages buyers to purchase their products on a regular basis. However, the overriding principle in the economics of markets is competition, and under these conditions most customers will respond to additional marginal benefit from competing suppliers and buy from the latter. These switches are normal in a competitive market but they are unlikely to engender good personal relationships between providers and their clients.

It is most likely that the selling organization will emphasize the benefits to be gained from purchasing their product and expect no more than a calculative involvement from their customers. Lack of loyalty and switching from one supplier to another is normal in these transactions. This focus on market exchanges has resulted in a concern for one-off sales, short time-horizons, a grudging acceptance of the needs of customers and a product orientation among manufacturers.[14]

This situation exists in consumer markets but things are different in industrial markets, where relationships tend to be long-standing.[15] Everyday experience tells us that relationships take time to develop. When we meet a new person or group for the first time we are rather unsure of ourselves and we spend some time getting to know the other party. We do not know how they will react, so we tend to be cautious in expressing opinions and try to find out how the other party views the world. After a time some behavioural norms emerge, the ebb and flow of conversation increases considerably and we may begin to disclose quite personal information about ourselves because we know that the other party will not take advantage of us.

David Ford[16] indicates that similar interactions between buyers and sellers emerge in industrial markets. If a firm is contemplating finding a new supplier, it will make enquiries in appropriate quarters about possible suppliers. If a source looks promising, a meeting will take place when each side will outline its needs, but since there is no history to the relationship the arrangement will be provisional. With the onset of exchange the parties will discover whether expectations are met and, if they are, a stronger commitment to the agreement will develop. With further successful exchange the level of trust will increase and affective bonds may develop which will allow the partners to deal effectively with the difficulties which so often arise in long-term relationships. It has been shown that if organizations want to be successful in international industrial marketing, they must forge close links with their buyers or suppliers.[17]

In recent years a number of marketers have recommended that even in consumer markets organizations should build lasting relationships with important customers with a view to accomplishing repeat sales and the purchase of a range of products offered by the supplier. In doing so these writers are emphasizing the interdependence between buyer and seller and the benefits of a long-term, as opposed to a one-off, relationship. However, it has been made clear that relationship marketing is not appropriate in all situations. They suggest that if it is easy for a customer to transfer from one supplier to another, then relationship marketing is inadvisable. It is also unwise if the product or service is unsophisticated and if the customers have no great interest in long-term relationships.[18]

Relationships within organizations

While the focus on interdependencies between organizations and their outside contacts is a relatively recent occurrence, it has long been recognized that the vast majority of groups within organizations are strongly interdependent. Indeed, it has been suggested that organizations are 'networks of interdependent subunits that struggle to improve their own positions, but that need one another at the same time'.[19] Because people need one another, they must develop associations and it would seem natural to suggest that affective relations might develop between the parties which could enhance their capacity to perform effectively.

Interdepartmental relations

If we reflect for a moment on the bureaucratic organization, it becomes apparent, however, that the necessary cooperation between individuals and departments is likely to be less harmonious than formal management theory would suggest. There are considerable differences between departments in terms of their outlook, administrative arrangements, reward system and leadership styles; they may subscribe in public to the notion that all departments contribute to the goals of the organization but quite often means and ends are reversed; dependencies restrict actions and many departments want to do their own thing; and the monetary and other resources of the organization are not unlimited, with the result that competition for scarce resources is quite common.[20] Just as it took the serious troubles in the UK and US motor industries and the marketing problems of numerous firms to encourage managers to recognize the need for collaboration between organizations, it often requires enlightened and forward-looking senior managers to remind departmental managers that they are interconnected.

In general, a background of overt or covert political behaviour provides a backcloth for a situation in which managerial peers recognize their interdependence while harbouring thoughts of independence. Given their situation they are unlikely to be able to coerce others. Equally, it is improbable that they will be successful in using moral persuasion to elicit compliance from their peers. It is quite possible, though, that access to economic resources or privileged technical or administrative information will provide some managers with a power base and the most likely response of peers to this means of influence is calculative. This, together with the fact that they will interact on a regular basis in the pursuit of organizational goals, will mean that many managers will have an interest in developing good working relationships with their peers. Time and energy devoted to developing a good relationship should enhance their capacity to get things done.

Superior/subordinate relationships

Peer relationships are important but superior subordinate relations are probably the most common form of association in organizations. The bond between these groups will depend on whether the subordinates are managers, professionals or operators. The first two groups have considerable discretion and expertise, and senior managers will tend to use a repertoire of essentially persuasive devices to secure their willing cooperation. In many cases these groups will trade technical or administrative information to secure commitment. With operators the situation will be quite different. In bureaucratic organizations operators have very little discretion and their working procedures are tightly controlled. In this context relationships between managers and operators will tend to be poor and, following Fiedler's maxim, managers will adopt a directive approach to management. We must remember, however, that managerial power is never absolute and given the calculative involvement of most operators, there may be times when managers see merit in developing a reasonable working relationship with their employees.[21]

Family firms

The focus of this text is on SMEs and there is a special kind of small firm which is worthy of consideration: the family business. These ventures experience special relationship problems. In the discussion so far we have stated that, as part of their everyday duties, managers are connected with numerous others for work-related reasons. Personal relations are superimposed on work-related transactions. In the case of the family firms non-work relationships become established first. In the non-family firm managers may have a good relationship with a peer or subordinate but if they are faced with a decision between maintaining a relationship and advancing the business they will normally favour the latter. This is much more difficult in a family firm: broken family relationships cause untold misery. For example, owners of a family firm may face challenges to their managerial approach from those children who are working in the business and who are likely to take over in time. The owners' experience may indicate that these children's actions are misguided but the owners may not criticize them because they are family. In other instances, founders may accept the need to pass on their business to their successor but fear that the loss of the business will result in a serious void in their lives. As a consequence, many family firms are burdened with serious rivalry and conflict between founder and successor with resultant hostility, guilt and turmoil.

Serious conflict also arises between siblings. Brothers and sisters may become deeply suspicious of one another and resent the real or apparent favouritism being given to their 'rival'. Things can become even more chaotic if several family members have a stake in the business. As a family, all demand equal treatment, but they don't all make an equal contribution to the venture. Squabbles, rivalries and 'internecine warfare' over territories can tear the business apart.

What can be done to resolve these disputes? Several authors contend that, in spite of the real difficulties involved, the parties must face up to the issues, communicate and build an effective working relationship where these, and other problems, can be addressed and resolved.[22]

Developing relationships

Our discussion so far suggests that there are many instances in managerial life when it is useful to have a good relationship with a regular contact, but let us elaborate on the adjective 'good'. Are we to imply that there must be affection between the parties? Not necessarily. While it can enhance the quality of a relationship, a very close personal relationship can present difficulties in business life. As our short discussion on family firms revealed, if there are strong emotional ties between the parties, this can inhibit rational business decision-making.

It is much more important that the parties are not hostile towards one another and respect their associates. They must be prepared to listen to one another and most important of all, have the capacity to face up to and resolve the differences which arise between them. A good working relationship can be made if:

1. The parties can work together in making decisions and conduct their business in a reasonably open manner.
2. The principals do not feel emotionally drained after an encounter.
3. The individuals concerned do not dread the next encounter.
4. The parties can approach the interaction in a positive frame of mind.
5. Distorted perceptions and negative stereotypes are absent.
6. The parties do not deliberately distort the information that passes between them.
7. The level of communication is high and few barriers are placed in the way of those who are communicating.[23]

These are some general propositions on the necessary conditions for effective working relationships, but how do individuals go about developing a relationship with someone else in practice? In our discussion on relationship marketing we touched on some common-sense notions of relationship formation but there is literature on this topic and we shall draw on it in the discussion that follows.[24]

Interaction and relationships

Once an entrepreneur, marketer or manager accepts that it would be useful to develop relationships with customers, for example, a question arises as to which ones are worth contacting. In making this choice managers will tend to focus initially on those people they know something about. To discover how much merit there is in a particular relationship face-to-face communication is needed. By interacting, parties find out as much as possible about each other. Steve Duck argues that during discussions individuals engage in detective work to discover if the attitudes and behaviours of the other party accord with their own. They sift information and send cues but the very act of communicating 'has a positive effect on liking, and it modifies the effect of dissimilarity on its own'.[25]

In interactions, the parties gain information sequentially, and while they may have strategies for gathering information, day-to-day conversation is very important. Parties seldom develop relationships in a rational and logical manner; quite often it just happens. However, Duck argues that in gathering and giving information we use indirect approaches. If our approach does not meet with success, we can argue that our failure to get directly to the point, rather than rejection by the other party, caused the failure. In general, in an initial contact we let others know something about our thoughts and we glean something about theirs. Much of the exchange is vague, with lots of guessing, but everyday conversation allows us to convey many messages.

If, after their initial interaction, the parties deduce that a continuing relationship might bring rewards, they will continue their interaction, and many people use self-disclosure to develop a relationship. By disclosing sensitive information people indicate that they have an increasing degree of trust in the other party. Self-disclosure is also useful in that it encourages reciprocity. Self-disclosure is useful, but it has been suggested that unless people can agree on basic issues, unless they reach consensus, their relationship is doomed.[26]

Mutual appreciation, discussion and trust

To arrive at consensus it is vitally important that the other party understands your point of view, but it is equally important for you to appreciate theirs. After all, 'we are interested in others when they are interested in us.' Understanding others is vital but we should not underestimate the problems that are involved. One may empathize (put oneself in another's shoes) but fail to understand their viewpoint because their values, beliefs or perceptions are quite different from one's own. Misunderstandings are especially common in dealing with people from different cultures. For example, in Japan a paternalistic relationship exists between buyers and sellers; the former are more powerful but they do attend to the needs of sellers. An aggressive British salesperson who is unaware of this cultural norm would find life difficult in Japan. While not underestimating the difficulties involved, mutual respect and understanding help cement relationships. For example, it has been shown that they are crucial factors in promoting the successful transition from one generation to another in family firms.[27]

Misunderstandings can arise because of differing perceptions but they can also occur as a result of poor communication. We noted that conversation was an important ingredient in initiating associations but it is equally important in sustaining them. It is important to get one's point of view across to a contact and in doing so it is essential that the speaker uses appropriate language; is clear on the reason for the communication; holds the attention of the other party; and is satisfied that the words used and their meaning are understood.

Getting your message across clearly and effectively is important, but it is equally important to listen not only to the words, but also to the emotions or intentions behind the words. For effective communication it has been suggested that the listener must convince the speaker that s/he is paying attention. This can be done by facing the speaker squarely and maintaining reasonable eye contact. The listener must also intimate that s/he is following the speaker's argument; appropriate questions and short summaries of what has been said are useful in this context. These and other techniques are beneficial in convincing the speaker that she really is worth listening to.[28]

Effective communication is vital for a good relationship but, if anything, trust is more important. If someone is trusted, it allows one party to get on with their own business, safe in the knowledge that their contact will do as they said they would. In addition trust is often reciprocated, and when two or more parties can be sure that their partners are reliable, it removes a good deal of the tension that characterizes business relations. However, we should be aware that there are two aspects of trust: faith in the intentions of others and confidence in their ability.[29] People may be reliable in the sense of always doing what they say they will do but the inferior quality of their work may not inspire confidence. Others may regularly fail to do what they say they will do because they take on more than they can cope with, or are overoptimistic. These people are not dishonest but their behaviour does not engender a great deal of trust. They cannot be relied on and they will make life difficult for their partners.

Dishonesty is another matter. If one party deliberately deceives another, this will do considerable damage to a relationship; damage which is very difficult to repair. There are, however, occasions when behaviour is interpreted as dishonest but there is no intention to deceive. In these situations it is important for the two parties to have an open discussion on the matter, to explain behaviours and intentions and to reassure contacts.

Trust is vital for a good relationship but it is risky. Roger Fisher and Scott Brown caution against being too trusting.[30] If one party trusts another implicitly and the other fails to deliver trust, the trusting individual will be in an invidious position. Trust is normally built up over time and we tend to trust people who have indicated that they are trustworthy. It is important, therefore, to set up reporting mechanisms to make sure that what is expected to happen does in fact happen and the frequency and detail contained in reports from partners will depend on the risk involved in trusting another.

Mutual understanding, effective communication and trust are important ingredients for a good relationship, and empirical support for this line of reasoning can be found in studies of family firms. In particular it has been shown that when these aspects of relationships are present, the transition from one family generation to another proceeds without the tension and conflict which can occur during managerial successions.[31]

Additional matters affecting relationships

Through interaction, entrepreneurs and managers use a repertoire of methods to get what they want from others. However, in spite of their formal authority they use coercion sparingly as a means of influence. One reason for this reluctance is the damage it does to relationships. People resent threats and when faced with them develop a negative or hostile attitude towards their aggressors, are unlikely to trust them and will be reluctant to see things from their points of view. Steve Duck suggests that threats make many people 'do exactly the opposite of what they were requested to do'.[32].

In view of the resentment open threats generate, individuals sometimes modify their approach and coerce in a roundabout manner. In some instances one party will constantly badger the other, and then intimate that they will stop if compliance is gained. In others, they do not make an overt threat but point out that if you do not comply, because of the way things are, you will be punished. In other instances, a partner will suggest that you will feel guilty if you do not comply, that others will think poorly of you if you refuse, or that only nasty people would refuse to comply.[33]

If coercive strategies are risky, what are the best ways of influencing others? Duck notes that influencers must grab the attention of the target person and an important way of doing so is to be a credible source. Credibility is enhanced by the attractiveness of the influencer, expertise, similarity to the recipient or the extent to which the influencer agrees with the target's ideas. Interestingly, people who argue against their perceived self-interest are regarded as highly credible sources. In general, persuasive or incremental strategies work best in gaining compliance and in maintaining relationships. Getting a foot in the door by seeking a small commitment and then asking for more seems to work, as does regularly increasing the cost of doing something once the target person has made an initial commitment. An alternative is to make a large request and then scale it down to something more reasonable.[34]

These strategies are useful for gaining attention but they have to be reinforced by other means. Many people use logical arguments supported by facts, figures and expert knowledge. Some will be impressed by these methods but we must remember that while individuals do have a logical side to their makeup they are also influenced by beliefs, emotions and feelings. Rational, logical approaches to changing opinions do not always work because what appears logical to the influencer contradicts the strongly held values of the individual being influenced. When we fail to make progress in influencing others Roger Fisher cautions against rejecting their point of view completely. We must accept that they have a right to feel the way they do. Accepting that they are entitled to their opinion does not mean that we agree with them. However, if we dismiss their concerns as irrational, it will not be easy to continue working with them.

In these situations we should also be wary of stereotyping. Faced with a struggle to bring someone round to our own way of thinking, we may be tempted to categorize our partner's behaviour in negative, stereotypical ways. All relationships will have their difficult times but a tendency to stereotype is inimical to effective long-term relationships.[35]

When logical argument does not impress, another approach to influence is required. Behaviours are often a reflection of social cultural norms and the latter are a product of the values and attitudes of the individual. In this situation it is important to invite those being influenced to re-examine their values and beliefs to discover if they are still appropriate in the current situation. For example, a person who believes strongly in the freedom of the individual may reject all the statistical evidence which shows that wearing a rear safety belt in cars prevents loss of life. The individual in question may be encouraged to consider whether the additional cost of hospital care for seriously injured passengers restricts the freedom of those on NHS waiting lists to receive the medical treatment they need. This approach is essentially one of re-education. It is often a lengthy process but, unlike coercive or some rational approaches, it will be less likely to impair the relationship between the parties.[36]

Disagreements and disputes are common in any long-standing relationship and the parties must have the capacity to face up to conflict and resolve it. However, strong beliefs arouse strong emotions. Emotions energize and encourage people to challenge existing practices, but strong emotions can seriously impair the ability of one or other party to resolve disputes. Intense anger, or love, can cloud judgement and reduce the quality of decisions.

However, emotions should not be ignored or swept under the carpet. In effect, a good working relationship will ensue when the parties achieve a good balance between emotions and rationality. As a general approach Fisher and Brown suggest that when they are resolving a dispute the parties should be aware of their own emotional state and that of the other side and be prepared to discuss openly why they are feeling the way they do. If they are very upset, it makes good sense for them to take a break, go to a separate location and generally calm down before getting back together again. Apologies are useful – they sometimes defuse a conflict and disarm the other party. In general, associates should be aware of the importance of emotions, reflect on the emotions exhibited during a discussion, anticipate occasions or events which are likely to generate strong feelings and be prepared to deal with them in an open way.[37]

A model of relationship marketing

In this chapter we have argued that in many instances managers have a vested interest in developing effective relationships with their contacts and we then proceeded to examine some crucial behaviours in relationship building. It seems appropriate, therefore, as we bring this chapter to its conclusion, to take a specific instance where relationship building is recommended and review the methods by which the latter is achieved. Let us proceed and examine the model of relationship marketing developed by Larry Crosby and his associates. These authors argue that the quality of the relationship between the salesperson and the client is very important in determining both the effectiveness of the salesperson's endeavour and the likelihood that the customer will continue to deal with the salesperson in the future. Furthermore, relationship quality is determined by the approach the salesperson adopts when dealing with the customer, the salesperson's expertise and the degree of similarity between the salesperson and the client. For effective interaction with customers three behaviours are regarded as essential: (1) the salesperson must interact on a regular basis, including times when s/he is not selling directly; (2) during interactions the salesperson discloses information of a personal nature and seeks reciprocity; (3) the salesperson must initiate and encourage present and future cooperation between the parties. When we reflect on our discussion on building relationships, these issues were raised as important precursors of effective relationships.

Similarly the lifestyle, the social stature and the appearance of both salesperson and customer, together with the perceived product expertise of the salesperson, were regarded as important determinants of the quality of a relationship. Let us say a little more on what the latter means. In brief, Crosby and his colleagues argue that if the customer has faith in the intentions of the salesforce and confidence in their ability to meet their needs over time this will produce an effective working relationship between the parties. A good quality relationship between the parties, coupled with the salesforce's expertise and personal similarities between the parties leads to an acceptable level of current sales coupled with an intention to continue with the relationship in the future.

In testing their model Crosby *et al.* found that the manner in which the salesforce conducted themselves had a marked impact on relationship quality, which in turn influenced anticipated future interaction. However, salesforce's expertise and similarity were moderately or weakly linked with relationship quality, although they did have a direct impact on current sales effectiveness. Overall, this specific model of relationship building provides substantial support for our general proposals on those behaviours which lead to the development of effective working relationships.[38]

Summary

In this chapter we have argued that relationship building and maintenance is a crucial aspect of the work of entrepreneurs, marketers and managers. These people are vitally involved with people as purveyors of information, generators of business ideas, consumers with needs to satisfy and key organizational resources. Managers, entrepreneurs and marketers need the willing cooperation of their personal contacts and associates to gather the information they need and to assist with the production of goods and services. Relationship building is particularly important in the modern era because managers have limited power over others. In essence, managers must create cooperative associations with strategic collaborators, suppliers, customers, peers, subordinates, etc. to release the full creative and productive potential of these individuals.

A good working relationship is a means to the end of accomplishing superior business performance but conflict-ridden relationships are common in organizations. They are most damaging for large, entrepreneurial and family firms. Furthermore, disruptive relationships have a tendency to degenerate into self-defeating cycles of dysfunctional behaviour which are difficult to break out of. It is better to avoid such degenerative cycles in the first place and relationship skills are essential if this state of affairs is to arise.

However, good working relationships do not emerge spontaneously. Parties need to recognize the essential ingredients of good relations and the behaviours which are necessary for success. They need to understand others and accept the legitimacy of their positions and seek, through reasonable open discussion, to resolve differences. Skills in communication, influence, persuasion, conflict resolution and negotiation coupled with a degree of flexibility and charisma are essential for the important task of working with others to accomplish organizational goals.

Learning questions

1. There are those who argue that owner/managers and managers are powerful people with the authority to get work done by others. They see relationship building as the latest gambit designed to challenge the managerial prerogative. What is your opinion on this?
   Prepare an outline text for a presentation on the topic for the next meeting of your board of directors.
2. Consider the situation faced by a medium-sized entrepreneural firm and indicate whether they would be well advised to build long-term relationships with their suppliers.
3. 'A properly designed organizational structure will achieve the appropriate coordination between sub-units. There is no need to develop good relationships between units'. Discuss.
4. 'When it comes to relationships you either have what it takes to form them or you don't'. How would you respond to this statement?
5. Outline the essential elements of relationship marketing and comment on its likely effectiveness for: (a) a service organization; (b) a mass production manufacturer; and (c) a manufacturer of basic chemicals.

Notes and references

1. Hales, C. (1993) *Managing Through Organisation*, London: Routledge, p. 43.
2. See, for example, McGregor, D. (1960) *The Human Side of Enterprise*, New York: McGraw-Hill; Peters, T. J. and Waterman, R. H. (1982), *In Search of Excellence*, New York: Harper & Row; and Bigelow, J. D. (ed.) (1991) *Management Skills*, Newbury Park, CA: Sage.
3. Huczynski, A. and Buchanan, D. (1991) *Organisational Behaviour*, Hemel Hempstead: Prentice Hall.
4. Etzioni, A. (1961) *A Comparative Analysis of Complex Organisations*, New York: Free Press.
5. Fiedler, F. E. (1967) *A Theory of Leadership Effectiveness*, New York: McGraw-Hill.
6. Fisher, R., Ury, W. and Patton, B. (1991) *Getting to Yes*, New York: Penguin Books.
7. Johnson, R. A. (1993) *Negotiation Basics*, Newbury Park, CA: Sage, pp. 68–93.
8. Kotter, J. P. (1982) 'What effective general managers really do', *Harvard Business Review*, November–December, pp. 156–67.
9. See Mintzberg, H. (1983) *Power in and around Organizations*, Englewood Cliffs, NJ: Prentice Hall, pp. 207–8 for a discussion on accommodating the needs of others.
10. This quotation is from Smith, A., *An Inquiry into the Nature and Causes of the Wealth of Nations*, cited in Robinson, J. (1962), *Economic Philosophy*, London: C. A. Watts, p. 53.
11. Carlisle, J. A. and Parker, R. C. (1989) *Beyond Negotiation*, Chichester: John Wiley.
12. *Ibid.*, p. 14.
13. Slovin, M. B. and Young, J. E. (1992) 'The entrepreneurial search for capital: An investment in finance'. *Entrepreneurship, Innovations and Change* 1, pp. 177–94.
14. Christopher, M., Payne, A. and Ballantyne, D. (1991), *Relationship Marketing: Bringing quality, customer service and marketing together*, Oxford: Butterworth-Heinemann.
15. Biemans, W. G. (1992) *Managing Innovation Within Networks*, London: Routledge.
16. Ford, D. (1980) 'The development of buyer–seller relationships in industrial markets', *European Journal of Marketing* 14, pp. 339–53.
17. Ford, D. (1984) 'Buyer–seller relationships in international industrial markets', *Industrial Marketing Management* 13, pp. 101–12.
18. See, for example, Christopher *et al.* (1991) *op. cit.*; Crosby, L. A., Evans, K. R. and Cowles, D. (1990), 'Relationship quality in, service selling: An interpersonal influence perspective', *Journal of Marketing* 54, pp. 68–81; or Jackson, B. B. (1985), 'Building customer relationships that last', *Harvard Business Review*, November–December, pp. 120–8.
19. Mastenbroek, W. F. G. (1993) *Conflict Management and Organisation Development*, Chichester: John Wiley, p. 10.
20. See Handy, C. (1985) *Understanding Organisations*, London: Penguin Books, pp. 222–56.
21. See Mintzberg (1983) *op. cit.*, pp. 151–62 for a discussion on ideology and pp. 130–4 for some details on the power of operators.
22. See Levinson, H. (1971) 'Conflicts that plague family business', *Harvard Business Review*, March–April, pp. 90–9; and Handler, W. C. (1991) 'Key interpersonal relationships of next-generation family members in family firms', *Journal of Small Business Management* 29, pp. 21–32.
23. Dutton, J. M. and Walton, R. E. (1965) 'Interdepartmental conflict and co-operation: Two contrasting studies', *Human Organisation* 25, pp. 207–20.
24. Two major sources are Duck, S. (1992) *Human Relationships*, London: Sage; and Fisher, R. and Brown, S. (1988) *Getting Together: Building a relationship that gets to yes*, Boston: Houghton Mifflin.
25. Duck (1992) *op. cit.*, p. 161.

26. Van de Ven, A. H. (1976) 'On the nature, formation and maintenance of relations among organisations', *Academy of Management Review* 1, pp. 34–6.
27. See Fisher and Brown (1988) *op. cit.*, pp. 64–83 for a discussion on mutual understanding. They attribute the quotation in this paragraph to Publilius Syrus. For family firm transitions, see Handler (1991) *op. cit.*
28. Bolton, J. E. (1986) *People Skills*, Sydney: Prentice Hall.
29. Cook, J. and Wall, T. (1980) 'New work attitude measures of trust, organisational commitment and personal need non-fulfilment', *Journal of Occupational Psychology* 53, pp. 39–52.
30. Fisher and Brown (1988) *op. cit.*, pp. 107–31.
31. Handler, W. C. (1989) 'The family venture', in Timmons, J. A., *The Entrepreneural Mind*, Andover, MA: Brick House, pp. 115–61.
32. Duck (1992) *op. cit.*, p. 161.
33. Maxwell, G. and Schmitt, D. R. (1967) 'Dimensions of compliance-gaining behaviour: An empirical analysis', *Sociometry* 30, pp. 350–64.
34. Duck (1992) *op. cit.*, cites the work of Petty, R. E. and Cacioppo, J. T. (1981) *Attitudes and Persuasion: Classic and contemporary approaches*, Dubuque, IA: W. C. Brown, and Eagly, A. H., Wood, W. and Chaiken, S. (1978), 'Causal inferences about communication and their effect on opinion change', *Journal of Personality and Social Psychology* 36, pp. 424–35 in support of his conclusions on influencing others.
35. Fisher and Brown (1988) *op. cit.*, pp. 149–65.
36. See Chin, R. and Benne, K. D. (1969) 'General strategies for effecting change in human systems', in Bennis, W. Benne, K. D. and Chin, R. (eds.), *The Planning of Change*, New York: Holt, Rinehart and Winston.
37. Fisher and Brown (1988) *op. cit.*, 43–63.
38. Crosby, Evans and Cowles (1990) *op. cit.*

Chapter 10

The marketing and entrepreneurship interface

Objectives

After reading this chapter the reader will understand that there is a strong interface between entrepreneurship and marketing. A common foundation and focus will be recognized in the context of SMEs. Although differences at a certain stage will be recognized, the emphasis throughout is on the similarities and how entrepreneurship impacts on marketing practice.

Introduction

It is acknowledged that SMEs have their own particular characteristics which affect the way they operate and which largely determine their preoccupations and concerns. Indeed, this view of small businesses is so commonplace that to many it is obvious. It can be said also that small business owner/managers conform to a number of stereotypes, such as being concerned mainly with the problems of the immediate future rather than consideration of the longer-term future; being essentially pragmatic as opposed to accepting new concepts; and preferring to tackle problems and decisions themselves as they occur, rather than working to clear procedures and programmes.

But what are the implications of these characteristics for formal and normal marketing planning approaches, especially when it is recognized that entrepreneurs tend to have a restricted knowledge of marketing planning practices? Experience suggests that an intuitive marketing approach exists in SMEs within every industry sector. That is to say, marketing activity is founded largely on traditional industry practices and experiences. Any attempts at formulating marketing plans using recognized marketing theory and terminology would seem to be limited and dependent on the depth of experience and knowledge of the owner/manager. Often, in many SMEs, marketing planning activity may be limited to planning for selling within a narrow industry perspective. The broader scope of marketing planning seldom features understanding or relevance, perhaps because of lack of knowledge.

Characteristics of SMEs

It is widely accepted that SMEs have characteristics different from larger companies. Sometimes these differences are ascribed simply to the factor of relative size but, while this may be true it is not always the most significant factor. Rather, the real differences are likely to concern objectives, management style and marketing. Clearly, SMEs have different characteristics from those of large companies. In addition to size, there are a number of qualitative characteristics which serve to underline the differences. These attributes are summarized by Schollhammer and Kuriloff[1] as:

Scope of operations. Small firms serve predominantly a local or regional market rather than a national or a international market.

Scale of operations. Small firms tend to have a very limited share of a given market, they are relatively small in a given industry.

Ownership. The equity of small firms is generally owned by one person, or at most, a very few people. Small firms tend to be managed directly by their owner or owners.

Independence. Small firms are independent in the sense that they are not part of a complex enterprise system such as a small division of a large enterprise. Independence also means that the firm's owner/managers have ultimate authority and effective control over the business, even though their freedom may be constrained by obligations to financial institutions.

Management style. Small firms are generally managed in a personalised fashion. Managers of small firms tend to know all the employees personally, they participate in all aspects of managing the business, and there is no general sharing of the decision-making process.

It is this last characteristic of small firms' management style that dominates much of the literature and is often cited as the single most significant factor influencing the development of a business. Indeed, there is much evidence to support the argument that the calibre and experience of management are the most important factors in determining business success.

The entrepreneurs' experience and management style will often mean that their approach to marketing will be different from professional marketing managers in large companies. For example, it is not uncommon for owner/managers in SMEs to have negative attitudes to marketing, a perception of marketing as a cost, to view distribution and selling as uncontrollable problems and, most significantly, to believe that their personal circumstances are so unique that general rules do not apply (Cohn and Lindbore). This antipathy is often manifested in the reaction to the use of marketing jargon or terminology. In fairness, however, it should be acknowledged that many of the marketing approaches employed in large companies as a matter of course have very limited relevance for SMEs — hence much jargon and terminology is meaningless and redundant to them. The Boston Matrix, for example, in emphasizing comparative market-share with the nearest competitor, has little practical value for the average SME with its few products, limited distribution and unmeasurably small market share.

The 'Ah, but it doesn't apply to me' response to a new concept or approach is often heard from entrepreneurs, who live and breathe their businesses. They are totally involved in them and, as a consequence, they tend to develop tunnel vision and a very rigid approach to their own circumstances. It is very difficult for them to look at their businesses from a different point of view or to draw parallels with other similar, although not identical, situations. In practical terms entrepreneurs are more likely to accept marketing ideas if they are jargon-free and can be easily related to their own situation. This will not necessarily ensure a conversion to marketing, but it may create a circumstance for conversion.

Marketing constraints on SMEs

Looking at the characteristics of SMEs from a marketing perspective, three broad types of constraints on marketing may be identified.[2] These are:

1. *Limited resources*, e.g. limitations on finance, marketing knowledge and time, may all contribute to limited marketing activity *vis-à-vis* to large companies and large competitors.
2. *Specialist expertise* may be a constraint because managers and entrepreneurs in SMEs tend

to be generalists rather than specialists. Traditionally, the owner/manager is a technical or craft expert; even today s/he is unlikely to be an expert trained in any of the major business disciplines. In addition, marketing expertise is often the last of the business disciplines to be acquired by an expanding SME. That is, finance and production experts (if the company is a manufacturing unit) usually precede the acquisition of a marketing counterpart.

3. *Limited impact* in the marketplace may be a constraint because SMEs have fewer orders and fewer customers and employees than larger companies. Consequently, the impact of an SME's presence in an industry, geographical area, or whatever, is likely to be limited as a result of its size alone. Similarly, because of limited resources and lack of marketing expertise, the impact on the media through advertising and publicity will often be negligible in relation to large company activities.

Marketing receptiveness of SMEs[3]

The constraints outlined above will have a significant impact on the way marketing is performed in SMEs. SMEs cannot expect to perform marketing at the highly sophisticated (and probably expensive) levels used by larger companies. Although this kind of marketing is beyond the scope of most SMEs, there is still a need, perhaps even a greater need, for an SME to perform marketing of some kind. There is an unshakeable logic which says that marketing is important to SMEs. The basis of this is that all SMEs must grow in order to survive. Some might argue that not all SMEs are growing and this may be true when considering the movement of sales or profits only. However, all firms experience change. Some products or markets will eventually, or inevitably, decline or die. These must be replaced by new products or markets. In order to fill the gap left by old products and markets the new ones must have growth.

Therefore, an SMEs growth, if you like, its ability to cope with change, is determined by *new* sales. These new sales may come from existing markets and customers and/or from new markets. In order to generate these new sales, an SME must employ some form of marketing activity, most probably a combination of products, price, promotion and distribution. Hence the importance of marketing to SMEs. However, it must be acknowledged that in some circumstances marketing is deemed to be peripheral to an SMEs requirements. Why is this?

Take a moment to consider how entrepreneurs *use* marketing. It can be argued that entrepreneurs will grasp general marketing concepts, approaches and theories and use them as they are described in the general sense. Therefore, the marketing mix in many SMEs will often be described under the headings of the four Ps (products, prices, promotion and place). Such a general use of this particular marketing concept is both wasteful and inappropriate, and consequently is not seen to function effectively. Indeed the four Ps, as first envisaged by McCarthy, were intended to serve as a convenient description of a complex set of interactions. Thus, this *use* of marketing is inevitably deemed peripheral to many business activities, since it does not appear to fit, nor have any significant impact on performance.

A second circumstance for marketing peripherality can lead to a lack of marketing credibility. Any SME may enjoy sales and profits growth without in fact *planning* any marketing activity and consequently, difficult and time-consuming formal marketing planning will be deemed unnecessary. Why should an entrepreneur learn to plan his/her marketing when business is growing without it? However, advocates of formal marketing planning would argue that by engaging in it, SMEs will actually perform better than they might otherwise do. In the circumstances just described, marketing planning has a credibility gap between apparent good and satisfactory performance and a theoretical and hypothetically better level of performance (Figure 10.1).

In addition to the credibility of marketing planning, entrepreneurs are not always *receptive* to marketing. While profits and revenue are growing the entrepreneur may not be receptive to formal marketing planning. However, in a circumstance where there is need for growth and expansion – for example, heavy investment in new plant and equipment financed on the basis of future growth or surplus capacity required to be utilized – what happens if profits and revenue level off? Previous and current selling activities are no longer effective. It is at this point that an entrepreneur will become receptive to marketing (Figure 10.2).

Similarly, where a firm enters a crisis, perhaps because of over-dependence on one large customer who is no longer able or willing to continue trading with the SME, the withdrawal of the customer's business will plunge the SME into a crisis of survival. Planned marketing can be seen as the saviour and subsequent provider of future success.

In conclusion it can be said that marketing *is* important to an SMEs growth, but where marketing is performed at a general level it may be deemed peripheral. Where growth is buoyant, formal marketing may have a credibility gap, and often the

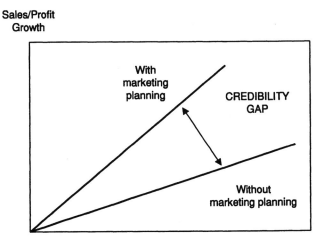

Figure 10.1 Credibility of marketing planning.

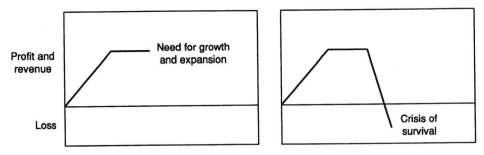

Figure 10.2 Entrepreneurs' point of marketing receptiveness.

importance of marketing is only realized, or even sought, when a firm *needs* to expand or is in a crisis of survival.

Scope of the marketing/entrepreneurship interface

The key points of the interface between entrepreneurship and marketing are opportunity, innovation and consequential change (Figure 10.3). Let us consider these three issues to gain insight into the nature of the relationship between these two areas and determine where the similarities and differences lie.

Even from its earliest pioneering days the SME owner must persistently be focused on opportunity, committed to continuously doing new things and be comfortable with the consequential change that attends effective action in the growth-oriented areas of entrepreneurship and marketing. The attitudes and focus of activity needed to accommodate these issues are both entrepreneurial and marketing in nature. We can say this because 'change', as the ultimate outcome of such effective action in both areas, is perhaps the key common denominator (Figure 10.4).

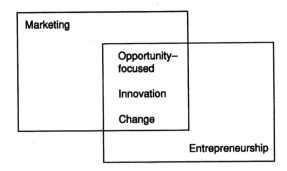

Figure 10.3 Key issues in the marketing/entrepreneurship interface.

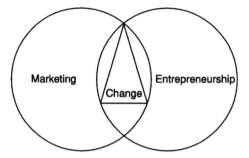

Figure 10.4 The central focus of marketing/entrepreneurship interface.

The successful adoption and implementation of a market extension strategy by a growing SME is essentially entrepreneurial. Such a successful action will have an impact on the enterprise, which may change it out of all recognition. In the early pioneering days of the enterprise there may be little to differentiate the two areas of activity. The constant change arising from the entrepreneur's commitment to continuous growth may, however, create pressures of its own which have, as we shall see, the potential to drive a wedge between entrepreneurship and marketing.

Entrepreneurship and marketing: some similarities

In the start-up period

In any new venture start-up, when products, markets, organization structure, management style and so on might be described as simple and uncomplicated, it is suggested that there is very little to differentiate marketing and entrepreneurship, at least in practice. The characteristic traits and behaviours that help us to understand entrepreneurship and the entrepreneurial process, the energies and power that drive the early start-up scenario, are similar to if not the same as those that we would expect to see in relation to the marketing activity, such as it is, at this early period of development. For example, the start-up prompt or focus is an opportunity, the origins of which lie in the marketplace. This market-focused approach is characterized by informality, extremely limited planning, if any, and limited risk and uncertainty, because the markets, and the product range too, are small and customers are few and probably well known. Resources will also be limited at this time and control mechanisms and management structures will be very simple (Figure 10.5). The factors that influence decisions made in such a scenario and how they impact on those decisions will be relatively limited, because things are so simple and uncomplicated.

We are suggesting that the way small business owners approach the sort of decision-making that will determine the progress of their enterprise will reflect their entrepreneurial character, which in turn will influence in particular the way in which

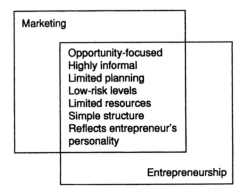

Figure 10.5 The early marketing/entrepreneurship interface.

the entrepreneur approaches the marketing of the enterprise in these early days. Marketing decisions will be characterized by the same informality, and in the same reactive, opportunistic and essentially short-term way (see Figure 10.6).

Rapid changes in technology, in social and cultural norms and in economic circumstances, changes in lifestyles, markets and products – all have created substantial scope for entrepreneurial opportunity for those with the vision to see their potential before anyone else has and who can take action to exploit them. Timmons suggests that in circumstances of environmental change characterized by chaos, confusion, inconsistencies, lags or leads, knowledge and information gaps and sundry other vacuums in the external environment, opportunities abound.[4] They exist or are created in real time in what he calls 'a window of opportunity'. Entrepreneurs are seen to have a vision of how things not only are but how they might be and are sensitive to the windows of opportunity that are opening and are likely to remain open long enough to be usefully exploited. The starting point for opportunities ultimately is what customers and the marketplace want; successful entrepreneurs understand this.

If the owner/manager is to succeed in developing the enterprise s/he needs, in addition to an entrepreneurial orientation, a very clear market or marketing orientation as well.

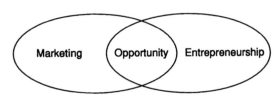

Figure 10.6 Opportunity interface.

The linkage of innovation

Innovation is about doing something new or differently, it is about activities that bring about change in some given social system. In the context of a commercial enterprise it might be seen as any renewal opportunity identified and implemented that strengthens the enterprise's position against its competitors, that allows the enterprise to maintain a competitive advantage in the long term. Innovation may be an entirely new practice or product, something no one has seen before, new to the market, or a derivative of some existing good or service. The innovation process is the management of ideas from creative conception, through filtration and the identification of the few ideas. The one idea that promises the greatest potential is then identified and developed through to ultimate commercialization. Change inevitably follows in the wake of innovative activity; the two are inseparable (see Figure 10.7).

An innovative idea is valuable if it works in the context of the company, in terms of its employees, facilities and access to resources, the company's markets and customers and the company's widening range of products. Invariably, an idea with some potential is unlikely to be highly radical. Scope is most often in the identification and development of ideas which a company has already developed or derived from something already in existence, i.e. a product that has already done well in one market might, with some development, work well in another. A marketplace similar to the company's current one might be receptive to the introduction of its existing lead product. Such innovation is continuous in character. These step-by-step, tinkering type developments, often in response to needs identified by a company's customers, have been presented as evidence of the SMEs obvious market orientation.

Contrary views suggest, however, that the SME owner committed to this tinkering approach is myopic, tied to short-term planning horizons; the owner and the company are in effect prisoners of their customers or their markets. The argument is that, for the most part, their customers actually do not know what they want except in very limited or marginal terms. However, conventional marketing wisdom places its weight squarely behind this market-pull school of thought. For longer-term strategic planning, though, greater recognition of the technology-push model is needed. In this case the emphasis of the innovation process is on identifying more inventive new ideas, ideas that are perceived as being discontinuous in character, quantum leap innovations that go beyond the customer, seeing things in ways that even the

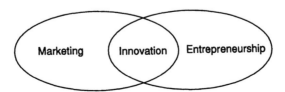

Figure 10.7 Innovation interface.

customer has yet to see them. The risks and uncertainties of such an approach are apparent and may explain why so many small firms appear to stick doggedly to continuous, incremental and essentially short-term marketing innovation strategies. It is at about this point that the practices of entrepreneurship and marketing begin to diverge.

The functions of entrepreneurship and marketing

Entrepreneurship and marketing are attitudes, ways of thinking and of behaving, ways of doing. Their scope to influence the establishment and development of new ventures is comprehensive, determining the way in which people approach their jobs and responsibilities, how they acquire resources, manage people, promote their enterprise or produce products.

The entrepreneurial process reflects this way of thinking. It is made up of the entrepreneur, the opportunity identified as valuable and the resources needed to exploit that opportunity. The entrepreneur's function in the process is to manage the best possible fit between the opportunity and the resources available, often in an environment that is subject to constant and radical change.

Managing such a marketing-oriented process requires the entrepreneur to undertake a number of key functions. The entrepreneur is the key visionary, the one to identify and evaluate the opportunity. This function demands all the entrepreneur's ability to be creative and innovative, his/her intuition and judgement. The acquisition of resources is the next major function. For the most part it is unlikely that the entrepreneur will have any substantial assets. The entrepreneur will be required to persuade backers to part with financial capital or human resources to back an idea perhaps with no tangible characteristics. The entrepreneur has to sell a vision of what might be and so will need strong negotiating skills, persuasiveness and perhaps a little wilfulness in the approach to the challenge. But supporters know that no one entrepreneur has all that is needed to make a success of an enterprise. They want to see that all the skills are available to increase its potential for success. The entrepreneur needs to function as a leader, building an entrepreneurial team that can fill the gaps in the skills deficit, motivating team members, inspiring them; this suggests not only social skills but authority too. The entrepreneur needs to give meaning and direction to the enterprise; this means some planning activity and flexibility in the face of changing circumstances. Additionally, the entrepreneur needs to keep an eye on the operational activity of the enterprise; this suggests a coordinating and controlling role. And since s/he must remain opportunity-focused, always mindful of the need for new ideas, the entrepreneur has a role to play in keeping up-to-date and knowledgeable about what is happening in the environment both inside and outside the enterprise. This suggests a commitment to a networking function as a particularly entrepreneurial approach to information and confirmation management. This issue is discussed in detail in Chapter 14. Figure 10.8 illustrates the functions of entrepreneurship and marketing.

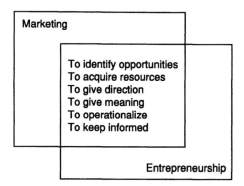

Figure 10.8 The marketing/entrepreneurship functions of the interface.

Entrepreneurship and marketing: some differences

Differences between entrepreneurship and marketing practice begin to emerge when the new venture starts to build a profile in its market and shows results for all the entrepreneur's efforts. In Chapter 1 we introduced the idea of the entrepreneurial firm as being one that is committed to the pursuit of continuous growth and development. This is what entrepreneurship really is.

The enterprise that settles down and seeks to limit its growth and development has, to all intents and purposes, ceased to be entrepreneurial. Management will be highly structured, as predictable as possible, scientific rather than organic. The new venture that begins to enjoy some successful growth also enters a period of transition. New markets, new products, many more customers, additional plant and equipment, new employees with increasingly formal and specialized training and skills – all combine to create new pressures within the enterprise.

Events begin to unfold in an uncontrolled and unexpected way. Time becomes increasingly compressed for considered decision-making, creating increasing levels of ambiguity and uncertainty about what is likely to happen next. There is increasing pressure to formalize activities and responsibilities within the enterprise. Others in the organization will have views on how the venture might be further developed and will see opportunities for growth. The founder entrepreneur will increasingly find not only that there is less and less time for creative activity but that others now have a contribution to make. People within the organization, once so comfortable with the simple structure of the early days, will find themselves uncomfortable with the lack of clarity as well as the confusion arising from the challenges of new roles, responsibilities and expected goals. The entrepreneur too will be under pressure to acknowledge the desire for greater clarity and to recognize the valuable contribution that others now joining the entrepreneurial enterprise can make. But the entrepreneur will experience a natural inclination to maintain autonomy and control and to avoid the pressure to delegate.

As the demands from markets and customers grow the simple collaborative culture of the early days gives way to increasing specialization and a systemization of operating mechanisms and controls. Plans and planning in a formal sense become commonplace, particularly in relation to marketing, in which the company is now increasingly sophisticated. Strategies reflecting long- and short-term dimensions are developed, the emphasis is on structure, discipline, systems and sequential steps, on formality.

While marketing as a specialist function in the enterprise becomes increasingly formal and systemized, what has happened to the spirit of entrepreneurship, which played such an important role in the early days of the venture? Entrepreneurship still remains the realm of the haphazard, the creative, the opportunistic, the reactive, the short-term, the informal. What appears now is that marketing and entrepreneurship are moving in opposite directions, the differences between the two become more and more apparent.

Entrepreneurship and marketing: the impact of innovation

Entrepreneurship and marketing and the marketing-oriented entrepreneur are focused on innovation and change. Really skilful entrepreneurs see things in a way no one else does. They perceive opportunities in the marketplace which perhaps are not yet fully formed but are currently no more than shapes and patterns arising from a new technology, fashion or trend, a possible cultural shift. To develop an enterprise around such an idea requires all those traits and behaviours we have discussed above. It is innovation with a quantum leap; idea generation that transcends the customer and comes up with new products, new markets, new uses and users, providing customers with products they never knew they needed or missed. Examples abound: the microwave oven, the Sony Walkman, the compact disc, the personal computer – the list is endless. These 'discontinuous innovations' are the very essence of skilful entrepreneurship.

However, here again a difference with marketing as it is practised in many firms emerges. The determination to stay close to customers, to meet their every need as far as the company's product is concerned, makes the company a prisoner of its current customer base and makes the customer the only real innovator in the relationship. Tying the company so closely to the customer is a low-risk strategy and essentially short-term in outlook. The company's marketing philosophy is myopic rather than expansive and long-term; it has become as much a barrier to real growth and opportunity as an overcommitment to efficiency. In this way marketing is potentially out of step with the skilful practice of entrepreneurship.

As the company grows and pressures build on the founding entrepreneur(s) to consolidate and systemize the management of the enterprise, their own entrepreneurial ability and commitment may be eroded. Having risked so much to get this far, the temptation to control that risk and face it less often is great. The literature refers to a 'comfort level'. In such circumstances entrepreneurship is evaporating in the organization as things settle down. It may take some new entrepreneurial effort to get things moving again.

The impact of entrepreneurship on marketing

Entrepreneurial activities and characteristics have impacted on marketing activity in SMEs. Indeed, it is possible to determine that marketing activity in SMEs is in fact entrepreneurial marketing. Such entrepreneurial marketing has a distinctive marketing style, which is characterized by the following:[5]

- *The stage of development* of the firm will have a significant bearing on the marketing activity. A young firm is likely to perform relatively simple marketing, whereas a mature SME is likely to have refined its marketing activity to a relatively sophisticated level.
- *Restricted in scope and activity*: because of their small size, the influence of the stage of development, and their limited resources, SMEs are restricted in the amount and kind of marketing activity in which they can engage.
- *Inherently informal*: SMEs do not have formal organization structures or formal systems of communication. They may have no systems at all when it comes to taking decisions on marketing.
- *Simplistic and haphazard*: because of their small size and marketing limitations, etc., and because of the influence of the entrepreneur, marketing decisions are likely to be simple and *ad hoc* in the context of formal marketing.
- *Responsive and reactive to competition*: because the SME cannot make a large impact in its marketplace relative to larger competitors, this competition tends to influence much of the market decision-making of SMEs. Rather than acting proactively, small firms tend to be reactive to the competition's marketing activity.
- *Opportunistic*: one of the inherent advantages of SMEs' marketing is the ability to react quickly and to change direction or introduce new concepts and activity. SMEs therefore tend to seize quickly on new opportunities as they occur in the market.
- *Short term*: for all these reasons and because SMEs tend not to have long-term plans or horizons, most of their marketing decisions are short-term.

These characteristics impose a fundamental marketing style on SMEs which should not be ignored; indeed, this style must be exploited. Once we have recognized these characteristics, we can move one step further towards performing effective marketing in SMEs.

Summary

While we have emphasized that entrepreneurship and marketing have a strong interface it must be recognized that they are two distinct concepts. Entrepreneurship is founded on traits and behaviours, whereas marketing is framed by approaches and techniques. From this perspective they have substantial differences at certain stages of an SMEs development and operation. However, in terms of basic concepts, philosophies and attitudes, entrepreneurship and marketing have a common bond. By recognizing this bond it is possible to envisage a meaningful and powerful concept of entrepreneurial marketing which is entirely suited to SMEs. The challenge that remains is how to harness this bond of commonality and enhance the marketing performance of an entrepreneurial-led SME.

Learning questions

1. What are the major marketing limitations of SMEs?
2. When are SMEs most receptive to marketing planning?
3. What are the fundamental similarities of entrepreneurship and marketing?
4. At what point might entrepreneurship and marketing diverge?
5. Generally, how does entrepreneurship impact on marketing?

Notes and references

1. Schollhammer, H. and Kuriloff, A. (1979) *Entrepreneurship and Small Business Management*, Chichester: John Wiley, p. 179.
2. Carson, D. (1985) 'The evolution of marketing in small firms', *European Journal of Marketing* 19 (5), pp. 7–16.
3. Carson, D. (1993) 'A philosophy for marketing education in small firms', *Journal of Marketing Management* 9, pp. 189–204.
4. Timmons, J. A. (1990) *New Venture Creation*, 3rd edition, Chicago: Richard Irwin, pp. 181–96.
5. Carson, D. and Cromie, S. (1989) 'Marketing planning in small enterprises: A model and some empirical evidence', *Journal of Marketing Management* 5 (1), Summer, pp. 33–50.

Further reading

Cohn, T. and Lindbore, R. A. (1972) 'How management is different in small companies', *An AMA Management Briefing*.
Joyce, P. *et al.* (1990) 'Barriers to change in small business: Some cases from an inner city area', *International Small Business Journal* 8 (4), pp. 49–58.
Piercy, N. (1991) *Marketing-Led Strategic Change*, London: Thorsons.
Simmonds, K. (1985) 'The marketing practice of innovation theory', *The Marketing Digest*, pp. 146–60.
Simmonds, K. (1986) 'Marketing as innovation, the eighth paradigm', *Journal of Management Studies* 23 (5), pp. 479–95.
Vrakking, W. J. (1990) 'The innovative organisation', *Long Range Planning* 23 (2), pp. 94–102.
Witcher, B. (1985) 'Innovation and marketing', *The Marketing Digest*, Winter, pp. 171–86.

Chapter 11

Entrepreneurial management

Objectives

After reading this chapter the reader will have an overview of the pioneering SME. We shall consider some of the factors that determine whether or not an SME continues to be entrepreneurial, and the reader will have an insight into the impact of being entrepreneurial on the SME. The chapter aims to give the reader an appreciation of the implications of managing an entrepreneurial enterprise and defines an entrepreneurial management approach.

Introduction

In Chapter 5 the issues pertinent to managing an SME were discussed. Some of the focus was on the characteristics of the SME, the turbulence of the environment in which SMEs operate, their relative lack of power in such circumstances and the necessary management practices. In Chapter 4 we discussed the concept of entrepreneurship and the numerous approaches that help us to understand entrepreneurial managers.

The entrepreneurial firm, though, can be distinguished from any other SME by its consistent focus on opportunity and its commitment to continuous innovation and change. However, any enterprise will be entrepreneurial only because its management is consistently entrepreneurial. In terms of its character and culture the enterprise reflects the personality and behaviour of its management. As in lifecycle models though, entrepreneurship can emerge, grow, mature and decline. The challenge of managing in an entrepreneurial small firm is to plan and organize to maintain that entrepreneurial effort to develop an entrepreneurial character within the enterprise that once initiated becomes a force in itself, driving the enterprise along a path of change and growth.

In this chapter we shall discuss how this focus on opportunities and the commitment to continuous innovation and change impacts on the SME. We consider what the implications are for managing such an enterprise. Some further thoughts on entrepreneurial management, considered first in Chapter 5 are offered in conclusion.

The entrepreneurial new venture

Lifecycle models give us a useful framework for characterizing the entrepreneurial SME and for understanding what makes it entrepreneurial. When a new venture is launched, the action is entrepreneurial, the period is pioneering. An opportunity in the marketplace has been identified and action taken to recruit the resources needed to exploit it.

These early stages are characterized by informality in relations between actors in the enterprise, by limitless energy on their part, and a high tolerance of the equally high levels of uncertainty and attendant risk that pervade these pioneering days in particular. Yet there is boundless zeal on the part of those involved and a determination to succeed. There is little structure, few specialist skills and extensive role ambiguity, with people in the company prepared to do any job. The new venture will have little in the way of resources, be they plans, skilled people, finance or current and accurate sources of information, the latter being especially critical for effective decision-making at this stage. Control and communications will tend to be highly informal, unstructured and based on the existence of strong personal relationships and on the charisma and even the magnetism of the founding entrepreneur. This will be reflected in leadership style, which in this pioneering stage will tend to be highly centralized, personalized and authoritarian in character. The founding entrepreneur is likely to experience problems with delegation and the sharing of the enterprise with others, so great is the need at this time for independence in the management of the new venture.[1]

Luckily, though, there will be few customers and the new venture will be operating in only a small number of localized markets, with few products, so the management of this new venture will be relatively simple. The founding entrepreneur alone makes the decisions on how to take the enterprise forward. The founder is involved in everything to do with the running of the business and is of necessity a generalist when it comes to managing the new venture. While the firm remains small and simple in terms of activity in its chosen market the founder can continue to play 'small business' and even make a reasonable living. So long as the enterprise does not appear to be so successful so as to attract the predatory attention of potential competitors, then all should continue well. The challenge to new business owners is keeping the business ticking over at an acceptable level to meet their material and personal needs.

Whether owner-managers who wish to contain their enterprise to a definite size, either in terms of number of employees or level of turnover, are still entrepreneurial is open to debate. One approach we suggest to understanding an individual's *degree* of commitment to entrepreneurship is to consider the degree of entrepreneurship on a continuum (see Figure 11.1). This commitment reflects their focus on opportunity and their willingness to accept the impact on them and on their enterprise of successfully managing that opportunity. The continuum suggests that some SME owners are reluctantly entrepreneurial, are, or indeed may become, essentially resistant to change, accepting it only because they must. At the other extreme the individual entrepreneur is represented as proactively keen to pursue any opportunity and to acquire and manage whatever resources are necessary to exploit it fully. Somewhere in between the individual's commitment to entrepreneurial activity can be seen as a response to opportunities that present themselves.

Influences on the entrepreneurial effort

As the enterprise begins to grow it will need to maintain an entrepreneurial character. Whether or not this happens depends wholly on the entrepreneur. It is the entrepreneur's attitude to growth and her/his appreciation of the impact that successful growth will have on the new enterprise that will be the crucial determining factors.

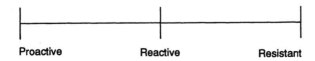

Figure 11.1 Entrepreneurial continuum.

A number of issues will have a bearing on their decision to remain proactively entrepreneurial or to exercise a degree of control over the amount of growth and change that the enterprise undergoes. First, SME owners may desire to remain independent and maintain ownership of their enterprise. Second, they may be driven, after the initial taxing effort to launch the venture, by an impulse to simplify life by keeping the enterprise small and more easily manageable. Thus they may attempt to limit the number of customers with whom they deal. As a consequence, the number of employees and external associates can be kept to a minimum. Keeping the business small will also mean that the informal rules defining the nature of relationships with people inside and outside the venture can be kept simple. The level of uncertainty and risk too can be kept to more manageable levels. Third, SME owners may harbour a genuine concern about their ability to manage successfully in a fast-growing, increasingly complex enterprise.

The challenge of entrepreneurial growth

Owner/managers' desire to maintain ownership of their enterprise and to remain independent operators will have a significant bearing on their commitment to growth. However, the individual owner/managers can never embody all the skills, the know-how and know-who, nor have access to all the resources necessary to expand the small firm on a continuous basis. Real entrepreneurial growth in an enterprise is only possible when entrepreneurs share their vision of the enterprise's potential with others who can bring to the venture new ideas, specialist skills, energy and commitment that make the achievement of that vision a real possibility. In return for their involvement, such people want to have a say in how the venture develops and grows.

The degree to which owner/managers want their enterprise to grow and develop will be reflected in their preparedness to share the management of their enterprise with others, both from within and outside the enterprise, who can help in a material way. This will have implications for the style of management in the enterprise, recruitment policies and teambuilding activities, the generation and maintenance of an appropriate climate that encourages entrepreneurship, and the development of relationships beyond the enterprise.[2]

Keeping SME management simple

The pioneering stage of the new business venture is recognized as the most chaotic, uncertain and risky period, with only a third of enterprises surviving beyond the first eighteen months. Not surprisingly, many owner/managers, having got beyond this period and established a viable business of sorts are reluctant to expose themselves or their enterprises to further risk and uncertainty by seeking ever more growth. The often overwhelming temptation is to keep life simple by keeping the business small.

Thus, the number of external rules and regulations and the level of risk and uncertainty are kept to acceptable and tolerable limits.

Ability to manage growth

Growth will have an impact on the small firm. It will change the nature of the informal roles and relationships that characterized the very early pioneering days and increase the level of complexity in terms of the rules and regulations needed to control more efficiently the increasingly larger enterprise. Many small business owners feel a genuine concern about their ability to manage in such rapidly changing, increasingly complex circumstances, in particular when they have to give leadership and guidance to employees who may have higher levels of current, specialist knowledge and training than the owner/manager. The problem is how they can manage these people and maintain an entrepreneurial thrust, which may often appear to be detrimental to the more formal backgrounds of the new staff.

Maintaining entrepreneurship

Continued entrepreneurship is not enough, though, for potential growth if this means simply 'more of the same'. The energies, the vision, the competencies required to address the challenges of starting a new venture differ substantially from those required to take that venture on to a consistently growth-oriented track. What is needed if the pioneering enterprise is to have any real chance for growth is a maturing entrepreneurship which, while remaining opportunity-focused and innovative, is professionally competent in managing the growing enterprise, in giving leadership, in sharing a vision of its potential and in building an entrepreneurial team to achieve it.

Such entrepreneurship will be unconstrained by debates about ownership but will see in growth a potential for a different type of independence, one built on an increasingly strengthened profile and competitive position in an industry and marketplace. It will be undaunted by the complex challenges that attend growth from both inside and outside the enterprise, indeed it will seek to tackle them in a typically positive and innovative way. Finally, it will be an entrepreneurship that will have developed the necessary professional management skills that will relieve the lead entrepreneurs of any lingering concerns they might have regarding their personal ability to manage the growing enterprise beyond its pioneering stage.

The stages of entrepreneurship beyond the pioneering stage can be illustrated as a lifecycle (see Figure 11.2). The key elements of the model are the entrepreneurial effort, the entrepreneurial scenario and the return on the entrepreneurial effort. The model seeks to represent the relationships between these elements and give a basis for understanding the challenge of maintaining the entrepreneurial effort. This, we suggest, is reflected in the energy, zeal and level of commitment of the individual to

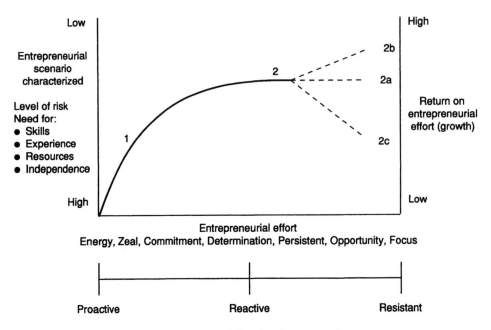

Figure 11.2 Entrepreneurial effort over the lifecycle of an enterprise.

establishing and building an enterprise by constantly focusing on market opportunities and innovative activity. The entrepreneurial scenario is characterized by the level of risk, uncertainty and chaos attending the launch of the new venture and the individual's need for skills, knowledge, experience and personal independence, not to mention adequate resources to launch the venture. Finally, the return on entrepreneurial effort reflects the degree to which the venture develops and grows over time as a consequence of the entrepreneur's efforts and changing circumstances.

From the model let us consider three points. At point (1) the entrepreneurial effort is highest at the outset of the venture and the entrepreneurial scenario is probably at its most adverse. The level of risk and uncertainty too is high, as are individuals' needs for skills and experience. Their desire to maintain their independence will be particularly significant at this time too. Their need for resources is also going to be high, as indeed will be their difficulties in gaining access to them. The return on entrepreneurial efforts in these early days is at its lowest. Yet entrepreneurs have a vision of how things might be and they are hungry enough proactively to seek ways to fulfil their ambitions.

At point (2) the model suggests that towards the late growth/early maturity stage, the level of entrepreneurial effort has arrived at a mid-point. The circumstances here are characterized by relatively low risk and a degree of sophistication and professionalism in the management of the enterprise. Access to resources is less problematic, the enterprise has a presence in the marketplace so it is easier to acquire whatever is needed for any new innovations. Individual entrepreneurs now are more reactive in their outlook. They and the enterprise may be less hungry for change and new opportunities, which characterized the early days. The return on current entrepreneurial effort is more than satisfactory and life for the entrepreneur is rewarding. Why spoil it?

As with lifecycle models generally we have a framework for gaining an insight into the options facing the SME at this time. To take action to extend the maturity stage (at point 2a), to seek to bring the enterprise on to a venture renewal track (at point 2b) or to do nothing and, in an entrepreneurially dynamic environment, risk losing everything (at point 2c).

Pressures for change

The truly entrepreneurial enterprise does not stand still. Constantly in search of new opportunities, entrepreneurs' focus primarily on the external environment of customers, competitors and markets — after all, the growth of any enterprise is achieved through effective action in the markets for its products. The successful pursuit and exploitation of opportunities emanating from the external market, however, will have an impact on the existing SME by creating pressure for internal change.

In recent times research has sought to spotlight the crucial importance for managers of adopting strategies for the internal market similar to those adopted so successfully in the company's external markets. There can be little doubt, though, that the successful implementation of marketing strategies in the organization's external market will impact on the existing organization bringing about changes of all kinds; for example, in the way resources are allocated, how information is communicated, the roles people play and in the very structures needed to ensure the continuous and successful delivery of externally focused marketing strategies.[3]

Any failure to manage these change processes and maintain a good fit between what is happening in the firm's external and internal environments will undermine the successful implementation of those strategies for growth. Once again, change and the management of change as a consequence of successfully adopting and implementing marketing-led strategies are key issues and lie at the heart of understanding the entrepreneurial energies at work within the enterprise. They are critical to understanding the challenge of management in the entrepreneurial small firm. These entrepreneurial energies force a transition or transformation in the fabric of the organization and a consequential change in the way things are done by the people who work there, including the lead entrepreneur.[4]

The transformation characterized

The entrepreneurial enterprise goes through a transformation with each successfully implemented, marketing-led growth strategy. In the pioneering stages the company is close to its few customers. Relationships, communications systems and decision-making are all informal. There is a great deal of ambiguity about the roles and tasks people play in the enterprise, control systems and accountability are unclear, the level of specialist or management skills are limited and the fortunes of the enterprise remain firmly under the personal guidance of the founder entrepreneur, who is the sole source of entrepreneurial thinking and energy. Chaos and unpredictability typify these early days.[5]

However, with each success comes pressure for change, forcing a transformation on the new venture and the people in it. This period will be characterized by a rapid succession of dilemmas or challenges which will have implications for the ongoing management of the enterprise. First, there will be the sense that the challenges confronting the growing venture are getting too big and that things are getting out of hand. As a consequence increasing pressure is exerted on existing communication systems and organization structures. The pressure also begins to open up gaps in the skills mix of the existing staff members and exposes deficits in the lead entrepreneur's management competencies. Increasing confusion emerges and not a little resentment over people's roles and responsibilities during the transition. Crisis management, 'fire-fighting', and an increasing loss of focus characterize this period, leading to pressures for new systems, clear structures, more formal controls and greater accountability. And with the emergence of specialist skills comes pressure too for increased decentralization and a greater sharing of power.

The threat to entrepreneurship in the growing venture

One possible victim of entrepreneurial success is the culture within the enterprise for entrepreneurship itself. The successful application of pressure for greater stability in the venture as a reaction to constant change undermines the acceptability of change as part of the emerging culture. In addition any strict definition or clarification of people's roles and tasks in the venture, reinforced by the emergence of specialist functions and supporting structures (with implied routes for promotion), undermines the early culture of collaboration and the sharing of ideas. The new commitment to tighter operating mechanisms and control systems compromises the potential for initiative and reduces the scope of people in the enterprise to take risks, to act entrepreneurially.

Implications for management

With mounting pressure for greater stability and structure in the enterprise, the lead entrepreneur faces a fundamental management challenge in order somehow to maintain the entrepreneurial character of the venture and to ensure it remains focused on opportunity and growth. This can only be done if founding entrepreneurs are prepared to share the management of their enterprises with the people who work for them and if they create a climate within the enterprise that is essentially entrepreneurial in that it encourages those employees within it to be opportunity focused and innovative too.

Specifically, they must give leadership, they must provide vision and develop it in others in the enterprise, they must build and manage entrepreneurial teams and provide appropriate organizational structures in the enterprise to facilitate their work. They must plan for change and act as a catalyst in the enterprise to ensure that things do happen, that goals are clearly identified and action is taken to achieve them. Ultimately, they must acquire the appropriate skills to manage the changes occurring in their enterprise, and gain access, through effective networking, to the necessary resources to implement them.[6]

Giving leadership

SME owner/managers must play the critical and pivotal role of the lead entrepreneur in the enterprise. Therefore, they must provide vision and direction to those working in the enterprise and such structure as is needed, without crushing initiative, to ensure things get done. They must build entrepreneurial teams within the enterprise and encourage members to be creative and innovative in the resolution of problems or the exploitation of opportunities. They must protect the innovative, empower colleagues, secure resources and encourage a climate within the enterprise, as it grows, that is tolerant and committed to planned change.

Providing vision

As lead entrepreneurs, the owners of growing SMEs must provide a focus for those working for them and a vision of the venture's longer-term direction, notwithstanding the twists and turns that characterize its progress *en route*. They also need to encourage those who work with them to accept ownership of that vision and to identify their own progress and development over the longer run with this vision.

Building entrepreneurial teams

Building entrepreneurial teams within the growing enterprise is a further critical management activity of lead entrepreneurs within the entrepreneurial small firm. As the enterprise undergoes a transformation the attendant pressures highlight the growing skills deficit within it. New specialist skills, undoubtedly considered unnecessary in the pioneering days, are now urgently needed as the challenges facing the growing enterprise become more complex. Identifying the nature of such gaps and selecting and recruiting the best possible people available to fill them becomes an essential activity for management in the entrepreneurial SME if it is to remain entrepreneurial. Critical too are the steps taken to create an environment within the enterprise which encourages those carefully selected people to stay with it as it continues to develop and grow. Good people don't stay in an organization long if their value is not recognized and rewarded. Consequently, the entrepreneurial manager has a key role to play in motivating entrepreneurial people within the SME, in empowering them and encouraging them to take initiatives and in offering protection to the very innovative, who consistently challenge and disturb the status quo.

Providing structure

Organization structures are often seen as the very antithesis of entrepreneurial activity and potential, however, the provision of some sort of loose structure in the enterprise becomes essential as it grows. The lead entrepreneur must play a core role in this critical activity if the innovative efforts of the people within the enterprise are not to be misdirected and squandered.

Furthermore, with constant and rapid growth, confusion and resentment can begin to build as people employed in the organization, both original employees and new recruits, become increasingly unclear about their changing roles and the nature of the relationships that exist between them. The pressure will mount for clearer definitions of people's relationships with each other within the organization.

The provision of some structure clarifies the roles and responsibilities of people in the venture, ensuring an integration, balance and direction to their activities. People know what is expected of them and where their efforts contribute to the continued progress of the enterprise.

Planning for change

The truly entrepreneurial enterprise strives to anticipate change opportunities and to become increasingly proactive in its commitment to innovation and continual renewal. Dissatisfaction with the status quo, therefore, characterizes the culture of the business, and the entrepreneurial manager plays the central role in nurturing and maintaining an environment within the enterprise which sustains such a culture. Planning for and managing change within the enterprise becomes as fundamental a part of the manager's thinking as the very definition of what business the company is in.

It calls for practice in creative problem-solving and imagination in decision-making, for experimentation and adaptability and the involvement of everyone in the enterprise in the pursuit and accommodation of continuous change.

Ensuring things happen

The innovative owner/manager in the entrepreneurial SME plays the key management role of ensuring things get done within the enterprise. As a primary catalyst they must be able to commit considerable time and effort to the development of the enterprise and to be able to draw from those working with them comparable levels of effort and commitment. The lead entrepreneurs must act as role models; indeed, within the enterprise they must be energetic, adventurous, action-oriented but able to manage the attendant stress of such a commitment to achieving goals in a positive way.

Acquiring skills and resources

The management of a truly entrepreneurial SME means managing an enterprise which is, by design, experiencing continued growth and development. This growth is a consequence of the management's opportunity focus and continuous commitment to innovation and change. In the pioneering period, when customers and employees were few in number and the demand for resources was small, relationships were relatively uncomplicated and simple to manage. The entrepreneur worked with employees on the shopfloor and managed the strategic progress of the small firm by the 'seat of his pants', gut feeling and intuition. He/she saw an opportunity, felt it could work and pursued it. He/she was happiest at the cutting edge of operations in the enterprise, doing things, solving problems, looking up now and then to see how – and, indeed, where – things were going.

Relationships within and beyond the enterprise become more complex as it grows in size, in terms of the numbers and types of customers, markets and products it addresses and the type of skilled people it must employ or be in contact with if it is to remain entrepreneurial. The lead entrepreneur must be prepared to change role within the enterprise, from one who is at the sharp end of innovative activity in the business to one who manages it in others, giving focus and guidance to those doing it.

Conclusions

To give leadership, sell a vision, develop and motivate entrepreneurial teams, encourage an opportunity focus in others and maintain the entrepreneurial effort of the enterprise calls for a whole new array of competencies. To manage effectively in the entrepreneurial SME business owners must seek to develop these in themselves. This critical issue of developing entrepreneurial competencies, and in particular the planned management of personal contact networks, is extensively developed in Chapters 14 and 15 as innovative responses to managing in the entrepreneurial marketing-oriented SME.

Summary

In this chapter we have considered the entrepreneurial small and medium-sized enterprise, how it might be considered to be entrepreneurial and how it might differ from SMEs which are not. The primary focus was the propensity of the SME to seek out opportunities for change and to accommodate the impact of those changes on its culture, structure, roles, relationships and control mechanisms. The characteristics of the entrepreneurial scenario, the entrepreneurial effort and the return on entrepreneurial effort highlight the implications of managing in such a dynamic environment. Effective management in these conditions has implications for management styles, orientations and competencies.

Learning questions

1. What is an entrepreneurial SME?
2. In what ways does the entrepreneurial SME differ from one that is not?
3. Discuss the likely impact on the pioneering new venture of a continued commitment to entrepreneurship.
4. What are the key characteristics of the entrepreneurial transformation?
5. What factors determine whether or not an SME remains entrepreneurial?
6. Discuss the implications for the entrepreneur of managing this entrepreneurial transformation.

Notes and references

1. Timmons, J. (1990) *New Venture Creation*, Chicago: Richard Irwin.
2. Kao, J. J. (1990) *The Entrepreneurial Organization*, Englewood Cliffs, NJ: Prentice Hall.
3. Piercy, N. (1992) *Marketing Led Strategic Change*, London: Butterworth-Heinemann.
4. Miner, J. B. (1990) 'Entrepreneurs, high growth entrepreneurs and managers: Contrasting and overlapping motivational patterns', *Journal of Business Venturing* 5, pp. 221–34.
5. Stewart, V. (1983) *Change: The challenge of management*, Maidenhead: McGraw-Hill.
6. Lessem, R. (1986) *Enterprise Development*, Aldershot: Gower.

Further reading

Greiner, L. E. (1972) 'Evolution and revolution as organizations grow', *Harvard Business Review*, July–August, pp. 64–73.

Moss, Kanter, R. (1985) *The Change Masters*, London: Unwin.

Scott, M. and Bruce, R. (1987) 'Five stages of growth in small business', *Long Range Planning* **20** (3), pp. 45–52.

Part Three

Chapter 12

A general framework for developing entrepreneurial marketing

Objectives

After reading this chapter the reader will appreciate that entrepreneurs are likely to have a learning perspective based on experience rather than structured theory. The reader will recognize that formal marketing techniques must be adapted to suit the entrepreneur and the SME. It will be recognized that entrepreneurial learning can be enhanced by the utilization of appropriate competencies and networks and that these dimensions must be seen in the context of a holistic framework.

Introduction

This chapter sets out a framework for entrepreneurial marketing. There are two broad aspects here: that of adapting established marketing techniques to suit the SME environment and that of introducing new concepts to aid marketing in SMEs. The framework allows the entrepreneur to employ both aspects in the development of the

SME's marketing activity. When adapting marketing techniques the emphasis will be on matching marketing techniques to the SME circumstance. In relation to ntroducing new concepts in developing marketing, the focus will be on the concepts of marketing competencies and marketing networks.

Learning and entrepreneurs

In order to understand the need for advocating a framework for entrepreneurial marketing we should remind ourselves of the problems referred to in this text. We have indicated that formal management approaches are sometimes inappropriate for SMEs and entrepreneurs. Similarly, we have suggested that formal marketing techniques may also be inappropriate because of (1) the inherent characteristics and behaviours of entrepreneurs, and (2) the size of SMEs and the resources available to them. The general thesis has been that management must be inherently entrepreneurial in nature, and combined with this marketing techniques must be appropriate for SMEs. If we accept this, then we have a strong argument for an approach that overcomes these problems, and hence a framework for entrepreneurial marketing development.

However, we must also recognize that if such a framework is to be accepted and implemented, entrepreneurs must be able to absorb the framework. This recognition is, of course, inherent in the proposed framework, but it is based on an understanding of the entrepreneurial learning process. Let us reflect for a moment on the basis of this learning process.

How do adults learn? What foundations do they rely on to enable them to learn and to accept new ideas, concepts and techniques? It must be recognized that individuals come to learning with different perspectives. We can categorize these as academically strong/weak and experientially strong/weak. Clearly age (i.e. young or mature) may have a bearing on these perspectives. Let us consider these perspectives through some general propositions, which are nevertheless fundamental to adult learning.

Proposition 1a. People with a strong academic foundation tend to view marketing from its theoretical perspective. That is, they tend to focus on the value of theory because it is what they know and understand and perhaps even believe.

Proposition 1b. People with a weak academic foundation tend to view marketing from the non-theoretical, practical perspective. That is, they tend to focus on the practical realities of marketing as they perceive them perhaps because they have experience of practical marketing.

This issue of experience leads us to another proposition.

Proposition 2a. Those people who have strong experience tend to focus on making marketing work. That is, they *use* their experience by applying it to problems of marketing.

Proposition 2b. Those people who have weak experience of marketing tend to rely on relating or applying theory to practice. That is, they tend to *use* theory as it is stated rather than taking account of the situation in which it is being applied.

In this context, the aspects of academic strength and weakness and experience strength and weakness have little to do with intelligence. It is more likely to be determined by the age of the individual and the length of time an individual has been away from an academic institution and the amount of experience gleaned since. This assumption allows us to state a number of other propositions.

Proposition 3. People with strong marketing decision-making experience tend to be older, and people with weak marketing decision-making experience tend to be younger.

Proposition 4. Older people tend to have a low academic foundation and younger people tend to have a high academic foundation. This is because older people have been separated from academic study for some time, whereas younger people have recent contact with academic study.

Proposition 4 allows us to relate to propositions 1b and 2a and generate our next proposition.

Proposition 5. The older a person and the more experienced they are, the greater the tendency that they will rely on experience to the detriment of academic foundation.

Therefore, they become intuitive decision-makers rather than taking decisions based on theoretical and logical dimensions. This is on the basis that older people (with experience) have difficulty relating back to theoretical and logical dimensions. Thus, they tend to describe marketing in terms of their own experience. Similarly, we can combine propositions 1a and 2b for our next proposition.

Proposition 6. Younger people, with strong academic foundation, tend to describe real marketing in theoretical terms and have difficulty relating to pragmatic dimensions of marketing.

What are the consequences of our discussion so far? It is clear that the degree of business and marketing experience or lack of it, age and nearness (or otherwise) of academic foundation combine to influence the receptiveness of individuals to marketing learning and the way that they will perceive marketing, either theoretically or practically.

If, in general terms, we classify entrepreneurs as being older and therefore low on academic foundation and strong on experience, what are the implications for their learning and improving their marketing performance? It is likely that they will find it difficult to learn new concepts which are too academic. Indeed, their experience will make them question the validity of such theoretical concepts.

We can summarize this discussion by suggesting that entrepreneurs' strengths in terms of learning can be listed as follows:

- They are informal in the way they do business.
- They focus on practical dimensions.
- They are weak on recent academic foundation.
- They are strong on experience.
- Their experience causes them to question theories.

- They do 'real' marketing intuitively.
- They focus on experience regardless of theory.

These points go a long way to helping us understand why entrepreneurs do not accept formal marketing techniques because they could easily be deemed to be too academic. Equally, if any learning is to take place, the topic must take account of the characteristics of the entrepreneurs' experience circumstances if it is to be accepted and used.

This, therefore, is the justification of our framework for developing entrepreneurial marketing. The framework does indeed take account of the entrepreneurs' experience dominance by introducing new concepts which have foundations in the inherent characteristics of entrepreneurship. The framework also recognizes that marketing techniques which are perceived as being too academic and formal are unlikely to be accepted by entrepreneurs. Therefore, marketing techniques must be adapted to match the characteristics of SMEs and the inherent characteristics of the entrepreneur. The general framework is outlined in Figure 12.1 and explained in more detail below.

Adapting marketing

The objective here is the adaptation of formal marketing to suit the characteristics of entrepreneurs and in doing so take account of the characteristics of SMEs. Let us

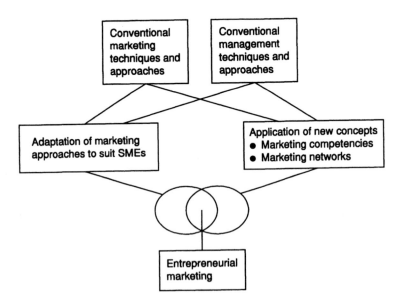

Figure 12.1 A general framework for developing entrepreneurial marketing.

look at some examples of how this can be done and conceptualize the outcomes of the adaptation process.

We shall begin by reminding ourselves of the inherent marketing characteristics of SMEs. You will recall that we identified three broad constraints on marketing. These were:

1. Limited resources, particularly in relation to marketing knowledge and the actual time available to do marketing activity, as well as the obvious restrictions of capital available for doing marketing.
2. Lack of specialist expertise, because there is unlikely to be room for a specialist concentrating on only one functional aspect such as marketing.
3. Limited impact on the marketplace, because of the above and because of the relative smallness of the SME relative to the overall market size.

In this context let us now consider some marketing adaptations.

First, the *adaptation* of formal marketing to suit the characteristics of entrepreneurs. We have discussed earlier that a normative model of marketing planning is inherently formal, follows sequential and structured steps and requires discipline and short- and long-term time-spans. Because it is all these things, it is inherently unsuited to entrepreneurial decision-making characteristics. However, it is a proven technique of marketing management decision-making and should therefore merit use in SMEs' marketing decision-making. Thus, what needs to be done is to match this technique to suit the characteristics and capabilities of the entrepreneur. This can be done simply by stripping a technique such as the marketing planning process down to its two inherent component parts – external considerations and internal considerations (Figure 12.2). By doing this, entrepreneurs need not be concerned

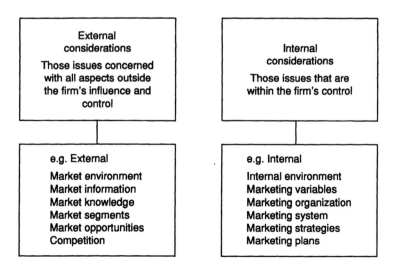

Figure 12.2 Adapted marketing planning process.

with the rigours of the technique, but the integrity of the process is maintained by addressing these two issues. Thus, entrepreneurs need consider only those *relevant* issues outside the firm's influence and control, and all those issues that are within the firm's control. In doing so, the entrepreneur is implicitly following a marketing planning approach, albeit loosely, but in such a way that is compatible with the entrepreneur's characteristics.

The entrepreneur is inherently considering the marketing environment in the broadest sense while implicitly taking account of opportunities and threats, competition, market segments and gleaning knowledge and information. Similarly, in considering internal issues the entrepreneur is implicitly including all aspects of marketing, albeit not in grandiose and jargonistic terms, but in a way that suits the firm.

A second consideration in matching small firms and marketing is to take cognizance of the stages of marketing development of the firm. The basis of this lies in accepting the concept of the evolution of marketing in small firms. This can be divided into distinct stages of marketing development (Figure 12.3). In the early days marketing in many small firms will simply be that of reacting to customer enquiry and demand. This is acceptable until sales/profits level off or decline. At this point entrepreneurs will begin to tinker with marketing techniques, for example, try a little advertising, produce a brochure, go to an exhibition. The essence of this marketing is that it is uncoordinated and wasteful, and may be only moderately effective. Its limited impact will eventually lead to sales/profits levelling off at only a marginally higher level than before. The entrepreneurial stage of development is where entrepreneurs concentrate all or most of their time and energy on marketing activity. Such a concentration increases the overall level of marketing activity and enables a substantial learning

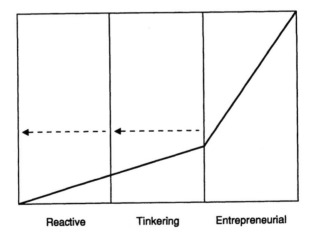

Reactive   Tinkering   Entrepreneurial

Figure 12.3 Stages of marketing development.
Source: Adapted from David Carson (1990), 'Some exploratory models for assessing small firms' marketing performance: A qualitative approach', *European Journal of Marketing* 24(11), pp. 1–51.

curve on marketing performance to develop. Eventually, the firm will mature enough to employ a professional marketing expert who can proactively develop the overall marketing performance of the company.

If the logic of these stages is accepted, it becomes obvious that an SME is at its most vulnerable at the reactive and tinkering stages. It is here that the firm may succumb to any number of environmental adversities because it is ill-equipped to deal with these in any meaningful sense. It is incumbent on an entrepreneur to recognize that the reactive and tinkering stages need to be contracted and that this can best be achieved by becoming immersed in sound marketing appropriate to SMEs. This can be done by adapting appropriate marketing techniques to suit the entrepreneur's capabilities.

Another approach is to encourage the entrepreneur to do marketing in the situation specific. This goes back to the earlier point that much of marketing in SMEs is done at the level of general concepts, approaches and theories. But this means that it is explicitly not matching the situation-specific characteristics of the SME and its market (Figure 12.4).

In doing marketing entrepreneurs must take full account of increasingly specific characteristics in relation to their firm. Thus, to begin with, the characteristics peculiar to SMEs must be taken fully into account; equally, the type of marketing in terms of goods, services or other types of marketing is important. In addition, industry-specific characteristics and norms must be considered. Finally, the

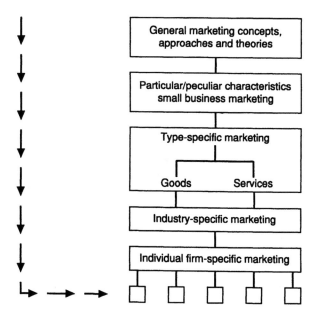

Figure 12.4 SME situation-specific marketing.

characteristics of the individual firm and its position in relation to other firms must be taken into account.

The argument here is that in any way and in every circumstance SMEs must be matched to specific marketing, and that useful marketing is *unique* to the individual entrepreneur and the firm.

When you have recognized this unique marketing dimension, and related it to the 'stages of marketing development' referred to above, then it is possible to formulate the notion that the level of marketing activity undertaken by an entrepreneur will be influenced by these. One can argue that entrepreneurs will do marketing in various degrees at different levels of activity depending on a multiplicity of circumstances. For example, an SME which does *little or no marketing* is likely to be largely reactive to customer enquiry. It will have little or no knowledge of its customers and where they come from; any knowledge it does have and any marketing it carries out will be fragmented, haphazard and disjointed, the latter done without any clear purpose in mind. Compare this with an SME that undertakes marketing as an instinctive activity. Such marketing will be *implicit and simple marketing*. Such a firm will do marketing as a natural part of business activity but its marketing remains fragmented, owing to a lack of resources, lack of knowledge of marketing activities in general and the necessity for this knowledge at all.

A third level of marketing activity can be classified as that which is *explicit and sophisticated marketing*. This occurs where companies perform marketing activity as part of a coordinated and integrated programme, with clear objectives and purpose. This need not be explicitly stated, but will reveal itself in the way a firm describes a situation and in the breadth of marketing activities utilized.

New concepts

What we have described so far accepts the principle of matching SMEs and marketing. The adaptations of marketing illustrated above all acknowledge the resource constraints of SMEs. The adaptations are also true to the basic principles of the marketing approaches and techniques on which they are based. In essence, therefore, what we have is the basis of part of our framework for marketing in SMEs. However, we must now acknowledge the influence of the entrepreneur in such marketing and in doing so, take cognizance of entrepreneurial characteristics so that we can complete our framework for entrepreneurial marketing in SMEs. We have positioned ourselves to argue that the best way of doing this is to address the concepts of competency and networks. By utilizing these proactively, we can argue that they are indeed new concepts of entrepreneurial marketing. Both new concepts have been defined and have been positioned within the broad scope of management, in both the context of management skills and management relationships. Both new concepts will be discussed in some depth in the following chapters. Our aim here is to state simply why they are important and to outline their purpose in developing entrepreneurial marketing.

Entrepreneurial marketing competencies

The importance of management competency skills has long been recognized by writers in the field. Indeed, skills development among manual workers has been the focus of much training in industry for many years. It is only recently, though, that the concept of developing management skills, or competencies has become genuinely fashionable. Previously, the development of management competencies was viewed in tandem with a thorough appreciation and understanding of the functional techniques of management.

Until recently writers on management competency development have been concerned with defining the scope of management competencies and then exploring how appropriate competencies can be learned by managers. Not surprisingly, the scope of management competencies is very broad and wide-ranging. Competency skills can be deemed to be important in all aspects of management, ranging from behaviourial skills such as motivation and leadership, to analytical skills such as problem–solving and situation analysis, to organizational skills such as delegation and responsibility. It is possible to identify a significant number of management competencies across the whole domain. When it is broken down to this level of category it becomes a daunting task to think of how such a range of competencies can be developed within a management framework. Of course, management trainers have tended to concentrate on developing those competencies deemed to be most important in any given circumstance.

Because of the need to concentrate on most important or most useful competencies, there has been a tendency to focus on those competencies that cover most aspects of management. It is easy to see that such competencies will be general in nature. For example, at a general level all management is concerned with motivation and direction, authority and delegation, planning and control. Consequently, the competencies which come closest to such concepts are those that have received most attention in management education and training.

We have argued elsewhere in this text that marketing and entrepreneurship have as their common bond management. It seems appropriate therefore that competency development at the general level will adequately serve entrepreneurs and marketers in improving their performance efficiency. However, we have argued more strongly and consistently that management techniques and approaches must be adapted to suit the characteristics of entrepreneurs and marketers if they are to become more effective. Therefore, if our argument is sound, management competency development at the general level is unlikely to enhance the performance of the marketing entrepreneur meaningfully. What is needed, therefore, is the identification of those competencies that are most appropriate to entrepreneurial marketers.

Having determined which competencies are appropriate, it is important to outline how these can be developed and utilized to best advantage. It is this issue that is the subject of Chapter 13 and the final chapter in this text.

Entrepreneurial marketing networks

It has long been recognized that networks play an important part in managers' everyday life. Dynamic managers thrive on making new contacts and maintaining and utilizing existing contacts for the purposes of securing business or moving deals forward. The concept of a business network and its importance to doing business is well documented in the literature. Business networks pervade all aspects of business, regardless of industry or company size.

However, if we consider the characteristics of SMEs and the entrepreneurs who run them, we can begin to appreciate the importance of networks. As we have seen, SMEs have limited resources and this means that they cannot enjoy the benefits of large-scale management decision-making. An example is manifested in the marketing area whereby an SME is unlikely to be able to have large-scale advertising and promotion or employ many sales staff. Similarly, an SME is unlikely to commission market research consultants to carry out a large survey of consumers.

What does an entrepreneur do to compensate for this lack of capability?

One principal way in which an entrepreneur will compensate for the lack of resources is to do what comes naturally to the entrepreneurial character, that is, network personal contacts. The personal contact network (PCN) is a well-known phenomenon of entrepreneurship, and is entirely inherent to the entrepreneur's approach to doing business. The PCN has been described in a whole manner of different guises, ranging from its density to its diversity, the psychological and geographical distances between its members, and its uniqueness (or otherwise) to an individual entrepreneur. Whatever the description there is one factor common to all networks and that is that, generally, they are informal. That is, an entrepreneur does not set out to establish a network; instead, such networks evolve from being in business. An entrepreneur will consult many people in the process of taking decisions; such consultations will, more often than not, occur as part of informal conversations and they will occur as *part* of the exchange; the entrepreneur is unlikely to have set out to introduce a topic so as to glean information. Such conversations may happen with people who are part of the network, family members or people as diverse as the bank manager, business competitor or supplier.

So, given the importance of the personal contact network to doing business in SMEs an interesting question to ask is whether this powerful tool can be harnessed to improve marketing decision-making and performance. If this is to be done it will be necessary to follow a logic similar to that for competency development in marketing, that is, we must identify those components of the network that are most conducive to progressing marketing thought on the part of the entrepreneur. The logic here is to argue that there is such a thing as a marketing network within the PCN. In some cases this marketing network may be the PCN in its entirety; in other cases it may be only a few people who are more directly involved in aspects of marketing. Whatever the case, the underlying point is that the PCN will be used for different purposes. The entrepreneur will raise issues of different concern and take cognizance of the views of the network. Given that SMEs are generally marketing led because they are growing and developing, then it is probable that many of the issues raised with the PCN are marketing issues.

If we accept that PCNs play an important part in helping and perhaps shaping the marketing decisions of an SME, then we should look for ways in which we can harness such a resource. If PCNs are used informally and, in some cases can be used semi- or subconsciously by the entrepreneur, then in these circumstances we have an under-utilized resource. Our aim in addressing this issue as an integral part of our 'framework', then, is to harness this resource by using the marketing network *proactively* and *formally* rather than subconsciously and informally.

Entrepreneurial marketing framework

Let us take a moment to explain a little more carefully the component parts of the framework illustrated in Figure 12.1. There are four essential components which combine to make up the framework: there are conventional management *and* marketing techniques and approaches, the adaptation dimension, and application of the new concepts of marketing competencies *and* networks. These are considered under the following headings.

Conventional management and marketing techniques and approaches

It should be recognized that there are few entirely new techniques and approaches to management and marketing. Instead, we contend that most conceptual thought progression is evolutionary in nature in that new ideas and concepts feed off old established dimensions and often set them in a new context. Thus most contemporary thinking in relation to management and marketing is firmly rooted in the established and conventional thought processes of the past. This should be viewed as a rich heritage built on long-established thought processes. Of course, as the management and marketing literature matures and develops, it is natural that it will begin to explore new avenues. The situation specifics of these new avenues or contexts mean that conventional techniques and approaches, which in the past may have held credence in more general contexts, become inappropriate when set in a highly specific context.

It is in this circumstance that entrepreneurial marketing is positioned. However, in our framework we recognize that we must consider, as a foundation, appropriate management and marketing techniques and approaches, *at a general level*, and then *use* these techniques either by adaptation or in a new setting.

Adapting conventional approaches and applying new concepts

As we have discussed above, our framework, while being founded on general techniques and approaches to management and marketing, combines the adaptation of these approaches and at the same time acknowledges the influence of entrepreneurs' inherent characteristics. In doing so it recognizes the importance of networking and the decision-making competencies of marketing. The framework, therefore, is about combining the adaptation of marketing techniques and approaches with the proactive utilization of a marketing network and concentration on appropriate marketing decision-making competencies.

The consequent culmination of these combinations forms the essence of entrepreneurial marketing, that is, marketing that is entirely suited to SMEs' resources and entrepreneurs' characteristics. The importance of marketing competencies and marketing networks is recognized in the following chapters. Similarly, while we have given some illustrations of the adaptation of marketing techniques and approaches we shall apply this adaptation in some detail in relation to devising an entrepreneurial marketing plan in Chapter 15.

Summary

We have argued that entrepreneurs have a particular way of learning which must be addressed if meaningful development of individuals is to occur. Having recognized this we have put forward a framework for developing entrepreneurial marketing. This framework accommodates the notion that formal management techniques and approaches, and in particular those that relate to marketing, must be adapted to suit the characteristics of entrepreneurs and SMEs. Equally, we argue as part of our framework that new approaches must be taken to improve marketing decision-making and performance. Our argument here is to perceive the concepts of management competencies and networks as new concepts of entrepreneurial marketing.

Learning questions

1. Why do conventional management and marketing techniques and approaches need to be adapted to suit SMEs?
2. How do the characteristics of SMEs impact on marketing activity?
3. How do the characteristics of the entrepreneur impact upon marketing activity?

Further reading

Carson, D. (1990) 'Some exploratory models for assessing small firms' marketing performance: A qualitative approach', *European Journal of Marketing* **24** (11), pp. 1–51.

Hills, G. E. (1989, 1990, 1991, 1992, 1993) *Research at the Marketing/ Entrepreneurship Interface*, Proceedings of the University of Illinois at Chicago Symposium on Marketing and Entrepreneurship.

Chapter 13

Marketing Competencies for Entrepreneurs

Objectives

After reading this chapter the reader will have an understanding of the scope and nature of entrepreneurial marketing management competencies in the SME context. In addition, the reader will be introduced to an approach to marketing competency development which takes account of the factors that characterize the entrepreneurial small firm scenario.

Introduction

This chapter begins with a brief review of our definitions of management, marketing and entrepreneurial marketing competencies. In particular, it examines the entrepreneurial marketing management competency spectrum as posited in Chapter 7 and explores how the elements of this spectrum impact on and manifest themselves in the marketing activities of SMEs. In addition the chapter explores the nature of these entrepreneurial marketing competencies, looking at such issues as competency interactions, in particular how certain competencies are interrelated and may be even interdependent. It addresses competency development and the sub-components and sub-elements that make up various competencies. Having explored the nature and makeup of entrepreneurial competencies we subsequently address the dimension of entrepreneurial marketing competency development in the SME context. In particular, the focus of such competency development seeks to create means by which the small firm entrepreneur can engage in the self-development of marketing competencies.

Management competency defined

Management competency has been defined by Boyatzis[1] as 'an underlying characteristic of a person which results in effective and/or superior performance in a job'. In addition, this text has acknowledged a definition of management competency which stresses competent management behaviour that is observable and demonstrable. A competent manager is an effective manager and management competencies are therefore the relevant qualities and management skills that lead to effective job performance. In relation to skills, it is worth restating that a management skill implies an ability which can be developed, not necessarily inborn, and which is manifested in performance, not merely in potential. This is an important aspect and one to which we shall return, given that this chapter also suggests an approach to competency development.

There are many management competency spectra and Chapter 7 presented a synthesis of these. It is worth noting that the range of competency frameworks available suggests that there is no general agreement in the field of management science about competency definition. What the existence of such frameworks does do, however, is suggest that there may be tasks and techniques common to all managers, but that these need to be applied to specific individual circumstances and situations before their appropriateness as descriptions of managerial competency can be assessed.

Marketing competency defined

If a management competency is the skill or ability that leads to observable and demonstrable effective and/or superior job performance, then a competent marketing manager is someone who possesses the relevant qualities and management skills that lead to effective performance of an enterprise's marketing activities. There is undoubtedly a varying degree of overlap in relation to the competencies required for the effective performance of both management and marketing tasks. The extent of this overlap will depend on the scope of management decisions for which the marketing manager has responsibility and how this impacts on other functional areas of the enterprise. It will also depend on a range of factors, including the background of the person performing the task, the task itself and the organizational environment.

Since marketing management focuses on decision-making in relation to an enterprise's marketing activities, we need to readdress briefly those general management competencies that are most appropriate for the marketing management function. We have debated this issue fully in an examination of management and marketing competencies in Chapter 7, where we suggested that there is a marketing management competency spectrum which is more appropriate to and consistent with good and effective marketing management decision-making. This spectrum of marketing competencies comprises vision, creativity, leadership, communication, motivation, initiative, intuition, adaptability, analytical skills and judgement. In essence, what is recognized is that many of the core generic management competencies are equally if not more applicable in the context of marketing.

Entrepreneurial marketing competency defined

So far we have explored the nature and characteristics of entrepreneurs and how these characteristics impact on the marketing activities of entrepreneurial owner-managed SMEs. Small firm characteristics have also been considered and the way these affect SME marketing activities has been examined. Consideration of such parameters enables the postulation of a set of marketing management competencies that would appear to be more suited to effective and/or superior marketing management decision-making in the SME context. As a consequence, in Chapter 7 it was suggested that there was an entrepreneurial marketing management spectrum dominated by the competencies of judgement, experience, knowledge and communication. To this spectrum we can add other entrepreneurial marketing management competencies such as motivation, planning and vision. Such a spectrum, it is argued, should be viewed as an integrative mix of attributes which, when used in a balanced way, will lead to improved decision-making in relation to the marketing activities of entrepreneurial owner-managed SMEs.

What is important here is to take a closer look at each of the entrepreneurial marketing management competencies within the spectrum and to establish the extent to which they manifest themselves in respect of SME marketing activities and, in particular, in respect of SME owner/managers' marketing decision-making.

Judgement competency

The judgement competency is crucial in the entrepreneurial marketing management decision-making processes. Entrepreneurs make marketing decisions based on a high degree of personal judgement. The competency is usually detectable in relation to marketing decisions affecting issues such as opportunity analysis, customer dimensions, product ranges and levels of service provided, etc. Inherent in this competency, for example, is the ability to identify a market opportunity and to be able to assess such an opportunity in the light of scarce company resources and perhaps to weigh up this opportunity against other attractive alternatives that might present themselves.

For many entrepreneurs however, judgement in respect of marketing decision-making seems to come as second nature, based on hunch, intuition and experience from finding themselves in similar circumstances over a number of years in the business. Therefore, SME entrepreneurs often exhibit high levels of product knowledge when it comes to making decisions about product modifications, for example, or customizing products or services for particular clients.

It can be seen that judgement, therefore, is closely related to the competency dimensions of experience and knowledge and many combinations of and interrelationships between these competencies are frequently evident and reflected through the manifestation of this particular competency in the marketing decisions of entrepreneurial SMEs. These dimensions will be explored below.

Experience competency

Experience is a key entrepreneurial competency. Although experience tends to be a dominant competency in the context of entrepreneurial marketing activity it is more usual for the competencies of experience, judgement and knowledge to be used together. A good example is that in times of heavy workload and pressure accurate prioritization of customers' orders without fear of customer dissatisfaction can occur. This entails a high level of knowledge of one's business, the firm's ability to satisfy customers and the ability to make sound judgements in such a scenario. Thus it is clear that these two important competency dimensions combine quite comfortably under the banner competency of experience.

The experience competency is usually evident in relation to a particular field of business – knowledge of who the main players are, for example. A more important aspect of the competency in relation to marketing is apparent in a high level of entrepreneurial confidence that individuals' wealth of experience enables them to predict how customers might react in certain circumstances, whether favourably or unfavourably. This type of expression of a key competence is refreshing in that it illustrates something more than an awareness of experience, being indicative of an ability to use, enhance and enrich experience through proactive marketing activity.

This asserts that the experience competency has a dynamic dimension in so far as it can constantly be refined and enriched with each experience. Indeed, one can contend that with the benefit of prior experience many entrepreneurial owner/managers are competent to deal with many marketing decisions, especially in relation to recurring events.

Knowledge competency

Knowledge is the fourth of our entrepreneurial marketing management competencies. Knowledge here refers in particular to knowledge of products and service ranges, markets, competitors, industry activity, emerging market trends and customers. It is fair to contend also that this competency is an essential dimension of the entrepreneurial marketing decision-making process. Typical SME entrepreneurs are highly competent to discuss their individual product ranges or to elaborate on each market segment in which they operate. SME entrepreneurs are generally competent to discuss markets, not only in geographical terms but also in terms of product usage and the breakdowns of each individual product line. They will talk knowledgeably about competitors and competitor activity. The key issue, however, is the fact that possessing this knowledge enables them to be more effective in relation to entrepreneurial marketing management decisions.

Evidence also indicates that entrepreneurs often attach importance to possessing the knowledge competency through an expression of their own shortcomings in aspects of marketing such as promotion or setting prices. Such individuals, it is suggested, feel less competent to take marketing decisions or engage in marketing activities in these areas about which they are less knowledgeable.

Communication competency

Communication is an essential competency for entrepreneurial marketing. The competency can be viewed from the two dimensions of communication in the SME context, that is, internal and external dimensions. Internally, the competency of communication is typically evident in the emphasis on staff and levels of staff awareness, staff confidence and entrepreneurial confidence. Externally, the key indicators of entrepreneurial style marketing communication emphasize customers, markets, suppliers, competitors and, of course, the formal actors of the entrepreneur's personal contact network. It is worth mentioning that both internal and external communications in SMEs can be viewed in many cases as proactive uses of the entrepreneur's personal contact network.

Entrepreneurs generally place a high degree of emphasis on the need for good communications internally and externally. Differences in the degree of emphasis are usually detectable though, and are generally dependent on the background of the individual entrepreneur. Those entrepreneurs who exhibit a strong sales orientation place more importance on external communications, especially those with customers. Others place a high value on internal communications and typically emphasize the need for healthy interaction with and among their staff. Such SME owner/managers believe that this proactive use of internal communications leads to improved business performance through better staff relations and see good internal relations as a mechanism for gathering vital information on key activities, for key marketing decisions and to stimulate innovation.

Finally, it can be asserted that communication is vital in relation to the whole process of entrepreneurial marketing decision-making. It can be argued, however, that when one considers the nature of communication in respect of SME marketing activities, it may depend on a range of component skills – e.g. knowledge, confidence, the ability to listen and to use simple and uncomplicated language, and the ability to use experience, judgement and knowledge. These sub-elements of the communication competency are notable; recognizing their existence is important in that such an understanding of competency makeup and building blocks can be used to aid entrepreneurial self-development of expertise.

Other predominant competencies

Additional entrepreneurial marketing management competencies such as motivation, planning and vision need to be examined briefly in terms of how they are evident in SME marketing activity.

> *Motivation.* Motivation is a vital entrepreneurial marketing management competency. As discussed in Chapter 6, entrepreneurs are a highly motivated group. Such motivation, however, manifests itself as job satisfaction, confidence, stamina, commitment, energy, a positive attitude and an unusually high level of task orientation in relation to performance of marketing activities.
>
> *Planning.* The ability to plan is also an important entrepreneurial competency. It is worth noting, however, that more so than any other competency planning can be broken down easily into component parts. Sub-elements can be identified as comprising organizing, opportunity analysis, implementation skills, analytical ability, judgement, experience, intuition, motivation, adaptability, etc. The planning competency, in other words, is a constellation of the other competencies discussed above.
>
> *Vision.* This is a key entrepreneurial marketing management competency. Entrepreneurship after all is characterized by vision and closely allied to the future focus dimensions of the entrepreneurial personality. Vision, in addition, is closely linked to judgement and planning, but it can none the less be viewed as a stand-alone competence. Typical entrepreneurial statements such as 'You always have to look ahead' typify this competency. In other instances vision is linked to innovation and creativity and the propensity to identify, grasp and exploit market opportunities or other opportunities for company development.

It is not being suggested here that entrepreneurial marketing management competencies are confined to those key issues addressed above. Such spectra, however, comprise many of the same elements and sub-elements as those discussed in this text.

The nature of competencies

We can now make a number of key points. First, there is a high level of interaction between the various competencies highlighted. The degree, level and extent of such interactions however, depends closely on the particular entrepreneurial marketing competencies in question and the nature of the specific marketing tasks to be undertaken.

In addition, our examination of marketing competency enables us to suggest, with a high degree of certainty, that entrepreneurial marketing competencies tend to be found in clusters or constellations with one particular competency dimension being dominant. The dominant competency will once again be dependent on the nature of the specific task being performed. These observations are critical to our understanding of marketing competency, especially so when considering issues pertaining to entrepreneurial marketing competency development. Each of these observations is therefore amplified below.

Competency interaction

An examination of entrepreneurial marketing competencies quickly supports the contention that they are not stand-alone entities. The highly interactive nature of entrepreneurial marketing competencies is clear when considering key marketing management issues. Take, for example, a few key marketing issues such as products, services, customers, markets, industry trends and specifics. These can all be assessed from the perspectives of knowledge, experience, judgement, etc. What is important is that the competencies must interact in relation to these marketing issues.

In certain circumstances issues relating to product/service and job specifics may lie largely in the competency domain of knowledge, whereas the parameters of market, industry activity and trends may largely lie in the domain of experience in other circumstances. Some specific parameters, however, are not indicative of any particular competence but rather are much more characteristic of the interaction between the two (or more) dimensions. This suggests that the ability to perform effective marketing activities in certain areas depends on having several key competencies.

Competency clusters

In assessing appropriate interactions of competencies it is useful to consider that competencies tend to be manifest in clusters of other competencies and skills. Indeed, each of the component parts of any entrepreneurial competency could be broken down into further clusters of competencies with the same key sub-elements recurring frequently (see Figure 13.1).

In this illustration the entrepreneurial marketing competency of judgement is the dominant one, but it does not stand alone in that it is closely related to the competencies of experience, knowledge, intuition, analytical skills and information

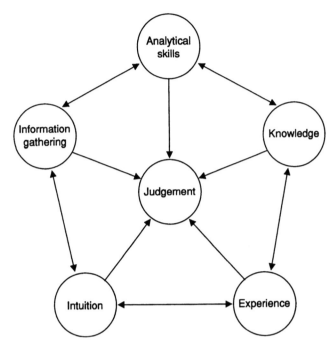

Figure 13.1 The 'judgement' cluster.

gathering. If the competency of knowledge was examined in the same way, then some of the competency elements, experience and information gathering for example, would undoubtedly recur. Such is the evidence of clusters of competencies interacting, that it is reasonable to assert that the predominant competency in any particular cluster depends on the marketing activity being undertaken and the specific environment in which an action occurs. This is illustrated in Figure 13.2, where we can see that the competencies of experience, knowledge and judgement are inseparable. This inseparability of competencies, it is suggested, is what actually results in effective performance of a specific job as opposed to acknowledging the possession of any one competency.

Having looked at the nature of entrepreneurial marketing management competency it is time to turn our attention to how these abilities might be developed in SME entrepreneurs.

Entrepreneurial marketing management competency development

First, it is important to accept that entrepreneurs and SME owner/managers have an inherent, common-sense knowledge of the marketing concept which can be realized

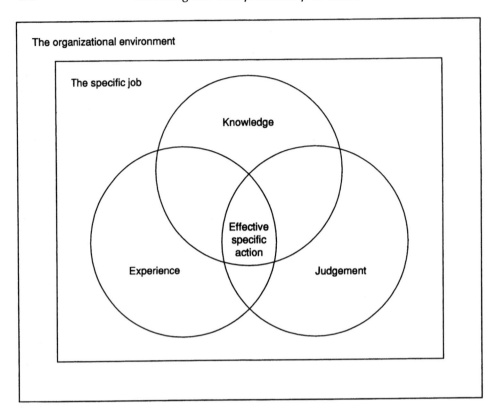

Figure 13.2 Competency inseparability.

through enhanced competency skills in marketing management. In addition, we must consider the nature of entrepreneurs and acknowledge that entrepreneurs engage in marketing, which is often implicit, often sophisticated but nearly always informal and not in line with the conventions of formal marketing. This means that there may be underlying dimensions of the entrepreneur which facilitate the self-development of these dimensions into marketing management competencies. Acknowledging this and having considered the nature of entrepreneurial marketing competencies and examined the nature of competency interactions and clusters, some suggestions can be made about ways in which these competencies can be developed. Account must be taken of these issues in addition to the issues already discussed; any focus on approaches to marketing competency development as a consequence need to be suitably tailored and sympathetic.

There have been many attempts to address competency development. A review of these techniques, however, suggests their inappropriateness for marketing management competency development. Nevertheless, one important dimension arising from previous work in this area is that it is clear that before developing competencies within any organizational system, the competencies needed must be identified and determined. It is also clear that the competencies to be developed are usually related to effective performance of a particular job within a specific organizational environment. Therefore, to be certain of effective competence development, competency frameworks need to be applicable to all jobs, job families and similar jobs with similar demands within the particular organization or enterprise. First and foremost, however, entrepreneurs must learn to recognize the competency that they wish to develop and understand how having this competency gives rise to effective and/or superior job performance.

The most effective approaches to marketing competency development in the entrepreneurial context, consequently, are rooted in some dimension of entrepreneurial self-assessment. This is important if individuals are to accept and acknowledge areas for personal development. Without self-assessment the entrepreneur is incapable of self-development as there is no self-recognition of competency weaknesses. In essence this means that entrepreneurs need to be able to recognize their own strengths and weaknesses in relation to marketing before being able to develop marketing skills in a positive way.

For self-development to occur in respect of marketing performance, entrepreneurs need to examine their own strengths and weaknesses when they carry out aspects of the enterprise's marketing activities. Some entrepreneurs, for example, regard themselves as very adept when dealing with customers; they pride themselves on the quality of such relationships. Others think of themselves as expert or highly qualified and capable as regards production processes and the quality of such processes. Others might regard themselves as having excellent judgement when it comes to making key marketing decisions and believe that such judgement is rooted in a vast reservoir of personal knowledge and experience.

On the other hand, some SME entrepreneurs readily recognize their own weaknesses. Experience indicates that those activities that entrepreneurs do not perform well are activities that they will tend to avoid in the day-to-day management of their enterprises. Specific to this discussion, some entrepreneurs regard themselves as weak in respect of various aspects of marketing activity. Some individuals feel that they do not communicate well with staff or customers. Others feel that they do not have a grasp of the financial side of their businesses; this might be rooted in self-doubt about their own analytical skills.

Entrepreneurial competency development, however, needs to go further than simply recognizing one's strengths and weaknesses and requires that the SME owner/manager fully explores these dimensions. This demands the entrepreneur to examine each strength and weakness thoroughly and examine the constituent and component elements of each. In other words, entrepreneurs must ask themselves why they are strong or weak at certain marketing activities. This enables them to focus on those sub-elements and aspects of each self-assessed strength which will be vital if they are subsequently to effect entrepreneurial marketing management competency development. Such a process is illustrated below in the case of an entrepreneur who, when exploring his own weaknesses, classes himself as a weak communicator. In particular, he classes himself as incompetent in relation to communicating with staff, customers and markets. When examining his strengths, however, he reckons that he possesses sound judgement, particularly in relation to decisions affecting the marketing development of his enterprise.

If one takes the two competencies being highlighted here – communication and judgement – and examines these in more detail (see Figure 13.3), it becomes clear that both are closely interrelated to a series of other competencies, competency sub-elements, characteristics and traits. In the case of communication the competency elements of information gathering, analytical skills and experience are evident. In the case of judgement the competency elements of discernment, experience and knowledge are evident.

What such a breakdown illustrates is that possessing the competencies of judgement and communication requires borrowing from other competencies/ characteristics and traits such as experience, decision-making and judgement. By breaking down these two competencies it becomes clear that there is considerable overlap between the two. The entrepreneur needs to focus on these areas of commonality. By doing this in the manner illustrated in Figure 13.3, entrepreneurs will recognize that they possess abilities they did not know they had. They move from a state of being unconscious/competent to being conscious/competent.

In this example an immediate impact on the entrepreneurs' ability to communicate can be effected. In this illustration their ability to exercise sound judgement in

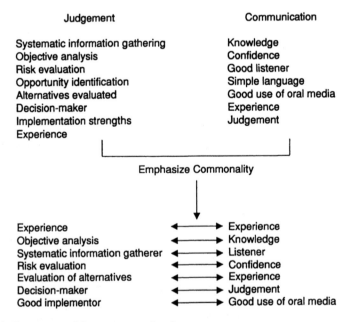

Figure 13.3 Entrepreneurial competency development.

relation to risk evaluation can be advocated as the potential catalyst for increasing personal confidence. Additionally, personal experience is common to the possession of sound judgement and to the ability to communicate; consequently, entrepreneurs are helped to realize that by concentrating on common strengths they can proactively address apparent weaknesses. This does not mean an immediate conversion of a former weakness into an entrepreneurial strength, but none the less it should still be viewed as a big stride forward in personal competency development. Much, of course, depends on the specific marketing management decision in question.

If, for example, an entrepreneur is considering the decision to launch an existing product into a new market, such a decision undoubtedly requires judgement (which in our example entrepreneurs possess) and the component elements of communication (which they feel that they do not possess). Experience is common to the possession of both competencies, objective analysis is not all that different from knowledge, systematic information gathering is allied to good listening skills, risk evaluation requires experience, making marketing decisions takes sound judgement and aspects of implementation of marketing activities require good use of oral media. Entrepreneurs realize that they actually do possess strengths of which they were unaware. These strengths allow entrepreneurs to begin to develop the sub-elements of the communication competency. Indeed, recognizing these competency sub-elements in the first place is a crucial step in their subsequent development. Here we see that by focusing and concentrating on natural strengths associated with judgement, entrepreneurs are actually honing their communication skills and abilities.

Through the application of the process as outlined above, entrepreneurs are helped to realize that all they need to do to develop their weaknesses is focus their strengths on developing the weaker areas. In this case the complementary skills are evident. These are experience, the ability to gather information, good decision-making ability and sound risk evaluation. Moreover, experience has shown that entrepreneurs are quick to realize and grasp an opportunity and do something positive if it will enable them to make better decisions – in this case more effective marketing decisions.

Other illustrations include recognizing that the vision competency in marketing may be developed by consideration of new domestic or international market opportunities; the creativity competency may be developed by consideration of new products and promotional ideas; and the communication competency may stimulate and enhance the company's message.

This approach touches on other issues relevant to the competency development debate. First, such competency breakdowns are dynamic in the sense that the composition of each breakdown changes and varies as a consequence of the specific marketing decision being taken. The competency sub-elements in the communication competency might vary from a circumstance of developing a sales lead to a situation involving information gathering in respect of competitors' activities.

This approach reinforces the other issues pertaining to the competency development debate. For example, it is clear from the illustration that competencies are highly interactive entities and that an emphasis on any particular dimension of competency will depend on the nature of the marketing decision being taken. Another issue which resurfaces here is the cluster aspect of competencies.

Summary

It is clear that a framework of marketing competencies exists which is more appropriate for marketing management decision-making in the entrepreneurial owner-managed SME. These key entrepreneurial marketing management competencies have been identified as judgement, experience, knowledge and communication. We can also comment on the nature of these competencies in that they are not stand-alone entities but interactions between, *and* clusters of, other competency elements. In the observable performance of any particular entrepreneurial marketing activity, one competency will be dominant. The competency that dominates will reflect the marketing activity being undertaken. In making a sale, for instance, one would anticipate the predominance of the communication competency in any cluster, whereas experience might come to the fore in, say, product development.

We also acknowledge that marketing competency can be developed. In an entrepreneurial circumstance a self-assessment and advancement approach to marketing competency development is offered.

The important conclusion, however, is acknowledgement of the existence of key entrepreneurial marketing management competencies and an acceptance that these can be developed. In an entrepreneurial owner-managed SME, therefore, self-development approaches to improving the competencies outlined in the entrepreneurial marketing management spectrum can result in effective and/or superior performance of the SME's marketing activities. If the SME entrepreneur focuses on using natural strengths and abilities to develop areas of personal weakness in respect of marketing, better company performance will follow. Essentially what is being offered is a means by which SME entrepreneurs can proactively develop key aspects of their marketing.

Learning questions

1. Select two marketing management competencies from the spectrum offered in this chapter. What are the ways in which these competencies interact in respect of the performance of a particular marketing activity?
2. How can entrepreneurs use the component elements of the judgement competency to develop their ability to analyze market opportunities?
3. What is the appropriateness of self-assessment and development approaches to marketing competency development in SMEs?

Notes and references

1. Boyatzis, R. E. (1992) *The Competent Manager*, New York: John Wiley.

Further reading

Quinn, R. E., Faerman, S. R., Thompson, M. P. and McGrath, M. R. (1990) *Becoming a Master Manager*, New York: John Wiley.
Whetten, D. A. and Cameron, K. S. (1991) *Developing Management Skills*, 2nd edition, London: HarperCollins.

Chapter 14

Networks for entrepreneurs and entrepreneurial marketers

Objectives

After reading this chapter, the reader will have covered the following objectives:

- To introduce the reader to the types of network available to entrepreneurs.
- To discuss the entrepreneurial nature of personal contact networks (PCNs).
- To investigate the particular significance of PCNs for marketing in an SME.
- To discuss those factors that determine the quality and potential of an individual entrepreneur's PCN.
- To consider the implications for the entrepreneur of developing his/her PCN.
- To introduce inter-organizational relationships (IORs) as a logical development from personal contacts.
- To examine the conditions that encourage IORs.
- To study models of IOR formation.
- To consider examples of inter-firm collaboration.

Introduction

Business people regularly make contact with numerous associates; these may include suppliers, customers, opinion-formers, competitors, government agencies, etc., and this allows them to conduct their business. However, while a business owner may initially set up unilateral contacts with others, as associations develop, the focal business person's contacts will, in all probability, make further contacts among themselves. The focal entrepreneur's suppliers may, for example, begin to supply others in the network. Therefore, networks encompass the totality of the associations or links between individuals, groups and organizations in a given social system, and it is likely that any modification in the nature of the contact between two or more associates will have a corresponding influence on other associations within the network.

In a business context associations can be instrumental, political, affective or normative. Entrepreneurs interact regularly with people and businesses in their environment to acquire resources, initiate action and dispose of marketable goods, and these exchanges have an essential economic component. However, these instrumental connections often create dependencies between individuals and they impact on the power of the interacting parties. In this situation highly dependent individuals will try to improve their own situation by persuading or putting pressure on others to modify their behaviour. Current relationships may also encourage friendship bonds and a sharing of values or beliefs between the parties. These bonds of affection can have a considerable impact on the way in which people conduct their business. In general, the frequency, nature and type of relationship between individuals or organizations influences the manner in which business is carried out between them.[1]

While networks generally define the type and totality of relationships between people and organizations, personal contact networks (PCNs) are seen as particularly relevant in the context of the entrepreneurial SME with its centralized, independent and personalized style of management. Personal contacts are also significant for marketing in the entrepreneurial SME from its pioneering days of intuitive marketing through subsequent periods of greater structure and control when marketing might be described as sophisticated. Such contacts play a critical role in maintaining the entrepreneurial efforts of those managing the enterprise's development and ensuring its continued commitment to opportunity and change.

With further development and maturity many organizations begin to consider the possibility of more permanent associations with their personal contacts. The complexity and volatility of the organizational world in recent years, coupled with a lack of resources in difficult economic times, has encouraged many firms to consider the benefits of working with their contact organizations and not against them. These inter-organizational relationships can lead to improved customer care, a sharing of information and a reduction in the costs of developing new products and services.

Defining a personal contact network (PCN)

A PCN can be defined as the relationships or alliances which individuals develop, or may seek to develop, between themselves and others. Individual behaviour is strongly influenced by the social context within which it takes place and not in isolation from it. Individuals may play a focal or central role in building both formal and informal relationships with people within their environs who are useful in assisting them to develop an enterprise in which they have a personal interest. The relationships that they establish and develop are unique to those individuals given their central role within it. Such a network is not a tangible asset that can be sold to another interested party; rather, it is intrinsically lodged in individuals themselves and in the personalized way they have nurtured and developed their relationships with those who form a part of their network of contacts.

Why PCNs are particularly entrepreneurial

PCNs are uniquely useful for entrepreneurs since the pioneering small firm is wholly dependent on the owner/manager for its direction and focus. Management in such an enterprise is characterized as being largely independent, highly centralized and highly personalized. Ideas for growth and development, its direction and how it is to be achieved, including the identification of the necessary resources, remain solidly the responsibility of the lead entrepreneur, who struggles to make and maintain a fit between the many components of the entrepreneurial process. To do so requires the sensitive use of entrepreneurial contacts in order to obtain the necessary knowledge and information. Entrepreneurs' use of personal contacts lends itself particularly well to this typically entrepreneurial way of doing business, which is largely unstructured, unplanned, intuitive, non-linear and time-compressed. Entrepreneurs' PCNs are aptly characterized by a high degree of informality and lack of planning which surrounds the management of the PCN and by its natural, almost subconscious development and use. Such personal networks act as a lubricant to the often overheated, chaotic and almost frenzied process by which the lead entrepreneur seeks to orchestrate that fit between an opportunity identified and the resources needed to exploit it.[2]

Entrepreneurs' personal contacts provide them with a source of accurate information and dependable guidance in a turbulent and dynamic environment. Because of the limited time, size and no track record they need to be able to access the support, information and guidance necessary for their enterprise's continued entrepreneurial development. Even with successful entrepreneurial action, which often forces the pioneering enterprise along an uncertain and risky transformational path towards growth, the need for personal networks remains strong. Such a transformation is often characterized by a rapid succession of dilemmas and challenges which change the character and culture of the firm and the roles and relationships of people working within it. Lead entrepreneurs play a critical role in effecting this transformation. Their decision to go for growth (or not) and what steps to take to achieve it will depend on their appreciation, understanding and acceptance of the most likely impact that growth will have on the enterprise and their role in it. The increasing complexities that attend such growth underline the central role of maintaining a dynamic network of personal contacts.

Entrepreneurial networks as a process

Entrepreneurial networking may be seen, therefore, as an activity in which the entrepreneurially oriented SME owners build and manage personal relationships with particular individuals in their surroundings. These are likely to be people who may be influential in determining the degree to which their enterprise is likely to become and remain committed to innovation, development and growth. The focus of entrepreneurial networking in the first place lies in providing entrepreneurs with a consistent supply of ideas for new products or markets which offer them and their enterprises real possibilities for sustainable growth.

In addition to providing them with insights into possible new opportunities they provide them with a means of accessing the resources necessary to exploit them. More often than not, though, entrepreneurs' need for resources exceeds their ability to acquire them. Entrepreneurs regularly pursue a number of opportunities and continuously evaluate their likelihood of real success. They must make tentative, short-term contracts for the supply of resources and, therefore need lots of likely backers who are prepared to support them in the expectation that they can realize an outstanding opportunity.

Accessing resources is no mean undertaking for someone with a vision or opportunity that might be exploited, but little understanding of how to do it. The shopping list of requisite resources can be extensive. Alongside finance, physical resources such as plant and equipment and additional human assets are essential. Lead entrepreneurs rarely possess all the skills and know-how needed to develop the firm; there will be gaps in any individual's portfolio of skills and teams are an effective means of filling this gap. Finding those resources and persuading those who own them to place them at the disposal of the entrepreneur is a critical aspect of networking. In making the fit between an opportunity and the necessary resources lead entrepreneurs need to employ all their persuasive and political skills to encourage people who are more powerful than they are to part with their valuable resources.[3]

An approach to networking which parallels this process is proposed by William Biemans. The elements of the approach include 'actors', 'activities' and 'resources'. Actors may be individuals, groups or organizations who perform activities and control resources. The activities they perform are categorized as transformational (activities that change resources through the use of other resources) and transactional (activities which link resources to each other). The resources in question are any human, physical or financial assets needed and acquired to carry out an activity. To make such processes work requires particular types of contacts to obtain the necessary knowledge and information and assets. These are issues which we shall consider in greater detail later in this chapter, when we look at factors determining the quality and potential of the entrepreneur's PCN.[4]

One final point worth addressing in relation to this process of entrepreneurial networking is that it is important to recognize that an entrepreneur's networks change and evolve in response to the increasing complexity attendant on entrepreneurially driven growth and development. The literature suggests that as the enterprise moves from launch, to new venture start-up through to becoming an established business with a recognized profile in its marketplace, the nature of its networking changes. The initial near-total dependence on social networks gives way to more business-focused networking and finally to strategic networking. The importance of broad social and inter-organizational networks are recognized as important for successful new venture start-ups and for their subsequent development.[5]

We must recognize that as the small entrepreneurial firm itself develops and grows, so too will the nature and character of the networks and networking within the enterprise and outside it. In its early days marketing in the small firm is conducted in a very chaotic, intuitive manner, but there is normally continued commitment to entrepreneurial development. As the enterprise develops, marketing activities move increasingly towards a greater level of sophistication. This has implications for the way in which entrepreneurs manage their networking activity. As they are urged to develop a competency in the planned construction of networks, so too it seems they must develop an ability in what might be called a planned approach to deconstruction too. As with most social systems, networks have lifecycles and they need to be maintained and renewed constantly. However, if they become obsolete, networks must be discarded.

The importance of entrepreneurial marketing networks

Marketing in an entrepreneurial SME has been discussed above in detail and it was suggested that the practice very much reflects the personality of the entrepreneur, that it is highly informal and *ad hoc*, relying, certainly in the early days, on the intuitive skills of the entrepreneur. This early unsophisticated marketing approach is seen as largely reactive in character. In addition, the enterprise they are developing emerges characteristically as one with a limited capability in obtaining quality information for effective decision-making and future planning, particularly in the area of marketing. With limited capability for processing information and with limited margins for absorbing errors, should plans not go accordingly, one can understand why much planning and decision-making are perceived by many small business owners as esoteric exercises more relevant to larger organizations than their own. However, identifying sustainable market opportunities and finding the resources to support them requires entrepreneurial contacts who can provide the necessary information and guidance. It also requires a confidence in networking practice to sell the vision of a venture idea, with a perhaps otherwise uncertain future, to potential, usually financial, backers. For the entrepreneurial manager of a small or medium-sized enterprise this is a challenge indeed. With a limited profile in the marketplace, an inherent desire for independence and to manage the business their own way, persuading others to put up the necessary resources to fund a venture requires sensitive political skills. Finding the right backers who can help or who know who can is important, as is finding information about that unique opportunity.[6]

Need for information

To succeed, the entrepreneurial SME owners need information on what is happening in the market to allow them to distil those opportunities that non-entrepreneurs fail to notice, to establish their likely potential and to ascertain the best way to exploit them fully. For example, entrepreneurs need information about what their customers want, what changes are happening in their market and how best to create and maintain a competitive advantage.

Conventional marketing wisdom in response to a company's need for quality information for effective decision-making and planning, emphasizes the importance of a planned programme in marketing research focusing on both secondary and primary sources of information. Any cursory consideration of the sources available indicates that there is any amount of material and, perhaps, paradoxically, that is the problem. As indicated above, the entrepreneurial small firm owner's approach to managing the enterprise might best be characterized as chaotic and opportunistic. The availability of time is one further resource which is often in short supply. Most entrepreneurial small firm owners who are characteristically action-oriented, simply do not seem to have the time, even if they have the skill, to search for appropriate data to uncover quality information for planning or decision-making. The challenge is to glean from the vast array of data those highly pertinent nuggets of information which pertain directly to the issue in hand. Gathering the data creates its own problems since information overload soon begins to make an impact.

Entrepreneurial small firm owners attempt to gather and absorb as much as possible 'on the hoof' as it were, given the many other demands for their attention and then, unless some better way of gathering information is available, an impromptu decision will be taken. However, decisions made in such circumstances and in such a way, against a backdrop of limited margins for error, greatly increase the level of risk attendant in the decision-making process. This makes it difficult to convince likely financial backers to support the business. Characteristically, entrepreneurs are moderate risk-takers, but decisions made on incomplete information, at best (or at worst on erroneous information) because the entrepreneur has little time, or like as not skill in planning for the necessary intelligence, must be suspect.

Successful entrepreneurial growth brings its own challenges. The advent of additional new products to the existing portfolio, the entry of the company into new markets, the introduction of new customers to the company's product add new complexities to managing the developing enterprise. The need for new and different types of information and ways of processing it increases. The entrepreneur needs to seek a more effective way of managing in these circumstances.

Need for confirmation

In addition to a regular and, from the entrepreneurs' point of view, more manageable supply of good quality, relevant information, entrepreneurs need a means to redress any doubt about the quality of decisions made. Entrepreneurs seek some means of confirming the validity of the decisions they are making, to establish their accuracy in so far as that can be done. So much is at stake: the future of the venture and the livelihood of the entrepreneur and those employed in the enterprise.

Consider the following scenario. The entrepreneur is planning to introduce a new product idea into the existing portfolio of products; the market has been particularly volatile and this opportunity has presented itself; it seems to offer real scope to develop the business. But it is going to cost a lot in terms of time, personnel and money. Should the entrepreneur go ahead? In such circumstances a decision like this is not easy to make, particularly when the firm has attained some reasonable degree of success in the past. Why risk what has been achieved? The ever-threatening 'comfort factor' lurks to undermine the continued entrepreneurial effort.[7]

The entrepreneur is often seen as a socially marginal person, one who is, to some extent, outside the cultural confines of the community. The entrepreneur seeks recognition through acceptance, perhaps in communities which revere professionalism, education and job security, where pressure in the environment is opposed to too much change and very much in favour of stability and predictable routine.

In general, entrepreneurs do not have all the skills needed to manage and develop their enterprises successfully. Any personal and honest analysis of their managerial strengths and weaknesses will tell them pretty quickly that this is so. Any comparison with the skills needed to manage and grow the enterprise will quickly identify the gaps that exist and that will need to be plugged if the venture is to continue to be successfully entrepreneurial. For example, an SME owner may have a background in engineering or production and have identified a product opportunity on which the enterprise has been built. But the ability to market the product may be relatively weak. In response and in a bid to develop the business, entrepreneurs may embark on a programme of focused technology transfer to compensate for and develop answers to marketing problems confronting the enterprise in its early stages. While things remain simple they may even be able to continue in this vein. As the enterprise expands and complexity increases they are faced with the need to update their marketing competencies, along with so many other necessary skills. But there are numerous pressures, not least lack of time. They might consider employing a professional marketing person, but perhaps the enterprise isn't large enough to afford that yet; then there is the question of sharing part of the enterprise with this emerging middle management. But it is largely recognized that teams build enterprises, lone entrepreneurs make a living. To grow, the business needs the entrepreneur to think in terms of a 'team'. A possible solution to the immediate problem of filling the gaps opening up in the required portfolio of competencies is for the entrepreneur to use a PCN and develop an 'entrepreneurial team' of contacts, on this occasion, outside the enterprise itself.

The critical point here is that the approach is planned for and worked through. The literature abounds with commentary on the specific weakness of entrepreneurial small firm owners in the area of marketing. The planned management of the entrepreneur's PCN offers an approach to addressing that weakness without necessarily compromising the entrepreneur's need for independence, in a way that is not time-consuming, while the relationship is mutually beneficial and perfectly legitimate.

Entrepreneurial networking

Confronted by the need for information and concerned to validate, if possible, a course of action, typical entrepreneurial SME owners seek feedback from people they know well. Any information about, and an endorsement of, an adopted position sustains morale and builds confidence. But entrepreneurs' approach to this networking activity reflects, to a critical degree, the chaotic, largely unplanned approach that characterizes their approach to managing and marketing their enterprises. Communication with members of their network will often be largely unplanned, opportunistic, highly informal and unstructured. It will be direct and verbal, focused on a specific issue of current importance to entrepreneurs and their enterprises.

An entrepreneur seeking to develop a new product or market, for example, will seek information from the network about the opportunity and its potential and/or the resources needed to exploit such a chance. They will formulate a decision on how to make progress with that opportunity, based on the feedback received, and may well return to the network members for confirmation of the value and validity of the chosen path. But as we suggested earlier, the entrepreneur will probably commit only limited time to this exercise, giving little thought to the approach being taken, who is consulted, why and to what end. However, once relationships have been established and seen to be of value, the sophistication in the way they are used may develop.

Entrepreneurial managers' preference is likely to be for face-to-face data collection, with the result that they employ their personal contact networks when gathering market information. It is through the continued use of those networks that they can further refine and develop the data collected and distil from it the intelligence needed to make decisions. The quality and potential of an entrepreneur's PCN is a function of a number of factors, which suggests that the entrepreneur needs to adopt an approach to networking which is better thought out and considered. The entrepreneur needs to be able to develop relations with people who are knowledgeable, empathetic, experienced, well connected and willing to help. We consider what some of those factors might be in the following section.

Factors determining the quality and potential of the entrepreneur's PCN

There are a number of important characteristics which define an entrepreneur's network. Foremost among these are density, reachability and diversity.

The density of the network refers to the number of contacts that exist between people in the network.

Allied to this is the degree of reachability that exists in the network, and this refers to the existence of 'pathways' between two people and the ease with which people in a network can make contact with one another. They may be direct, in that they define immediate and significant relationships with people who can have a particular impact on the enterprise, or indirect in that they define relationships with people outside the immediate network but contactable through it. The strength of the link in any network depends on the geographical, psychological and cultural distances between the two actors involved, how often the relationship is used, how mature it is, the degree of trust and the nature of past experiences between the two parties.

Diversity refers to the number of different sources from which information or assistance might be drawn and reflects the backgrounds of people in the network, their skills, knowledge, experience, additional access opportunities, and the like. The strength of these characteristics in any given network will ultimately determine the richness of the information being distilled from the network and the value of the advice and guidance available from its members. To network effectively, therefore, an individual must give thoughtful consideration to these issues and how they might best be managed. We look at some of these issues in more detail below.[8]

Characterizing personal contact networks

The entrepreneurial small firm owner needs to be able to access what we might describe as 'rich' information. By this we mean information that is current, accurate, focused, manageable and validated. Rich information is very much a function of the properties or characteristics of the source from which it has been acquired and the methods used to gather it. In an entrepreneurial contact network the focal person is the entrepreneurial SME owner and the network comprises those persons with whom the owner has *direct* relationships. *Direct ties* depict immediate and significant relationships with people who can have a particular direct impact on the enterprise. In addition there are *indirect ties*, which define relationships with people outside the immediate network but who can, if their role becomes significant, be contacted through it. Figure 14.1 outlines this property more clearly.

The entrepreneur is the focal person in the network with direct contacts with A, B, C and D. We said that they should be significant in terms of their relationship with the entrepreneur, and by significant we mean that they should be people who are knowledgeable about business issues generally and perhaps the entrepreneurs' industry in particular. They will be experienced in business, with a reputation or profile among people in the industry; they will have influence with the entrepreneur, people the entrepreneur can trust and in whose views, comments and guidance the

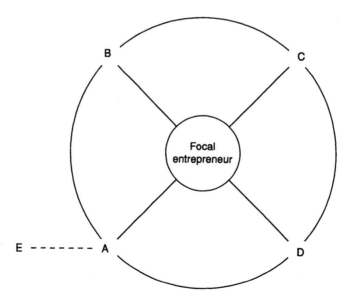

Figure 14.1 Entrepreneurial contact network.

entrepreneur has confidence. The entrepreneur, however, has an indirect tie with E through his direct association with A. Any decision to draw E into the direct network will be a function of many issues, not least the significance of such contacts to all parties concerned.

Let us look at this in more detail by considering a related and arguably complementary property of networking, the issue of *strong and weak ties*. Whether a tie between contacts in a network is strong or weak reflects the nature and consequent strength of the bond between the actors involved. The *strongest ties* are with people who share affection: family members, very close friends and relatives. These are people who are close to the entrepreneur; they know and care for one another. They have played a meaningful part in the entrepreneur's life for a very long time, often over a lifetime, and share a range of experiences and emotions. These emotions and interactions are vital in holding relationships together. Such relationships might be seen as largely unconditional, in that the actors give and receive without any recognizable or definable preconditions or expectations of reciprocity. These types of relationships are rooted in mutual respect and affection and are common in family and social relationships. These are the ultimate network for the lonely, otherwise marginal personality who is setting up an enterprise and who will need all the moral support and confidence-boosting available, particularly when things go wrong.

However, such non-business relationships need to be differentiated from the more commercially rooted relationships. As mentioned above, when introducing the idea of *direct ties* the entrepreneurial small firm owner needs to build *strong ties* with people who can give the information and confirmation needed to make decisions for the development of the enterprise. Additionally, though, these contacts may be bonded together by ties of mutual trust and confidence, mutual support and the valid expectation of reciprocity. The more people in the network are known to each other, usually over a long period of time, the stronger the ties between them. Such a network reflects the family/community network, although it can be argued that the former is more planned and the latter is more natural in evolution and development. *Weak ties* in a network, however, will be made up of casual acquaintances with people who are unlikely to know one another; however, the maintenance and nurturing of these ties is essential for an effective network. Where the entrepreneur relies solely on existing strong direct ties where everyone is known to each other and is mutually dependent on each other for support, information and guidance, we have what is called a *high density network*.

The opportunity in such a network for new thinking beyond the norms of the existing group of members is potentially limited as members endorse and support each other's views. The potential for a version of 'group think' must be strong. For a network to be truly useful it needs to have access to diverse opinions and varying perspectives. This introduces a further property of networks, the need for *diversity*. For a personal network to be effective, it needs a relative balance between strong and weak ties if the supply of information and the prospects of guidance and confirmation are to be rich and valuable.[9]

So the density of the network refers to the degree of interconnectedness between people in the network. Diversity refers to the number of different sources from which information or assistance might be drawn and reflects the backgrounds of the people in the network, their skills, knowledge, experience, and the like. The third key characteristic of networks introduced above is the degree of *reachability* that exists in the network. Howard Aldrich and Catherine Zimmer refer to the existence of pathways between two people and the ease with which people in the network may make contact with one another. For example, in Figure 14.1 the reachability between the entrepreneur as the focal person and E is very much a function of the strength of the tie not only between the entrepreneur and contact A but between A and E and A's willingness to act as a go-between. This introduces an additional characteristic of developing networks, particularly wider social networks: *the networking broker*. The entrepreneurial small business owner operates within some context or contexts, be it an industry sector or, say, a community or wider social system. Membership of this system bestows an identity and with it a legitimacy or standing, the strength of which is crucial for the usefulness of networking opportunities. *Networking brokers* play a significant role in any social system by linking the entrepreneurial PCN with people outside it who have complementary interests, by transferring information or resources and generally facilitating the interests of people not otherwise directly related to one another. A in Figure 14.1, for example, might be such a person.

Developing entrepreneurial marketing networks

What the entrepreneurial owner/manager requires is a competency in building networks which have the characteristics described. This needs to be done in a way that reflects the maturing character of the enterprise and the increasing complexities that attend effective entrepreneurial action. This necessarily poses a significant challenge to recognize the critical importance of networks to maintaining the entrepreneurial effort of the enterprise and to develop an approach to networking that is increasingly rational rather than wholly natural, that is more planned than unstructured and that is more formal than totally informal in character.

The entrepreneur must recognize, in adopting a more rational approach to network development and management, the importance of building quality into the potential of the networks. Entrepreneurs must thoughtfully seek appropriate levels of diversity and density in their relations with others and think strategically about the issue of reachability. David Carson[10] points out that entrepreneurs' personal contact networks provide them with one mechanism for developing a common-sense approach to marketing. He suggests that what is required is for them to use it consciously and proactively to help them make key marketing planning decisions to resolve problems. This ultimately is the challenge facing the entrepreneurial networker.

Relationships between organizations

We have noted that organizational leaders contact one another regularly, that the networks of personal contacts are extremely useful in gathering information about opportunities and resources and that the friendships which develop provide important support for individuals. They can test out their ideas on informed listeners and discuss matters of mutual benefit. However, in recent years organizations have been developing more formal associations and joint research projects, marketing alliances and systematic comprehensive associations between manufacturers are commonplace.[11] In contrast with these developments classical economists argue strongly in favour of independent firms which operate in a competitive market. Their basic argument is that competitive market forces are an effective mechanism for regulating the contact between organizations. In essence if organization (1) believes that an association with organization (2) will yield a greater return on investment than a linkage with venture (3), then (1) and (2) will develop their relationship, at least until such times that linking with a new organization will yield a greater rate of return. Contacts are made and exchanges occur so long as they facilitate the maximization of profit. However, we saw in Chapter 9 that this competitive, dog eat dog situation can produce some unwanted results. In the UK and US automobile industries in the 1970s, manufacturers demanded ever-cheaper parts from their suppliers and threatened that they would change suppliers if cost-cutting could not be achieved. Suppliers responded to these demands by cutting prices but with disastrous consequences for quality. We saw also in Chapter 9 that manufacturers, aware that fickle customers in a competitive world will quickly shift their loyalty to another product in pursuit of economic advantage, are concerned to build lasting relationships with customers. When we recognize that the customers for many firms are other organizations rather than the general public, we can see that permanent associations between transforming and client organizations are a distinct possibility.

While not denying that many sectors of the economy function in a competitive world it has been pointed out that organizations have always been embedded in semi-permanent networks of other organizations – sometimes called organization sets – which supply raw materials and act as markets and that these associations are a source of stability in a turbulent world.[12] However, inter-organizational relationships (henceforth referred to as IORs) are more common nowadays and we shall explore the reasons for this increase in collaboration.

Rationale for inter-organizational relationships (IORs)

Several authors have argued that many organizations do not have the resources they need to accomplish their objectives and that in these situations there is an incentive to cooperate to acquire the necessary resources.[13] For example, two organizations may have an interest in developing a new product but discover that, independently, they do not have sufficient money. However, by cooperating and pooling their financial resources they discover that the development process can be completed to the benefit of both parties. Similar arguments apply with non-financial resources. For example, two firms may develop a new service but find that the market is insufficient to occupy staff from both organizations fully. In this situation they can compete and let the winner take all, or share the work among staff from both organizations to the benefit of both ventures. It has been suggested that when organizations seek opportunities in their environment but discover that they cannot command sufficient resources to realize the opportunity, they begin to seek collaborative associations which will allow them to gain access to requisite resources.[14]

The situation just described is particularly relevant for small firms, restricted as they often are by limited resources. For example, a recent research study in Sweden showed that many businesses involved outsiders fully in the process of developing their new products.[15]

New knowledge and technologies

The need to marshall resources often gives rise to inter-organizational collaboration, but Alter and Hage suggest that recent events have given an even greater impetus to this trend. A key factor is the pace of change in today's world; it has been so rapid that it has revolutionized industrial structures. In a traditional market a firm might buy the best scientific and marketing talent and nurture a new product in the expectation that, even in a competitive market, its new product would provide them with an advantage over the competition for some time. However, if we consider areas such as microelectronics, biotechnology and genetic engineering, new knowledge emerges so quickly that today's new invention is superseded by an even newer product in a short time. This presents huge problems for innovative firms.

They can be sure that their competitors have similar or more advanced scientific and market information and that the lifecycle of their new product will be short. Speed, flexibility and responsiveness are the necessary attributes for the modern innovative firm and recent research confirms that collaborative associations with other organizations, including former competitors, are the only viable ways to acquire the necessary knowledge, share the developmental costs and spread the risks of new product development. They must also share the benefits. If not, competitive pressures will re-emerge.[16]

The organizational arrangements that can deliver these outcomes are not large, vertically and horizontally integrated, bureaucracies; indeed, these firms are rapidly removing their former acquisitions and creating smaller, organically structured work constellations which are linked in collaborative networks. Many small firms are flexible and responsive but they have a serious disadvantage – their decision-making is centralized and focused on the owner/manager. The generation of new knowledge, ideas, processes, etc. requires independent thought from experts to whom decision-making has been decentralized. Assuming that fiercely independent entrepreneurs can be persuaded to decentralize, the organizational form which can encompass flexibility, responsiveness, creativity and specialized expertise is the systemic network of small specialized knowledge-based firms.

Adaptive efficiency

Changes in technological knowledge can influence the supply of goods or services, but equally important changes are taking place in the marketplace. Customers are increasingly sophisticated and demanding and want quality goods and services geared to their specific needs. Alter and Hage point out that in previous decades efficiency was associated with the ability to produce large quantities of standard goods at low cost. Large bureaucratic performance organizations perfected the production of cars, televisions and the like, and this approach was referred to as 'Fordism'.[17] These authors argue that in today's world 'adaptive efficiency' is required. Customers want goods which are competitively priced but they are prepared to pay a premium for individualized, good quality goods and services. Cooperation between networks of small niche firms allows them to derive some of the benefits of large combined output along with the capacity to meet special customer needs and to modify products to meet the particular needs of customers. There is considerable research evidence to show that small firms are likely to act conjointly with others by entering into cooperative market agreements.[18]

Trust

Classical theories of economics assume that if people pursue their own self-interest, an invisible hand will guide economic activity for the general benefit of society. Organizations in the market are supposed to base their interactions on economic criteria only and to distrust those with whom they do business. Safety for individual firms is provided by the large number of competing suppliers and buyers. If one supplier seeks a disproportionate advantage a producer will simply engage a new supplier.

If a producer is to enter into an exclusive agreement with suppliers, customers or even competitors, then it is vital that a high degree of trust exists between the parties. Trust is a fragile commodity. It takes time for it to develop and a single action can destroy it forever. However, in spite of traditional economic theory there is considerable evidence that trust is part and parcel of business activity. Without it participants would constantly have to look over their shoulders and there is increasing evidence from Europe that relations between suppliers, manufacturers and customers in industrial markets are characterized by 'cooperation, trust and loyalty'.[19]

In addition, far from confirming that nice guys always finish last, research has shown that the most effective strategy for managing on-going exchanges is one of reciprocity. In other words, it is best for one party to start an exchange in a cooperative mode and to continue to do so as long as the other party cooperates. If the other person takes an uncooperative stance, the first person should retaliate immediately and only return to a cooperative mode if the other person does so.

Numerous trials on this kind of interactive exchange show that reciprocity is the most beneficial strategy for both parties.[20] Research into problem-solving and negotiation shows that, if the parties adopt a collaborative stance, they can often arrive at innovative solutions to problems that are beneficial to both sides. These outcomes are more effective than grudging compromises which merely split the difference between the demands of each party.

Bureaucratic organizations rely on a small group of thinkers and experts to design organizational practices and on a mass of unthinking workers to complete activities and tasks mechanically. However, in the newer innovative and complex ventures, which are likely to form IORs, highly educated individuals who will challenge the status quo are required. Fortunately, as a result of higher education for larger numbers of students, a tendency for people in modern societies to appreciate different cultures and values, and an increase in international travel, many countries have a pool of people with the skills to function effectively in complex, problem-solving organizations.

In general, new notions of efficiency, rapid changes in knowledge and markets and a highly educated populace who are prepared to trust their colleagues support the formation of collaborative IORs. While we started our discussion on IORs by emphasizing collaboration to acquire additional resources we have seen that significant changes in organizational environments can increase communication between organizations as they explore threats and possibilities for working together.

Examples of IORs

Our discussion to date has been quite general and we feel that we should present some examples of extensive IORs. One of the most developed systems of IORs occurs in sections of the Japanese motor industry. Major manufacturers like Honda and Toyota involve their suppliers fully in the design of components and in resolving the problems they encounter with the final product — the car. When parts malfunction they are not declared as rejects: they prompt a joint investigation by supplier and assembler to try to ensure that the difficulty does not arise again. Any cost savings that are made are shared between the suppliers and the manufacturers and prices for components are set collaboratively. In effect, suppliers and manufacturers operate as if they were part of the same organization and because the needs of the suppliers are being met they have every incentive to carry on cutting costs, improving quality and delivering parts to the manufacturer just-in-time.[21]

In Europe the completion of the integrated market in 1992 prompted several organizations to form IORs to allow them to share information, costs and markets to make them globally competitive. For example, DAF and Bava, two Dutch bus manufacturers, joined forces and then invited firms from Britain and Denmark to collaborate with them. Phillips, the Dutch giant, stated in 1990 that as part of their business strategy to increase competitiveness they would reduce the extent of their vertical integration and increase their cooperation with other organizations.[22]

Public services such as health and welfare have been decentralized in the United States since the 1950s but initial evaluations reported many problems. Services were fragmented and duplication was common. However, financial pressure on agencies and an insistence that there be no duplication of effort created a situation where agencies (1) cooperated to make the best of available financial resources, (2) specialized in the services they provided, and (3) developed client referral systems to meet the needs of clients with multiple problems. These developments reflect those that have occurred in many service areas in the United States and elsewhere and some of the most intricate IORs are to be found in the service sector.[23]

Forming IORs – the process

We have argued that a number of environmental variables have increased the likelihood of IOR formation, but it should be noted that environmental conditions do not determine organizational structures; they are determined by senior managers. The decision of a manager to enter into an IOR will, in all probability, be influenced by the factors discussed above, but s/he will have to be committed to the idea personally before interaction takes place. Andrew Van de Ven argues that a number of conditions must be met before senior managers will enter an IOR.[24] When entrepreneurs feel that they might want to collaborate with another organization to acquire resources or exploit an opportunity, they will need to know about the capabilities and activities of neighbouring organizations. They will have to develop some awareness of their strengths and weaknesses, the organizational culture and their goals. Most of this awareness will develop through communication with people who have information about the likely contact organization, most particularly personal contacts within the target organization. If contacts have known one another for a long time and if the parties are on good terms personally, this will speed up the flow of information. Personal contacts are important for this purpose but so is geographical proximity. Research indicates that organizations are more likely to make contact with a neighbouring organization than a distant one.[25]

Before an IOR becomes a reality there will have to be a measure of agreement among the participants on the ends they are pursuing and on the means of achieving them. Distinct organizations are likely to have distinct goals, but to work conjointly they will have to arrive at a joint decision on means and ends. This will entail discussion, understanding of each other's position and a degree of accommodation. If moderate consensus does not emerge it is unlikely that an IOR will come into being. We need to emphasize, once again, the importance of communication between the parties in developing an awareness of one another's capabilities and desires and in seeking agreement on collective goals. An effective personal network is indispensable for this purpose.

Communication, awareness and consensus are important but so is the business sector of the parties. Some authors suggest that organizations that provide very similar or very dissimilar services are unlikely to collaborate. In the former instance they will compete for a greater market share while in the latter they will pursue their own ends in their niche market. Andrew Van de Ven suggests, therefore, that collaboration is most likely among ventures with moderately similar domains. Others argue that cooperation is most likely when the collaborators are highly differentiated. In the latter case, however, the customers or clients served by the collaborating organizations will require a variety of services, and organizations will route clients to those providing additional assistance.[26]

If these conditions are suitable, then a degree of cooperation will emerge between agencies. This can range from tenuous links in which information is pooled and exchanged, through joint agreements on procurement or marketing to the fully integrated production network where the separate organizations behave like semi-autonomous divisions in a divisionalized organization. In all cases there will be exchange of one or more of the following: (1) friendship, (2) information, (3) resources and (4) products/services. Without these flows it is doubtful if an IOR will continue. In analyzing IORs it is important to be aware of the intensity and direction of flows. These variables allow us to recognize the leaders and followers.

If relationships continue for some time, the pattern of interaction and flows will stabilize and the IOR will develop recognizable structured elements. The major structural features are formalization, centralization and complexity. Formal IORs exist when agreements are concrete and written down. Centralization occurs when joint decisions are made by a small number of people such as a coordinating committee. Complexity refers to the number of agencies whose efforts have to be integrated. In general, increasing participating units increases IOR complexity.

When structural features emerge they indicate that there is a degree of permanence in the IOR but Alter and Hage point out that IORs can be vulnerable. If one or more parties pursue their own ends at the expense of the collectivity an IOR may well break up. If an IOR is to continue, it is important that the parties agree, and continue to agree, on means of achieving goals, on the capacities of the participating organizations and on the contribution each can make to the overall goal(s). In reality, just as departments within single organizations specialize, so organizations within an IOR develop particular abilities which should complement those of other ventures.

Power is another matter which must be monitored in an IOR. IORs comprise horizontally linked organizations and it is important that decisions are made jointly and that no organization begins to control proceedings. If this occurs, it is likely that the IOR will end. We must appreciate, however, that it is not easy to achieve power-sharing among independent ventures. With the best will in the world there will be many disagreements about activities, procedures and objectives. It is vital, therefore, that key individuals in a network develop the skills of negotiation, bargaining and compromise to allow them to find creative solutions to the problems they will face as a network of organizations.[27]

Relations between enterprise support agencies

To complete our discussion we shall illustrate some of the matters we have been examining with the help of a recent case study of inter-agency collaboration between small business support agencies.[28] This text has been addressing matters of importance to entrepreneurial SMEs but it is widely recognized that they experience many difficulties. As a result most governments provide support for SMEs, and in Northern Ireland this assistance is provided by approximately eighty state, semi-state and private enterprises offering advice, training, financial assistance, etc. While this support is welcome, some people believe that there is duplication of effort among agencies. When we examine the environment of these enterprise supporters we find that they are not well financed and are clear candidates for the pooling of financial resources. In addition, we find that following the huge increase in knowledge about SMEs in recent decades and the demand by small firms for customized assistance, enterprise supporters are increasingly responsive to and innovative when providing services to their clients. An additional factor is the high level of educational attainment of our enterprise supporters. If we review those conditions favouring IORs above, it would appear that conditions are suitable for collaboration.

Turning to the process of IOR formation we find that, because of the small geographical size of Northern Ireland and government-sponsored conferences, the enterprise supporters have a keen awareness about their fellow supporters and there is regular and effective communication among them. Given the level of communication and awareness among organizations we might have predicted a high level of consensus among agencies but this is not the case. There was only a modest level of consensus on the goals of enterprise support policy and the means of achieving objectives. On domain similarity we find that the agencies have a mean score on this variable of 2.7, where 2 means that respondents think their domain is similar to that of other contact agencies to a 'little extent' and 3 indicates they are similar 'to some extent'. Since agency domains are neither very similar nor very dissimilar this would suggest that there would be a considerable flow of resources between agencies.

As it turns out there is only a modest level of exchange between the agencies. In general, there is little exchange of tangible resources such as money, equipment or personnel; a little more willingness to trade clients and advice; and they are even more content to exchange social support and promote their organizations collaboratively.

The enterprise supporters' environment was quite conducive for integrated network formation but it did not happen and few IOR structural dimensions, such as the centralization and formalization of procedures and decision-making, emerged. In spite of favourable conditions the key decision-makers within agencies decided to act largely independently. This points to the importance of the willingness of the parties to create IORs.

Summary

Many associations in life are unplanned and coincidental and arise through social activity. Even in a business context associations may emerge in a subconscious and reactive manner. However, the planned development of networks, in a thoughtful and proactive way, may offer a useful addition to the pool of competencies needed by small firm owners. In contrast with managers in bureaucracies, who act as the custodians of resources under their control, entrepreneurs actively seek resources to capitalize on their business ideas. In their quest for information, resources and customers, entrepreneurs simultaneously explore many possibilities and a range of contacts, who are knowledgeable about these and related matters, are indispensable for the growth-oriented entrepreneur. Business know-how is essential for successful venturing but without large numbers of specialized employees who are expert in business functions, the entrepreneur needs to know who to turn to for expertise, assistance or information.

As organizations mature they often recognize that loosely coupled connections with others are not sufficient for continued business success. In the increasingly turbulent and complex business world of the late twentieth century permanent alliances between organizations are becoming necessary to acquire new knowledge, develop new markets and share the expense of purchasing scarce resources. In many spheres of endeavour permanent systemic networks of organizations, not autonomous firms, are seen as the structural formation which will guarantee the continued competitiveness of business organizations.

Learning questions

1. Discuss the two main networking approaches available to the entrepreneurial SME owner.
2. In what ways are the personal contact networks (PCNs) of the SME owner particularly entrepreneurial?
3. Evaluate the significance of PCNs to the practice of marketing in the SME?
4. Discuss the factors that will determine the quality and potential of the individual entrepreneur's PCN.
5. Discuss the implication for the entrepreneur of developing the PCN.
6. It has been contended that in a modern business environment independent firms are unable to maintain sustained growth. What are your views on this matter?
7. Comment on those influences from outside and inside organizations which might stimulate the formation of IORs.

Notes and references

1. See Johannisson, B. (1986) 'Network strategies: Management technology for entrepreneurship and change', *International Small Business Journal* 5, pp. 19–30; and

Mastenbroek, W. F. G. (1993), *Conflict Management and Organisation Development*, Chichester: John Wiley.

2. Dubini, P. and Aldrich, H. (1991) 'Personal and extended networks are central to the entrepreneurial process', *Journal of Business Venturing* 6, pp. 305–13.

3. Stephenson, H. H. and Gumpert, D. E. (1991) 'The heart of entrepreneurship', in W. A. Sahlman and H. H. Stephenson (eds.), *The Entrepreneurial Venture*, Boston, MA: Harvard Business School.

4. Biemans, W. G. (1992) *Managing Innovation within Networks*, London: Routledge.

5. Butler, J. E. and Hansen, G. S. (1991) 'Network evolution, entrepreneurial success, and regional development', *Journal of Entrepreneurship and Regional Development* 3, pp. 1–16.

6. MacMillan, I. C. (1991) 'The politics of new venture management', in Sahlman and Stephenson (1991), *op. cit.*, pp. 160–70.

7. Drucker, P. F. (1985) *Innovation and Entrepreneurship*, London: Heinemann, argues that a successful current product inhibits the drive for innovation.

8. See Aldrich, H. and Zimmer, C. (1986) 'Entrepreneurship through social networks', in D. A. Sexton and R. W. Smilor (eds.), *The Art and Science of Entrepreneurship*, Cambridge, MA: Ballinger, for an excellent analysis of network characteristics.

9. Granovetter, M. (1982) 'The strength of weak ties: A network theory revisited', in P. V. Marsden and N. Lin (eds.), *Social Structure and Network Analysis*, Beverly Hills, CA: Sage, pp. 105–30.

10. Carson, D. (1993) 'A philosophy of marketing education in small firms', *Journal of Marketing Management* 9, pp. 189–204.

11. See, for example, Jarillo, J. C. (1993) *Strategic Networks – Creating the Borderless Organisation*, Oxford: Butterworth/Heinemann; Gadde, L. E. and Hakaanson, H. (1993) *Professional Purchasing*, London: Routledge; and Biemans (1992), *op. cit.*

12. See Evan, W. M. (1976) 'An organisation-set model of interorganisational relations', in W. M. Evan (ed.) *Inter-Organisational Relations*, Middlesex: Penguin Books, pp. 78–90 and Trist, E. (1983), 'Referent organisations and the development of inter-organisational domains', *Human Relations* 36, pp. 269–84 for a discussion on the stabilizing influence of networks.

13. See Alter, C. and Hage, J. (1993) *Organizations Working Together*, Newbury Park, CA: Sage.

14. Van de Ven, A. H. (1976) 'On the nature, formation and maintenance of relations among organisations', *Academy of Management Review* 1, pp. 24–36.

15. Hakaanson, H. (1990) 'Technological collaboration in industrial networks', *European Management Journal* 8, pp. 371–9.

16. Lambourghini, B. (1982) 'The impact on the enterprise', in G. Friedrichs and A. Schaff (eds.) *Micro-electronics and Society*, London: Pergamon; Powell, W. W. (1990), 'Neither market nor hierarchy: Network forms of organisation', in L. L. Cummings and B. M. Staw (eds.), *Research in Organizational Behaviour*, Greenwich, CT: JAI Press; Alter and Hage (1993), *op. cit.*; Biemans (1992), *op. cit.*

17. Hollingsworth, J. R. (1991) 'The logic of coordinating American manufacturing sectors', in J. L. Campell, J. R. Hollingsworth and L. N. Lindberg, *The Governance of the American Economy*, New York: Cambridge University Press.

18. Pollack, A. (1992) 'Technology without borders raises big questions for U.S.', *The New York Times*, 1 January, p. 1.

19. Biemans (1992) *op. cit.*, p. 79.

20. Axlerod, R. (1984) *The Evolution of Cooperation*, New York: Basic Books.

21. See the discussion in Alter and Hage (1993) *op. cit.*, pp. 7–10 on cooperation in the Japanese and other motor industries.

22. See Biemens (1992) *op. cit.*, pp. 82–4 for examples of inter-firm cooperation in Europe.

23. See Alter and Hage (1993) *op. cit.*, pp. 10–12 for details of public sector cooperation.

24. Van de Ven, A. H. and Ferry, D. (1980) *Measuring and Assessing Organisations*, New York: John Wiley.
25. Schermerhorn, J. R. (1975) 'Determinants of interorganizational cooperation', *Academy of Management Journal* 18, pp. 846–56.
26. See Van de Ven (1976) *op. cit.* on domain similarity.
27. See Alter and Hage (1993) *op. cit.*, pp. 78–80 for a discussion on the necessary conditions for the continuation of IORs. See also Van de Ven and Ferry (1980), *op. cit.*
28. Cromie, S. and Birley, S. (1994) 'Relationships among small business support agencies', *Entrepreneurship and Regional Development*, 6, pp. 301–14.

Further reading

Andersson, P. and Soderlund, M. (1988) 'The network approach to marketing', *Irish Marketing Review* 3, pp. 63–8.
Gummesson, E. (1987) 'The new marketing – Developing long-term interactive relationships', *Long Range Planning* 20, pp. 10–20.

Chapter 15

The entrepreneurial marketing plan

Objectives

After reading this chapter the reader will have a clear understanding of how to develop an entrepreneurial marketing plan. The reader will appreciate the scope and parameters of an entrepreneurial marketing plan and the processes involved in devising it. The chapter is linked to a series of worksheets in Appendix A, which will allow the reader to build an entrepreneurial marketing plan that is unique to the individual enterprise.

Introduction

We have argued throughout this text that formal management approaches and techniques are inappropriate for entrepreneurs and SMEs. This is not to say that entrepreneurs do not manage, nor is it to say that some aspects of management approaches and techniques cannot be utilized for the benefit of an SME. Indeed, we have acknowledged that entrepreneurs take decisions just like any other managers, but that they do so in a way that is unique to them. Similarly, we have recognized that entrepreneurs do perform marketing, albeit in a way that is uniquely influenced by the entrepreneur. Remember also that we stated in Chapter 1 that the link shared by marketing and entrepreneurship is, in fact, management. The essence of our conclusion is that, while entrepreneurs may manage, take decisions and carry out a form of marketing, such management and marketing may be inefficient and most certainly could be improved. But how can this be done? What steps can an entrepreneur follow in order to develop a *usable* and *meaningful* marketing plan?

Underlying factors

When developing an entrepreneurial marketing plan it is important that it conforms to existing constraints and conditions. A whole range of constraints and conditions have been repeatedly referred to throughout this text, but we can distil them down to certain basic underlying factors. These encompass the following.

Any entrepreneurial marketing plan must take account of the inherent characteristics of marketing, which are about a positive approach to doing business in a changing environment and which takes as its focus the customer. Equally, the inherent characteristics of entrepreneurship must also be taken into account; these can be summarized as opportunistic exploitation of a change environment. Having debated these characteristics in some depth, we can say with some confidence that the characteristics of marketing and entrepreneurship are closely related, if not similar. This conclusion is confirmed when we set both dimensions in the context of SMEs, primarily in relation to the inherent resource constraints of SMEs but also by the fact that they have a limited impact on their market because of these resource constraints.

The framework for developing entrepreneurial marketing

In the context of the inherent and fundamental characteristics mentioned above, we have devoted this section of this text to setting out a framework for developing entrepreneurial marketing. As the reader will know, the key aspects of this framework are the notion of adaptation of management and particularly marketing approaches and techniques, and the application of new concepts. When we advocate adaptation of marketing approaches we are implicitly arguing that there is a proven merit in the formal or traditional approaches of marketing. If we take account of the inherent characteristics of entrepreneurship and SMEs, then we must adapt these proven concepts.

We have illustrated how this can be done in relation to aspects of marketing planning and decision-making, as these are most relevant to the ultimate aim of this text. The new concepts that we have concentrated on are, of course, the development, value and use of marketing competencies and marketing networks. These are chosen because they are inherent to good management practice and performance in the case of competencies, and implicit to the entrepreneurial decision-making processes in the case of networks.

There is one other underlying factor which we must recognize before we set out the process of developing an entrepreneurial marketing plan. Consider that we have repeatedly used the term context in connection with the adaptation process and in relating management and marketing concepts to SMEs. It is of primary importance that any marketing activity, whether entrepreneurial or otherwise, should be set in the context in which it is occurring if that marketing is to be truly effective and meaningful. So our description of the importance of moving general marketing concepts, approaches and techniques towards the situation specific of an actual marketing circumstance must be adhered to if entrepreneurial marketing is to be successful. Of course, situation-specific aspects are most likely to be implicitly inherent in entrepreneurial marketing because this is something that an entrepreneur will do naturally. Remember, we stated that entrepreneurs address issues that are of primary importance to themselves or their business. By doing this they are addressing the situation specific and therefore introducing a degree of context. However, we cannot rely on this happening intuitively; we must proactively and explicitly ensure that we take full account of all the factors that influence the situation specific. Therefore, an entrepreneur must not only take account of the type of marketing circumstance that pertains to the enterprise but also such factors as the inherent characteristics of industry, competition, market profiles, product differentiation, etc. Only by a proper and full assessment of *all* factors relating to a situation specific will entrepreneurial marketing be set in context.

Devising the entrepreneurial marketing plan

The entrepreneurial marketing plan will have as its foundations the individual's competency abilities and his/her use of the marketing network. Determination and techniques of application of these concepts have been described in detail in Chapters 13 and 14. Suffice to say here that the entrepreneur will have given consideration to the range of marketing competencies and determined his or her personal strengths and weaknesses in relation to them. It is implicit in developing the entrepreneurial marketing plan that entrepreneurs *know* their competency strengths and know how to use them to minimize competency weaknesses. By using these strong marketing competencies the entrepreneur will enhance the entrepreneurial marketing plan.

Similarly, it is assumed that a personal marketing network will have been identified by the entrepreneur. This will be made up of those individuals who can offer the best possible advice and guidance on aspects of marketing in relation to the SME. The network will be utilized proactively in the development of the entrepreneurial marketing plan. That is, the entrepreneur will purposefully and actively seek advice and guidance by presenting ideas and problems to individuals within the network, with a view to refining and finalizing the plan after carefully considering their response.

It has been assumed that the entrepreneur will make provisional decisions about the plan by naturally utilizing his or her marketing competencies; then, having determined an outline plan, will allow the marketing network to comment on and assess the viability of its proposals. If necessary, this process can be repeated until the entrepreneur is confident that the plan is appropriate and workable. This is an ongoing process: constant refinement and realignment of marketing activities in anticipation of, or in reaction to, market changes are natural aspects of the process.

Developing a statement of the entrepreneurial marketing plan

Having determined appropriate marketing competencies and networks and how best these can be developed and used, our task is to complete the framework by marrying them with the adaptation of marketing approaches and techniques.

Let us remind ourselves that the adaptation of marketing techniques must be done in the context of SMEs. SMEs do not operate in a vacuum, they exist in an interactive environment which can be hostile or friendly. When competitiveness is seen as hostility, entrepreneurs often perceive themselves to be under a major threat, and in such cases feel they cannot compete with the seemingly greater resources of the competition. This is particularly true in relation to larger companies. If there is substance to these comments, what can entrepreneurial SMEs do to compete effectively with strong competition?

Beating the competition

To beat the competition we must appreciate and understand, not only the inherent characteristics of SMEs but also the potential marketing advantages they might have over the competition in general and larger companies in particular. In order to determine these advantages, we must appreciate how they can be used to beat the competition through entrepreneurial marketing.

We have discussed elsewhere the inherent characteristics of SMEs as incorporating size, limited resources, flexibility, limited marketing expertise, lack of finance, a narrow product base, credibility and innovativeness. This is not an exhaustive list; there are undoubtedly many more characteristics that may need to be taken into account. However, we have tried, in Chapter 6, to encompass all factors by considering the characteristics from a marketing perspective and summarizing them as limited resources – including finance, marketing knowledge, time, etc.; lack of specialist expertise – because entrepreneurs tend to be generalists rather than specialists in any one field, including marketing; and limited impact on the market – because of fewer orders and customers, and as a consequence less of a presence in any industry or geographical area.

While these limitations may exist it does not mean that SME characteristics will not lead to or allow some marketing advantages. Marketing advantages might include: personal touch and more personal contact and service; specialist offers; employee loyalty; better/quicker delivery; flexibility; quicker decision-making; direct access to the top decision-maker; more intimate knowledge of the customer; local image, etc. While this too is not an exhaustive list, it is still extensive and impressive from a competitive viewpoint. The challenge is for an entrepreneur to give careful consideration to the advantages that offer the best opportunities for beating the competition.

A typical list of characteristics that might enable an SME to beat its competition at marketing might include:

● Consistent quality in relation to product, delivery and after-sales, all of which might lead to a good reputation.
● Personalized product/service.
● Flexibility of operations.
● Quick response, leading to speedy operations, opportunism and marketing innovation.
● Local market knowledge allowing greater impact in local markets.

There are substantial advantages in knowing the marketing characteristics of SMEs and evaluating them in such a way as to allow SMEs to compete favourably with large companies and competition in general. Readers may wish to consider how to beat the competition for themselves by completing worksheets 1.1–1.3 in Appendix A.

While there may be attractions in making a list of competitive advantages such as those outlined above, it is important that the entrepreneur does not forget the constraints and limitations imposed on marketing activity. Therefore, if entrepreneurs are to realize the benefits of marketing activity they must concentrate on those key issues that will enable this to occur. Having acknowledged this, an entrepreneurial SME may do well to concentrate on key customers and the best marketing opportunities in key market segments while positioning its strengths against the competition's weaknesses. These are issues which will be addressed later in this planning process.

Marketing information for SMEs

We live in an information age. Businesses in general are deluged with data on all aspects of their operations. Information put to good use will lead to knowledge, which in turn will enhance decision-making. However, as many entrepreneurs will agree, it can often feel as if there is too much information available across a wide spectrum of activity. Prior knowledge will enable the entrepreneur to assess what is good information and what is marginal to his/her needs. But regardless of prior knowledge, it is important that the entrepreneur knows where to get information and how to acquire it and use it to best advantage. We shall consider these issues while recognizing the inherent constraints and limitations of SMEs' marketing.

The key dimensions of marketing information in relation to SMEs are:

● Sources of marketing information in terms of *who* can provide it and *where* it can be found.
● The methods that can be employed to gather information.
● How information can be utilized and organized.

Readers may wish to answer these questions by completing worksheets 2.1–2.3 in Appendix A.

Completion of these worksheets will have generated a wide variety of sources of marketing information and methods for gathering and using it. The primary sources of marketing information of use to SMEs are likely to incorporate the following items:

● Media publications for general observation and awareness.
● Media editors and marketing information departments for specific information.
● Government sources and publications.
● Widely known and accepted consumer preferences.
● Industry key informants and trend-setters.
● Competitors.
● Customers.
● Suppliers.
● Internal information from sales profiles and employees.

This list is by no means exhaustive; there will be several other sources of information, many of which will be peculiar to specific markets and industries. For SMEs the most immediate problem is how to gather information within their inherent constraints. The question is: Which are the best low-cost, information-gathering techniques that an SME can effectively employ? These can be listed as follows:

● *Recording information from the environment.* This can generally be found in the popular media by referring to competitive activities, industry trends, economic changes, political decisions, new developments in the market, and so on.
● *Observation.* This can be done intuitively by maintaining an awareness of events surrounding an SME's activities. The references listed above can also be enhanced and enriched by general observation.
● *Information from key informants.* These informants are likely to be customers, suppliers, competitors' customers, employees, etc. The information gathered can be of a general

nature such as described above, or highly specific in terms of information about a competitor's products or views on an entrepreneur's own company and its products.
● *Internal record systems.* Such information can provide sales profiles; potential sources of enquiries, customer enquiries, and general requests.

There are many other techniques for gathering information; indeed, SMEs often devise techniques uniquely suited to their particular circumstances. Two points to emphasize are (1) that information gathering is a continual process and should be viewed as an integral part of normal marketing activity whether sophisticated or not; and (2) information should be gathered from as wide a variety of sources as possible. The principle here is that reliance on one or a few sources of information may be dangerous and certainly carries a greater risk of giving a misleading signal than information which indicates a strong signal but which is gathered from a wide range of sources.

Knowing customer expectations

One of the cornerstones of marketing is to satisfy customers by providing products or services which meet their expectations. It goes without saying that an SME's offerings must match its customers' expectations. However, these expectations can sometimes be very complex and diverse. What an SME must do is find out as much as possible about its customers. This means knowing precisely who they are and precisely what motivates them. Also, it means knowing how they like to make purchases and why they purchase from one source and not another. In particular, an SME should know its customers' expectations in relation to the performance of its products or services, and how this might compare with other competitive products or services. In other words, an SME must consider *why* a potential customer buys one firm's products or services in preference to another firm's products or services.

To this end it is important to consider the customers' perception of the SME's products or services; that is, to consider the product or service from the *customer's* perspective as opposed to the firm's perspective.

An SME must have a thorough understanding of how customers think and evaluate this with a view to providing what the customers want; in other words, satisfying customers through the firm's products or services. Let us attempt this by considering the following aspects.

Customer definition of an SME's product or service

In arriving at a conclusion to this definition we must consider *how a potential customer thinks*. To do this we must understand the importance of customer needs and expectations. These may cover a wide spectrum of issues, including economic factors revolving around price, availability, acceptability and convenience; and psychological or emotional factors such as value for money, the image of the firm and its products or services, impressions or expectations of how a product or service performs, and needs and wants in general.

It is possible to test how well an SME's customers are known by comparing a definition of a firm's product from the entrepreneur's view with *why* customers should buy this product. Often the answers vary considerably, because the entrepreneur sees the product from the perspective of features while the customer sees the product from the perspective of benefits in use. It is the latter that are important and must be the focus of the marketing and sales message, since it is *how the customer thinks* that is important. How can an entrepreneur bridge the divide and think like the customer? One way is to follow a simple process. This involves defining your product/service as though you were explaining it to someone else. Readers may wish to do this for themselves by completing worksheets 3.1–3.3 in Appendix A. An examination of the definition may involve discarding any of the following statements:

- The product is special, unique, different, the only one available, superior, etc.
- The price is good, cheap, better, etc.
- The quality is good, better, superior, etc.

A restatement of definitions *only* in relation to customer expectations may be necessary. That is, definitions should *only* include statements that *customers* would make or consider when buying the product or service.

Determining who the customers really are

One reason for defining a product or service from the customers' perspective is to help determine precisely *who* the customers are. The following questions may help to answer this:

- How many are there approximately?
- Are they increasing, declining or static in number?
- How old or how long established are they?
- Where are they situated?
- How much do they spend annually on your kind of product or service?
- Have they any special features or characteristics, and if so what are they?
- Has their behaviour changed over the past *x* years, and if so in what way?

Worksheets 4.1–4.4 in Appendix A offer the reader the opportunity to answer these questions for themselves.

Why should customers buy an enterprise's products?

Once an entrepreneur has determined who his/her customers are and defined the company's product/service in customer terms, it is possible to combine these two considerations and determine the reasons *why* potential customers should buy the company's products/services. It is sometimes useful to ask the question 'Why should customers buy my products?' and then seek qualification and justification for the

Table 15.1 Why should customers buy your products/services?

Is it because:

- You are better than the competition? If yes, how and why?
- Your products/services are unique? If yes, in what way?
- You are the only supplier? If yes, were there ever any other suppliers? What happened to them and why? Are there likely to be any other suppliers in the future? If yes, where will they come from?
- You know your customers personally? If yes, how did you get to know them?
- Your customer likes you? If yes, why and in what way?
- You are convenient to your customer? If yes, how and why is this important?
- You delivery quickly? If yes, how can you do this and how important is it to deliver quickly?
- You are better priced than others? If yes, in what way and why?
- You are reliable and dependable? If so, how and why?

answer by asking 'Is it because?' questions. Table 15.1 lists potential 'Is it because?' questions which cover most aspects of customer expectations. Worksheet 4.5 in Appendix A allows the reader to formulate some answers.

It is easy to appreciate that there are many answers to these very important questions, but it is imperative that the answers are known in as much detail as possible. The more precisely these answers are known the more certainty there is that an SME will be in control of its marketing. If these answers are not known, then it is highly likely that an SME will *not* be in control of its marketing and therefore be at considerable risk of competitor dominance. Also, by answering these questions the entrepreneur can go a long way towards constructing a marketing plan. *Knowing why* customers respond to different aspects of a firm's marketing activity allows an entrepreneur to strengthen the performance of these activities. Let us expand on these questions and consider how we can examine the major tools of marketing in relation to SMEs.

Marketing tools for SMEs

The actual tools of marketing employed by an SME are those that are most appropriate for the individual enterprise. Thus the tools used and the emphasis given in this use are likely to be *unique* to an enterprise and its marketing. What we shall give here is a broad description of tools of marketing considered from the perspective of an SME, the way in which these tools interact and the different emphasis that can be given to them are outlined in several case studies in Appendix B.

The process for determining appropriate marketing for an SME is simply to consider each marketing tool in three ways:

1. Make a list of the different ways in which particular marketing tools can be performed. The process at this stage is not judgemental, but simply to brainstorm as many ways or methods in which a particular function of marketing can be performed. The object is to create a comprehensive list of methods and by so doing stimulate consideration of issues which have previously been ignored or missed through too narrow a focus.

2. Evaluate the list of ways and methods in relation to the actual SME and determine the *best methods* that would serve the company most effectively. This means taking account of the market and *customer knowledge* gleaned from the previous considerations and exercises. By doing so the entrepreneur will not only be determining, with reasonable certainty, which are the best methods for the enterprise, but also will have the opportunity of assessing the *viability* of the various methods. In considering this it is useful to restrict these to a manageable number within the resources of the enterprise; therefore, it is unlikely that more than five methods can be justified. Indeed, there may be some benefits in this restriction as it forces a tight assessment to be made.
3. Having determined the best methods of marketing activity for the enterprise it is important that these are put to good and effective use. This requires an articulation not only of how marketing activities will be used but also a plan of the sequence in which they will be employed. In doing this the enterprise will have developed a coordinated and cohesive plan of marketing.

These three steps should be taken in relation to each important area of marketing. Thus the process might resemble something like the following:

Promotion and publicity decisions (Worksheets 5.1–5.3)
- Make a list of ways/methods of promoting and publicizing your businesses products/services.
- Make a list of the five *best* viable ways/methods for promoting and publicizing your business and justify these.
- Describe how the five best ways/methods you have chosen can *actually be used and implemented*. Your description should explain the *sequence* in which they might be used/implemented.

Distribution decisions (Worksheets 6.1–6.3)
- Make a list of factors that can be taken into account when distributing products. In other words, how do you distribute your goods?
- Make a list of the five best ways/methods for distributing your products and justify your choice.
- Describe how the five best ways/methods you have chosen can actually be used and implemented. Your description should explain the *sequence* in which they might be used/implemented.

Pricing decisions (Worksheets 7.1–7.3)
- Make a list of factors that can be taken into account when setting price. That is, how do you set price?
- Make a list of the five best ways/methods of setting price and justify your choice.
- Describe how the five best ways/methods you have chosen can actually be used and implemented. Your description should explain the *sequence* in which they might be used/implemented.

Selling decisions (Worksheets 8.1–8.3)
- Make a list of factors that can be taken into account when selling your products/services. That is, how do you sell your products/services?

- Make a list of the five best ways/methods of selling and justify your choice.
- Describe how the five best ways/methods you have chosen can actually be used and implemented. Your description should explain the *sequence* in which they might be used/implemented.

An integrated marketing plan

Having evaluated and justified your decisions in relation to each of the important aspects of marketing activity, it is now important to evaluate each one in relation to all the others. This means going through the process outlined in Figure 15.1.

The value of this exercise is that it enables integration and cohesiveness throughout the whole of the marketing activity.

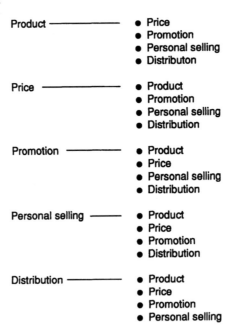

Describe your marketing activity by considering each aspect of marketing in relation to all other aspects. That is, consider how decisions in relation to each aspect impact upon all other aspects and how these aspects must match.

Consider the impact of:

Product ——————
- Price
- Promotion
- Personal selling
- Distributon

Price ——————
- Product
- Promotion
- Personal selling
- Distribution

Promotion ——————
- Product
- Price
- Personal selling
- Distribution

Personal selling ——
- Product
- Price
- Promotion
- Distribution

Distribution ——————
- Product
- Price
- Promotion
- Personal selling

Figure 15.1 Summary of a marketing strategy.

The marketing plan in relation to the market

So far we have gone through a process that has allowed us to give considered thought to knowing the market and knowing customers, and using this knowledge to determine marketing variables and how these integrate. What we must do now is assess these decisions against the market and assess how they will stand up to market forces. In planning terms this means evaluating the enterprise's marketing variables in relation to the company's strengths and weaknesses and the opportunities and threats emanating from the market. In formal marketing terms this means doing a SWOT analysis. Strengths and weaknesses should be evaluated against competitors, opportunities and threats in the market. Short- and long-term opportunities, and the enterprise's strengths and weaknesses and threats, should be evaluated against competitors and market trends, as well as against the enterprise's strengths and weaknesses. Worksheets 9.1–9.4 allow the reader to go through this process.

After consideration of all the aspects described in this planning process the entrepreneur will be in a position to describe the enterprise's marketing environment and its situation and position within this marketing environment accurately. The entrepreneur will also be able to define the products and services accurately and describe *how* each of the marketing variables integrates with the others. Worksheets 10.1–10.3 allow the reader to make this statement.

On completion of this final step in the process we will have completed what we have termed an 'entrepreneurial marketing plan'. In fact, the final three worksheets *are* the plan.

The discipline of going through this process will have considerably enhanced the company's marketing profile. But there will have been much greater benefits accruing which can be summarized as:

● The substantial learning experience of the process in itself.
● The amount of knowledge gleaned with respect to marketing issues.
● The ability to do marketing.

Perhaps the most important benefit is that the SME will have a marketing plan that is built on the foundation of entrepreneurial, marketing and SME characteristics that is entirely compatible with the unique characteristics of the firm. The benefits of operating to such a plan will be found in the enhanced performance of the firm.

Summary

This chapter has been concerned with implementing a framework for developing entrepreneurial marketing. The chapter represents the culmination of entrepreneurial marketing decision-making in that it offers the opportunity to articulate the thought processes surrounding the application of competencies and networks in the form of an action plan for entrepreneurial marketing. The reader will now understand marketing thought processes which are suited to SMEs and, if desired, will have completed a unique entrepreneurial marketing plan.

Appendix A: Worksheets for devising an entrepreneurial marketing plan

1. SMEs/Large Companies Marketing Interface

1.1 Characteristics of SMEs
1.2 The Marketing Advantages of SMEs
1.3 Beating Large Companies on Marketing

2. Marketing Information for SMEs

2.1 Sources of Marketing Information
2.2 Methods for Gathering Marketing Information
2.3 Using Information Methods

3. Knowing Customer Expectations

3.1 Defining the Product/Service
3.2 Customer Descriptions of the Product/Service
3.3 Defining the Enterprise's Customers

4. Who are the Enterprise's Customers?

4.1 Where and How Many Customers?
4.2 Definition of Customers: Variations
4.3 How Customers Think
4.4 and 4.5 Reasons Why Customers Buy

5–8 Marketing Tools For SMEs

Promotion and Publicity Decisions

5.1 Methods
5.2 Best Methods
5.3 Implementing Methods

Distribution Decisions

6.1 Factors to be Taken into Account
6.2 Best Methods
6.3 Implementing Methods

Pricing Decisions

7.1 Factors to be Taken into Account
7.2 Best Methods
7.3 Implementing Methods

Selling Decisions

8.1 Factors to be Taken into Account
8.2 Best Methods
8.3 Implementing Methods

9.   Devising a Marketing Strategy

9.1 Marketing Strengths
9.2 Marketing Weaknesses
9.3 Marketing Opportunities
9.4 Marketing Threats

10.   The Entrepreneurial Marketing Plan

10.1 Definition of the Enterprise's Market
10.2 The Enterprise's Market Position
10.3 Integration of the Marketing Variables

1.1 SME's/LARGE COMPANIES MARKETING INTERFACE

CHARACTERISTICS OF SME's

> List the characteristics of SME's
> That is, What makes SME's different to large companies?

-

-

-

-

-

-

-

-

1.2 SME's/LARGE COMPANIES MARKETING INTERFACE

THE MARKETING ADVANTAGES OF SME's

Make a list of the MARKETING ADVANTAGES of SME's

-

-

-

-

-

-

-

-

-

-

1.3 SME's/LARGE COMPANIES MARKETING INTERFACE

BEATING LARGE COMPANIES ON MARKETING

How can SME's BEAT large companies on Marketing?
Make a list of five good marketing approaches for beating large companies

-
-
-
-
-
-
-
-
-
-

2.1 MARKETING INFORMATION FOR SME's

SOURCES OF MARKETING INFORMATION

Make a list of SOURCES of marketing information.
Who can provide marketing information?
Where can marketing information be found?

-

-

-

-

-

-

-

-

-

2.2 MARKETING INFORMATION FOR SME's

METHODS FOR GATHERING MARKETING
INFORMATION

Make a list of the METHODS SME's can employ for
information gathering.
Think of both internal and external ways of gathering
information

-

-

-

-

-

--

2.3   MARKETING INFORMATION FOR SME's

USING INFORMATION METHODS

How can information methods be utilised and organised to best advantage?
Make a list of five ways in which these methods can be USED
(The list should be in the order in which to do things and how best to get information)

-

-

-

-

-

- -

3.1 KNOWING CUSTOMER EXPECTATIONS

DEFINING THE PRODUCT/SERVICE

Define the product/service as though you were explaining it to someone

-
-
-
-
-
-
-
-

3.2 KNOWING CUSTOMER EXPECTATIONS

CUSTOMER DESCRIPTIONS OF THE PRODUCT/SERVICE

Consider the definitions in 3.1 and discard anything that states that:

The product is special; unique; different; only one available; superior; etc

The price is good; cheap; better; etc

The quality is good; better; superior; etc

Restate the definitions ONLY in relation to customer expectations. That is, your definitions should ONLY include statements that CUSTOMERS would make or consider.

I am buying this product/service because it does the following for me:

-

-

-

-

-

-

-

3.3 KNOWING CUSTOMER EXPECTATIONS

DEFINING THE ENTERPRISES CUSTOMERS

Define who the enterprises customers should be

-
-
-
-
-
-
-

4.1   KNOWING CUSTOMER EXPECTATIONS

WHERE AND HOW MANY CUSTOMERS

Taking account of the definition of who the customers should be, answer the following questions and see if the definition of who the customers should be comes close to who the customers actually are

Approximately how many customers are there?

Are they increasing, declining, static in number?

How old, or how long established are they?

Where are they, geographically?

How much do they spend annually on your kind of product/service?

Have they any special features or characteristics and if so what are they?

Has their behaviour changed over the past x years and if so in what way?

4.2   KNOWING CUSTOMER EXPECTATIONS

DEFINITION OF CUSTOMERS: VARIATIONS

Compare the definition of the product/service with the reasons why potential customers should buy it.
Make a list of any differences and variations and explain.

DIFFERENCE/VARIATION: BECAUSE...

-
-
-
-
-
-
-

4.3 KNOWING CUSTOMER EXPECTATIONS

HOW CUSTOMERS THINK

How does your customer think?
What makes your customer tick?
Make a list of your customrs characteristics, buying patterns,
influences, etc

-

-

-

-

-

-

-

-

4.4 KNOWING CUSTOMER EXPECTATIONS

REASONS WHY CUSTOMERS BUY

Make a list of the reasons why potential customers should buy
your products/services

-
-
-
-
-
-
-
-

4.5 KNOWING CUSTOMER EXPECTATIONS

REASONS WHY CUSTOMERS BUY

Taking account of the list of reasons WHY potential customers should buy your products/services (4.4), answer the questions listed in Table 15.1.
Compare your list of reasons in 4.4 and amend as appropriate.

Why should customers buy your product?
Is it because...

-

-

-

-

-

-

-

-

5.1 MARKETING TOOLS FOR SME's

PROMOTION AND PUBLICITY DECISIONS

Make a list of ways/methods of promoting and publicising the enterprises products/services

-

-

-

-

-

-

-

-

5.2 MARKETING TOOLS FOR SME's

PROMOTION AND PUBLICITY DECISIONS

Make a list of the five BEST viable ways/methods for promoting and publicising the SME and JUSTIFY

VIABLE WAY/METHOD: JUSTIFICATION

-

-

-

-

-

-

-

-

5.3 MARKETING TOOLS FOR SME's

PROMOTION AND PUBLICITY DECISIONS

Describe how the five best ways/methods you have listed in 5.2
can ACTUALLY BE USED AND IMPLEMENTED.
Your description should explain the SEQUENCE in which they
might be implemented

-

-

-

-

-

-

-

-

6.1 MARKETING TOOLS FOR SME's

DISTRIBUTION DECISIONS

Make a list of factors that can be taken into account when distributing products.
How does the enterprise distribute its products?

-
-
-
-
-
-
-
-
-
-

6.2 MARKETING TOOLS FOR SME's

DISTRIBUTION DECISIONS

Make a list of the five BEST ways/methods for distributing your products and JUSTIFY

WAY/METHOD: JUSTIFICATION

-

-

-

-

-

-

-

-

-

-

6.3 MARKETING TOOLS FOR SME's

DISTRIBUTION DECISIONS

Describe how the five best ways/methods you have listed in 6.2 can ACTUALLY BE USED AND IMPLEMENTED.
Your description should explain the SEQUENCE in which they might be implemented

-

-

-

-

-

-

-

-

-

-

7.1 MARKETING TOOLS FOR SME's

PRICING DECISIONS

Make a list of factors that can be taken into account when setting price.
How do you set price?

-

-

-

-

-

-

-

-

7.2 MARKETING TOOLS FOR SME's

PRICING DECISIONS

Make a list of the five BEST ways/methods of setting price and JUSTIFY

WAY/METHOD:	JUSTIFICATION
-	
-	
-	
-	
-	
-	
-	
-	

7.3 MARKETING TOOLS FOR SME's

PRICING DECISIONS

Describe how the five best ways/methods you have listed in 7.2 can ACTUALLY BE USED AND IMPLEMENTED.
Your description should explain the SEQUENCE in which they might be implemented.

-

-

-

-

-

-

-

8.1 MARKETING TOOLS FOR SME's

SELLING DECISIONS

Make a list of factors that can be taken into account when
selling the enterprises products/services.
How do you SELL your products/services?

-

-

-

-

-

-

-

-

8.2 MARKETING TOOLS FOR SME's

SELLING DECISIONS

Make a list of the five BEST ways/methods of selling and JUSTIFY

WAY/METHOD: JUSTIFICATION

-

-

-

-

-

-

-

-

8.3 MARKETING TOOLS FOR SME's

SELLING DECISIONS

Describe how the five best ways/methods you have listed in 8.2 can ACTUALLY BE USED AND IMPLEMENTED.
Your description should explain the SEQUENCE in which they might be implemented

-

-

-

-

-

-

-

-

9.1 DEVISING A MARKETING STRATEGY

MARKETING STRENGTHS

Make a list of the enterprises MARKETING STRENGTHS.
This means evaluating your marketing variables and resources
and assessing them against the competitors and opportunities
and threats in the market.

-
-
-
-
-
-
-
-
-

9.2 DEVISING A MARKETING STRATEGY

MARKETING WEAKNESSES

Make a list of the enterprises MARKETING WEAKNESSES
This means evaluating your marketing variables and resources
and assessing them against the competitors and opportunities
and threats in the market.

-
-
-
-
-
-
-
-
-

9.3 DEVISING A MARKETING STRATEGY

MARKETING OPPORTUNITIES

Make a list of the MARKET OPPORTUNITIES that may exist for your enterprise to exploit.
This means evaluating both short and long term opportunities and assessing them against your strengths and weaknesses.

-
-
-
-
-
-
-
-
-

9.4 DEVISING A MARKETING STRATEGY

MARKETING THREATS

Make a list of the MARKET THREATS that may exist against your enterprise.
This means evaluating the threats presented by competitors and market trends and assessing them against your strengths and weaknesses

-
-
-
-
-
-
-
-
-

10.1 THE ENTREPRENEURIAL MARKETING PLAN

DEFINITION OF THE ENTERPRISES MARKET

Outline the main elements that describe your enterprises market
and its environment.
This means defining the market and listing the main
environmental elements that influence it

MARKET DEFINITION:

ENVIRONMENTAL ELEMENTS OF INFLUENCE:

-
-
-
-
-
-
-

10.2 THE ENTREPRENEURIAL MARKETING PLAN

THE ENTERPRISES MARKET POSITION

Describe the enterprises situation/position within its marketing environment.
This means taking account of the SWOT in 9.1 - 9.4 and describing your enterprises position in relation to your nearest competitor

-

-

-

-

-

-

-

-

10.3　THE ENTREPRENEURIAL MARKETING PLAN

INTEGRATION OF THE MARKETING VARIABLES

Define the enterprises products/services and describe HOW each of the marketing variables influence/impact upon them.

PRODUCTS/SERVICES DEFINED:

Influence/impact of PRICE

Influence/impact of PROMOTION

Influence/impact of PERSONAL SELLING

Influence/impact of DISTRIBUTION

Appendix B: Case studies of entrepreneurial marketing

Introduction

The purpose of this appendix is to illustrate, by way of four case studies, how entrepreneurial marketing can work for SMEs. The preamble to each case and the cases themselves are set against the general framework for developing entrepreneurial marketing as described in Chapter 12, and where appropriate, the aspects of networking and marketing competencies, as discussed in Chapters 13 and 14. One case centres on the markets for specialist musical instruments, two on the food market and one on travel and tourism. The basis for choosing the first case study reflects the importance of music, in particular popular music, in people's everyday lives. Similarly, the basis for the choice of the remaining three case studies is that we all buy food products and so each of us has experience of food marketing from the customer's perspective, similarly most of us go on holiday every year and have firm ideas about what we expect from our holiday choice. From this perspective it is easy for readers to understand some of the basic market positioning undertaken by marketers in these industries.

In the first case study the entrepreneur attempts to renew the enterprise's fortunes and rebuild the profile of his hand-made guitars in the critically important North American market. The importance of personal contacts in developing an entrepreneurial approach to resolving marketing problems is addressed. The second case describes the start-up stages of a 'goods' trading company and emphasizes how its lack of resources led to the adoption of the SME marketing approach. An added feature of the description is the fact that it addresses one of the key development areas of marketing, that is, an international context, which is built on the networking dimension and competency strengths of the entrepreneur. The third case study focuses on the marketing of fresh foods and processed foods. In the fourth case we are made aware of the obvious competency and network characteristics of the owner, but the concentration is on the specifically adapted marketing approach, based on the workbook approach, used as a consequence of the severely limiting SME characteristics.

When seeking to understand the evolutionary progression of these companies the reader should bear in mind the frameworks described in Chapters 12, 13, and 14. The reader will be able to observe how conventional management and marketing approaches have been adapted to suit the resource constraints and characteristics of SMEs. In particular, it will be possible to understand the influence of the inherent entrepreneurial characteristics of the owners and how they, either instinctively or proactively, use their networks and work to their competency strengths. The net result is entrepreneurial marketing, a kind of marketing that is uniquely different from conventional marketing but which is entirely suited to the entrepreneurially led SME.

This appendix describes the four cases with brief evaluations and explanations that link the events to the concept of entrepreneurial marketing.

1 Lowden Acoustic Guitars

Introduction

From the moment he took control of Lowden Guitars Andy Kidd knew that the United States, as the country that had exercised such a major influence on music styles world-wide, was going to be the one he had to succeed in. With this fact in mind, he had recently established a subsidiary company of Lowden Guitars in Forest City, North Carolina. The focus of this new company was to market and distribute the company's products throughout North America.

Since he had become involved in the company initially, quite by accident it seemed now, he had little thought of what the ups and downs of managing a small firm would be. The past four years had tested his determination, commitment and, at times, his very personal faith to the limit. Yet four years later he felt, while there was always room for improvement, that he had emerged strengthened. A widely travelled man, fluent in three European languages, with a network of friends world-wide he demonstrated a sensitive, easy-going attitude, tempered with a firmness that had stood him in good stead when there were tough decisions to make.

Historical background

The company was founded by George Lowden in the mid-1970s. Since his early twenties he had dreamt of designing and making the best guitar in the world, now it seemed that his dream had begun to materialize. As a perfectionist he was committed to pursuing the very best in quality in terms of design and materials available for his guitars. His approach resulted in the creation of a musical instrument with an international reputation for the very highest quality and workmanship. Indeed, so successful was he in establishing that reputation in those early days that demand for his guitars very quickly outstripped supply. As a one-man operation at the time he simply had to find some means to increase output. In a bid to address this challenge George, with the help and guidance of a German friend and colleague, granted a licence to manufacture his guitar to a small Japanese guitar factory with a reputation for making high quality instruments. For the next four years he strove, in association with his Japanese associates, to address the demands of his market. But the pressures of maintaining the exacting standards he sought for his guitars over such a great physical distance finally persuaded George of the need to bring production back to Ireland.

His determined and single-minded pursuit of a high quality, world-class guitar meant that his best efforts to develop his enterprise in any real commercial way remained constrained. Ultimately, limited cash and diminishing goodwill placed the future of the company in jeopardy. If the growing reputation for Lowden Guitars as a world-class instrument was to be maintained and further developed, the management of the company needed to be restructured. The company's next stage of development saw a rescue package emerge which put in place a new entrepreneurial management team headed by Andy Kidd. With the help of local enterprise agency funding and a supportive bank manager, new purpose-built premises were opened and equipped where a hand-picked team of skilled craftsworkers continued to produce the acclaimed Lowden Guitar, under the guidance of George Lowden.

The company's products – Lowden Guitars

The Lowden range of products provides a series of hand-made wooden guitars. All are designed and manufactured to the same exacting standards that typify the company's continuous quest for perfection. Each is designed with a particular type of player in mind. The 'O' Series, the original Lowden Guitar, is targeted at the 'finger style' guitarist. The 'F' Series, by design, is more suitable for either finger-picking or flat-picking playing styles. The 'S' Series, with features more akin to that of a classical guitar, is designed to appeal to ragtime musicians. The 'L' Series or 'stage edition', with its all-round smaller dimensions, is an ideal guitar for stage performances. Finally, the latest addition to the range is the 'D' Series or 'Lowden Dreadnought', which reflects the traditional style of the classical 'Martin' guitar.

A further dimension to the company's product planning strategy is a series of five-string electric guitars under the 'Goodfellow' brand. Consistent with Lowden's approach to guitar production, each is hand-made from the finest selected wood available. The variations in the range are defined by a solid mahogany body with a choice of various veneers. Custom options on these guitars include different hardware appointments, pick-ups and the like.

The company's markets

North America in particular and those countries influenced by its many musical cultures constitute the main target markets for Lowden products. The company seeks to address the needs of both professional and amateurs for steel strung acoustic guitars and, to a lesser extent, electric bass guitars. In addition, Lowden have sought to address the emerging trend towards a new style of instrument known as an 'electro-acoustic' guitar. Similar to the conventional instrument in looks and sound, this new guitar seeks to achieve a compromise between the normal acoustic performance and how it performs when amplified by means of a pick-up system fitted to it. A collaborative venture with the American company EMG, renowned for its pioneering work in electric guitar systems, has led to the development of a new acoustic pick-up system for Lowden's products.

Competition

Manufacturers of guitars can be divided into three categories;

1. Cheap, mass-produced instruments made in the Far East usually under many different brand names.
2. Well-made, mass-produced instruments, often featuring technological innovations such as plastic bodies or incorporating an integral pick-up as standard.
3. Quality hand-made instruments, using only solid woods and offering some sort of 'custom build' facility.

Competitors for Lowden's acoustic guitars are largely in the third group, though some of those operating in this sector may also have guitars manufactured for them, under licence, in the Far East. The two main competitors facing Lowden are 'Martin', which has a long-established reputation as arguably the original inventors of the acoustic guitar as it is known today and 'Taylor'. Both are US companies. There are few comparable European competitors.

Lowden's market position

Lowden's guitars are positioned very much in the upper end of the market. The premium price charged for the company's products places them in a small, essentially exclusive market sector which represents a relatively small and not necessarily lucrative proportion of the overall guitar market. Research suggests that the main concentration of demand for guitars is actually at the lower end of the market in the $200–$600 price range. The need for volume sales at low costs becomes essential. The most competitively priced 'Lowden', however, costs on average five times as much.

Getting Lowdens to market

Change in the management of the company meant a new policy of appointing agents in the company's markets over an earlier policy of using distributors. Thus Lowden in Ireland has itself become the main distributor in Europe addressing a large, well-established customer base, either directly or through agents. A subsidiary company, based at Forest City, North Carolina, has been established to manage marketing and sales activities in the all important US market.

Advantages of this approach are numerous. The company has been able to obtain much more competitive prices for its products as a consequence with net average selling prices increasing by some 50% over a three year period in the European market. Competition on prices in the United States remains particularly strong, and scope for price variations on models is limited. Variable exchange rates make for often more difficult circumstances. However, being closer to the marketplace and in more direct contact with customers has given Lowden's management much more reliable feedback on trends and tastes than had previously been available. The key challenge of the new policy has been to develop strong personal relationships with agents and dealers.

The Lowden appeal

Numerous successful musical personalities have enjoyed the value and quality of a Lowden guitar. In addition to their views being a testimony to the company's products, they are a key source of information on the design and development of new models. Yet, though increasingly acknowledged by more and more people, both the Lowden acoustic and Goodfellow electric bass guitar brands have yet to achieve significantly higher profiles in the company's chosen markets. Reluctant to go down the endorsee route to promote the company's product, Andy Kidd felt strongly that the company's guitars were of such quality that they were a promotion in themselves.

Lowden's management

Andy Kidd, the managing director of Lowden guitars, hadn't always sought to own and run his own production company. Indeed, town planning was the career he originally had in mind. After two years at a university however he began to have doubts. He was no academic after all. The course he was doing didn't excite him sufficiently, so he decided to try something else. Still in his early twenties there was still time to experiment. He left Ireland for England and a job as a recording engineer with a music company. Within a short time he was producing records. This whole experience set off what Andy saw as a latent creativity in himself and a desire to do the best possible job, whatever the limitations. He wasn't really interested in second-best efforts.

Although he knew of George Lowden as a consequence of his recording background, and George was a friend of his brother, it was only while living in England that he, quite by accident, came to be friendly with him. He shared an apartment with a musician friend who owned and played a particularly expensive Lowden guitar. From time to time, when Andy returned home to Ireland his friend asked him to bring his guitar to George for any minor repairs that were needed. As a consequence of these visits George and he became friends and Andy was able to keep up to speed on the Lowden story as it developed.

After three years in the recording business, Andy became freelance and moved to Scandinavia in search of new challenges. He subsequently returned to Ireland, a fluent Swedish and Norwegian speaker, and considerably more experienced in and knowledgeable of the music industry. On his return he established a recording studio of his own.

Over the next eighteen months he brought a wide variety of different groups to Ireland from abroad for recording sessions and soon started to travel to their home bases for rehearsals. He also sought to meet the demands of the local music scene for recording opportunities. However, the increasingly unsocial hours of these demands began to conflict with his personal life and plans to marry. He decided that some degree of stability was needed. He closed the recording studio and joined a local television company making commercials and corporate promotional videos. He became involved specifically in such creative activity as storyboard writing, developing concepts and writing background music, learning all the while the jargon of the promotions and advertising people.

Ever restless it seemed, Andy and his wife looked again to Scandinavia for a new home. As a possible business outlet he contacted George Lowden and offered to distribute his guitars there. As discussions developed he became increasingly aware that the originator and designer of Lowden guitars was struggling to hold his company together. Andy became concerned that Ireland might actually lose this classic product altogether if some positive actions were not taken quickly. Some crucial management skills and extra funds would be needed to meet the challenges and to this end and with nothing other than an ambition to keep the Lowden guitar in Ireland, Andy arranged a meeting between George Lowden and one of his closest friends, a person with extensive experience in production management. This colleague brought with him to the meeting a close contact of his own, an individual who was a qualified and experienced accountant. Andy nurtured the hope that by bringing these people together perhaps a package to rescue the company could be hammered out. At the meeting it was agreed that Lowden guitars definitely had a future. At this point in the meeting all eyes fell on Andy who had until then sought to maintain a neutral role in the proceedings.

With no experience in running a manufacturing business, little personal capital and never having borrowed money, Andy, not surprisingly, at first felt the very idea of managing Lowden's recovery was absurd. To whom could he go for help, for funds, for guidance? Initially, his friend's accountant came to the rescue, talking him through what was involved in approaching financial institutions and development agencies for funds.

Finance was available but evidence that a strong management team existed to support the enterprise would be necessary to convince lenders that the venture would work. Andy looked to his friends and acquaintances for help. He identified six people who all knew each other and with whom he mixed socially, who were successful in their own careers, in marketing and production or in the case of two in particular, were small business owners themselves. Andy would regularly turn to these friends and colleagues for guidance in the many decisions that had to be made in running the company. A number of key challenges threatened the ongoing success of the small firm. For example, improving the level of productivity and reducing the costs of distribution. In addition, the supply of guitars to the company's markets had now been interrupted twice in only eighteen months, once after the switch in production back to Ireland from Japan, and again during the period of transition when the new management structure had to be introduced into the company. Decisions in response to these challenges would not be easy any more than the actions necessary to put these decisions into good effect. As Andy stated.

> I would not have done any of these things if I couldn't turn to these people. On my own, I'd say I'd never have made it. If I'd been faced with looking at the facts and figures that I was able to pull together by myself before making decisions I'm sure I'd have got lost somewhere down the line.

In order to formalize his friends' involvement in the company each was appointed Director. Andy (mistakenly, as it was to turn out) sought, by making these appointments, to encourage them to become more involved in the practical, day-to-day challenges of managing the venture's renewal. One friend in particular left a job in a well-established engineering company to assume responsibility for production matters at Lowden.

Meanwhile, the constant need for investment funds in these early days to fund the relocation to and development of new premises was largely addressed by an extremely empathic and helpful branch bank manager who sought to accommodate Andy's efforts to re-establish the company. He had warded off pressure from central banking authorities for payments the company would otherwise have had great difficulty in making at that time.

For the immediate future Andy felt freer to address what he saw as the key marketing challenge of rebuilding the company's profile in the United States. Two major problems that he had to face immediately were how to rebuild the image of the company's products in the marketplace and how to address the issue of an inherited price structure for the company's products which reflected an outdated productivity level and an exchange rate which had long since ceased to be of relevance. The result of this latter issue was that some products in the Lowden range were actually being sold in the American market at less than cost. Once again Andy needed help in deciding how best to go about getting back into the US market and addressing these issues. He recalled from his past an old friend with whom he had worked when he had been involved in record production in England. Now a church pastor in up-state New York, Bill Davidson was glad to hear from his friend and only too happy to place the rather substantial basement of his house at Andy's disposal. Indeed, for the next eighteen months he even undertook to ensure that guitars arriving at his basement from the factory in Ireland found their way to those who had purchased them. To facilitate sales Andy had acquired an '800' number in the United States with the facility to transfer the calls to his home in Ireland. Early morning calls to his home became a regular occurrence, as was the surprise of those placing orders when they realized that they had got through to Europe with their call.

With this toehold in the market Andy had to find a way to increase the profile of the company and its products. One thing he was sure of was that there had to be a better way to get his products into the market besides using distributors. His experience in Europe had left him in no doubt that distributors' margins contributed to the inflation of the products' price. In addition, those margins posed an attractive target for Andy himself. Could he get around them and still address the needs of his market effectively? A network of dealerships around the country with whom he could relate personally was surely the answer.

To do this properly was going to require that Andy establish a US subsidiary of Lowden Guitars to include sales and marketing. The costs of doing this as well as meeting the added expenses of an expanded production level were going to require an additional investment of funds. Even the best efforts of his bank manager and friend would no longer be enough. Once again, he turned to his network of friends for help. Support came in the first instance in the shape of the company's German distributor, a long-standing associate of the company and friend of George Lowden, and second, and perhaps critically, given the company's ambitions to develop its profile in the US market, Ray Nenow. Ray was a man with considerable experience in the music industry in the United States and a personal friend of Andy's for some twelve years. In taking a share in the company he also assumed responsibility for marketing the company's products in the United States.

Progress in the US market was described as slow but sure. Having relocated himself and his family in North Carolina, Andy feels better placed to oversee that progress. Just at the moment though, he spends half his time in Ireland at the factory overseeing production.

Of the network of friends to whom he turned in the early days for guidance and support only one remained, representing the company's interests in the Far East. The continued pressure for funds to maintain the growth of the company eventually led to a requirement for the directors to increase their commitment but this time in the form of financial guarantees. Faced with the choice, the others opted not to continue their involvement. At about this time too, his friend, who had joined the company as production manager in the early days of the company's relaunch, decided it was time for him to reconsider his career in small firms and to move on in pursuit of new challenges. Andy bought the interests in the company of those who wished to sell out.

It was an often stressful period of change. Contacts with a local development agency and a local innovation programme, however, have provided a source for much of the funds needed to help sustain development in the company. George Lowden remains an associate of the company responsible for the design and development of new products. It has been an exciting first five years.

Case evaluation

This case study focuses on the importance of personal contacts to a relatively inexperienced entrepreneur anxious to rescue his ailing company and to effect a relaunch of its products in its chosen markets. The central importance of personal contacts as being particularly entrepreneurial in character is explored. Other important issues to note are the dependence of the entrepreneur on his extensive contacts, particularly social contacts initially, for sourcing relevant information for decision-making generally but marketing decisions in particular, the scope of personal contacts to help the entrepreneur to validate those decisions before implementation by bouncing them off network members, and the nature of change in the character and makeup of personal contacts approached by the entrepreneur as his enterprise develops and he begins to confront marketing challenges of increasing complexity.

2 Eaton & Caron (EC) Marketing

This case study describes the situation of a small agency firm, Eaton & Caron (EC) Marketing, doing business with the food distribution industry in Ireland. The entrepreneur, Paul Eaton, had established a network of relationships among all the major food buyers in Ireland. He had been selling a wide variety of food and related products to the food distribution industry for several years. He felt it was time to expand the business beyond its established but narrow parameters. He was stimulated by the onset of the Single European Market which came fully into effect on 1 January 1993.

Paul's new venture began in April 1992 with a visit to France and the Benelux countries with a friend. He travelled overland and purposefully called into a variety of supermarkets as he came upon them. He purchased a variety of products and carefully recorded details of packaging, description, price and source manufacturer or wholesale supplier. After several days it became obvious to Paul that Holland offered the best potential for sourcing products. His observations led him to a large general distributor which had its base in Holland, near Amsterdam. Paul was able to use his personal contact network back home in Ireland to identify a name and obtain a letter of introduction to the Dutch company.

The Dutch company was happy to supply products to Paul's trading company subject to normal trading and credit checks. It was agreed to run a trial on ten products which matched the profile of differentiated basic food products. The chosen products comprised a range of Dutch coffee and a selection of Belgium chocolate. Most of the ten products proved highly successful in the Irish market. Buyers were intrigued by the nonconformity of the products and consumers appeared to be attracted to the continental differentiation.

The relationship between Paul and the Dutch suppliers flourished, as might be expected given the mutual benefits experienced by both parties. Within three months the product range had expanded to incorporate four new ranges: pasta, biscuits, savoury snacks and beverages. The total number of individual products had expanded to 65.

Towards the end of 1992 Paul was again in Holland – his third visit in eight months. The relationship had developed to a stage were Paul felt comfortable to raise the issue of selling his Irish products to the Dutch market. His Dutch partners were immediately enthusiastic and placed telephone calls to potential buyers extolling the merits of Paul and his company and organizing meetings for Paul, who, simply by extending his visit, was able to follow up immediately. Agreements were made with two Dutch buyers for some of Paul's products. *Exporting had begun.*

Currently, Paul's company is expanding its export sales simply by servicing his new found agents in Holland. Sales of the Dutch imported products continue to grow. Paul is expanding his export activity into other European countries. He has visited major food distribution exhibitions in France and Germany, with a view to buying other European products. That is, by *importing* first and using his new relationship to develop export sales.

It is appropriate at this point to emphasize another phenomenon of entrepreneurial marketing: that of falling into a niche. As part of Paul's trawling for other suppliers his entrepreneurial instincts for opportunities has led him into new, peripherally related areas. Previously his company had concentrated on food products, but Paul had been intrigued by other product lines which fitted the scenario of familiar but differentiated products. So Paul has begun to distribute a range of confectionary products which show signs of expanding the business even more rapidly than previously envisaged.

Case evaluation

The key advantages of this approach to exporting are not only that it overcomes the known barriers to exporting but it is also compatible with the entrepreneurs inherent characteristics. There is also an inherent benefit for all parties:

- The entrepreneur utilizes a new source of supply.
- The entrepreneur gains additional sales in the local market.
- The foreign supplier establishes a beachhead in a new market.
- The entrepreneur begins to export through the mechanism of the personal contact network.

● The new foreign buyer is assured by the personal recommendation of a fellow countryman.

There is no doubt that these benefits are substantial, in fact, it is unlikely that Paul would have embarked on an exporting programme through the conventional approach. He would not have had the resources nor the confidence to research any new potential and foreign market.

However, this alternative approach is useful and best at the initial stage of exporting. If Paul is to develop his export programme in a controlled and efficient way, he must quickly conform to sound marketing practice. That is, he must begin to manage his exporting by establishing systems, policies, strategies and plans for the programme as a whole. He must begin to do *international marketing* as opposed to simply exporting on demand. But at least he can now do this from a position of confidence and successful trading.

Let us take a moment to consider the Eaton & Caron marketing story in the context of the general framework for developing entrepreneurial marketing, and specifically the exporting and international dimension in relation to SMEs.

It is accepted that conventional wisdom for developing export markets is, in the main, sound. That is, a newly exporting firm should identify a suitable market offering good potential opportunities and soundly research that market for suitable customers. Having once established a foothold, that market is therefore ripe for exploitation and development. Such an approach may have many trialists and many will succeed, however, it is not appropriate for many other firms, particularly many

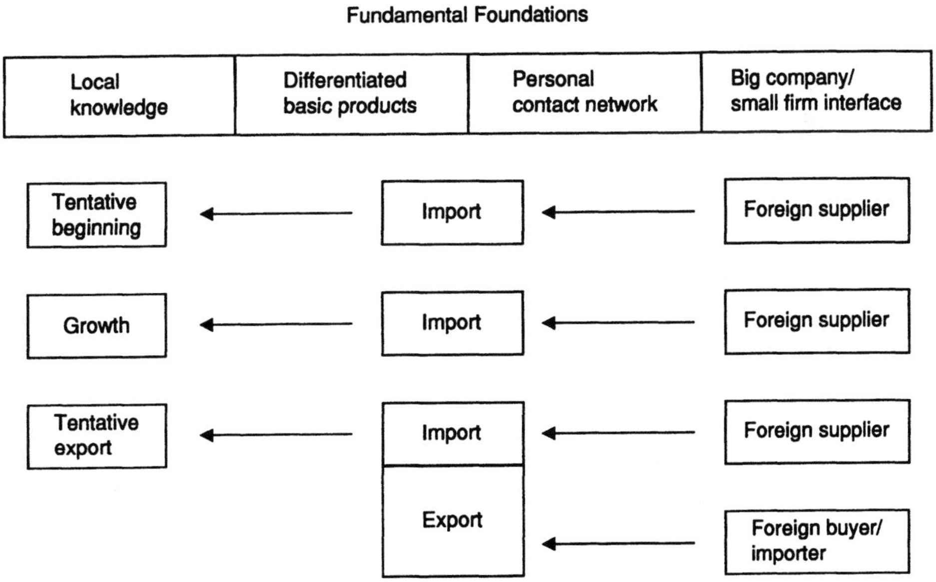

Figure A.1 Theoretical proposition for export development

SMEs. This case illustrates that there is another way to develop export markets. It shows what can be done to overcome the many barriers that many firms, particularly entrepreneurial led firms, experience.

The theoretical proposition, illustrated in Figure A.1, is designed to appeal to the entrepreneurial instincts of the entrepreneurially led SME which has never before exported but which may have been trading in a small market niche within its home market.

The proposition or 'new concept' is that:

> Entrepreneurially led small firms can best develop export markets by first *importing* products into their home domestic market and once having established a relationship with a foreign supplier can begin to use this suppliers networks for exporting products.

The fundamental foundations of this theoretical proposition stem from the following:

Local knowledge – that is, the intimate knowledge possessed by the entrepreneur of the local home market. The entrepreneur knows the wants and needs of his/her market, the type of products which are most in demand and an intuitive feel for new potential products.

Differentiation of established products – Consumers in today's developed economies know what they want, particularly in relation to standard, everyday, regular purchases such as basic food items or similar domestic products. Retailers pander to this comfort purchasing pattern by standardizing products and emphasizing strong brands. Thus, consumers are not very receptive to entirely new products but are curiously attracted to new variations of products they can easily recognize; that is, products that are differentiated through packaging or origin.

Both aspects of local knowledge and differentiated established products are simple representations of *conventional* marketing management approaches. The following comments on personal contact networks and SME relationships with large companies are illustrations of the utilization of new concepts and adaptation of conventional approaches to suit SMEs.

Personal contact networks – Recognition that entrepreneurs will be more comfortable doing business with personal contacts with whom they have developed a good relationship. Such networks are strong whether buying or selling.

Big company/small firm interface – Recognition that small firms must just as often do business with large companies as they do with other small firms. Such relationships can be either one of buying from or selling to, or both.

These fundamental foundations are more strongly biased, initially, towards *importing* rather than exporting. It might be argued that there is still a fundamental barrier in establishing the initial contact, but it is immeasurably easier to establish a contact when wishing to purchase than when wishing to sell.

Having established a tentative supplier contact, the entrepreneur can use his/her local knowledge to assess the potential of the supplier's products as appropriately differentiated but still easily recognizable products.

The entrepreneur can now use his/her selling skills in developing the new products in the local market. During this time the relationship between the entrepreneur and the supplier company personnel is growing and cementing. Both parties may visit each other's establishments as a natural progression of the trading relationship. It is during these visits that opportunities will arise for introducing the entrepreneur's products to the supplier. The supplier can be encouraged to introduce the product to some contacts in the foreign market on the basis that they might be interested.

Thus the network begins to widen and new contacts are made. Most importantly, the entrepreneur has begun to export in the most natural way possible, one that is wholly compatible with his/her inherent characteristics. The original supplier company is able to widen the contact network for the entrepreneur as is the new buyer contact. *Exporting has begun.*

Of course, it should be recognized that throughout this process success is heavily reliant on the *competencies* of the entrepreneur in taking the products to the market. Without the inherent entrepreneurial marketing competencies of knowledge, experience, communication and judgement, the concept would not achieve the same success.

3 Avondale Foods

Derek and Harry Geddis, two brothers, left horticultural college in England twenty years ago to return to their father's 20 acre farm in Ireland. As teenagers they both grew vegetables and sold them to local shops for pocket money. Even at this young age both had already decided that they wanted to work for themselves so on their return they immediately set about planting and growing produce to sell to local retail outlets and supermarkets which were just beginning to experience accelerated growth in the form of multiple retailing. At first they grew lettuce, cabbage, carrots and parsnips and using their father's car called on local shops offering their stock for sale. Much of this early business was on a barter basis with the brothers on occasions exchanging produce for cigarettes and food. The brothers traded under the name of Samuel Geddis and Sons.

The brothers were quite different individuals. Harry Geddis, the older of the two, was very technically minded with a natural flair for both horticultural technique and understanding machinery or indeed anything mechanical. He was a quiet individual and happier when not having to deal personally with customers and business contacts. His abilities none the less were to make a subsequent and major contribution to the business development. Derek Geddis by contrast had a personality that enabled him to generate an extensive network of friends and business contacts. He was a natural marketer, inherently customer-focused in both word and manner, possessing an ability to engender confidence in his customers and financial backers. Both brothers had complementary abilities. Derek's ability to get on with people and to make contacts easily meant that business soon began to grow and expand at a rapid rate.

Accelerated growth of the business brought with it its own problems. First, customers were looking for other products which the brothers did not grow. Second, an increased demand meant that the 20 acre farm was not big enough and had to be supplemented with the lease of additional acreage. To satisfy the demand for an increased product range the Geddis brothers began to plant other produce. The product range now extended to cover the full range of local vegetables demanded by customers. The increased product range and increased acreage meant that the brothers needed to possess a diversity of horticultural techniques which had potential negative implications for product quality. They firmly believed in producing the highest quality produce and felt that this could only be achieved through growers specializing in growing particular product lines. Furthermore, increased business meant that more time had to be spent in the fields sowing and harvesting and therefore insufficient time could be dedicated to managing the business or growing it in a deliberate direction.

From a marketing point of view several key developments paralleled this activity. First, while at college the Geddis brothers had noticed that English supermarket chains, which were developing rapidly, were featuring more and more prepacked produce as opposed to traditional loose produce. This prompted them to begin prepacking produce for retailers in their local market. This dimension of their business was innovative and such was the success that they had to expand their basic prepacking facilities at the farm. In addition, this resulted in the hiring of employees on a part-time basis to assist with the pre-packing activity.

Business continued to grow rapidly and the brothers were faced with some key decisions. They could go on hiring more staff and leasing more land. Although this appeared like a reasonable direction to take, it meant that the majority of their time was going to be spent working the land. Then Derek Geddis had an idea which was fundamentally to change the nature of the business. He knew that since they were located in a highly agricultural area a large variety of horticultural produce could be easily sourced. In addition his experience of supplying the local market to date provided him with the knowledge that the market was being serviced by an extensive network of farmers who delivered directly to food retailers. His regular communication with these other farmers through every aspect of his business equipped him with the knowledge that by and large farmers were uncomfortable in business dealings that involved setting prices on a daily basis, in dealing with customers, customers' complaints, coping with demand for prepacked produce and worst of all, having to take time away from the land to deliver to retailers, often on demand, at all sorts of hours.

Derek and Harry saw an opportunity to facilitate these other growers as well as solving their own problems and circulated all the farmers and growers that they knew and invited them to attend a meeting at a local hotel. First, they wined and dined the large number that attended and then proceeded to outline their vision of how the market should be developed. Essentially, they offered to take responsibility for the prepacking and marketing of the growers' produce and assured them of a fair return in exchange. This would mean that growers could concentrate on what they knew best and would mean only one delivery of produce to the Geddis brothers' farm. They did stipulate, however, that they were only interested in quality produce and offered horticultural support and assistance to those who required this. In addition they would indicate to growers which products to grow, which varieties and in what quantities. Most of those growers who attended the meeting were happy to participate in the scheme. This meant that the Geddis brothers could immediately turn their attention from growing produce to other important aspects of their business.

The increased volume of business that they had to handle had several implications for the business. First, it meant that there was an increased volume and range of stock to be prepacked. Second, there was a substantial increase in produce volume to be distributed and this required additional distribution capability. Staff were hired on a full-time basis and another delivery van and driver were employed. Meanwhile Harry Geddis continued to develop the prepacking of produce by adding a washing facility for vegetables and designing machinery to handle this process. Derek, capitalizing on his communication skills, continued to develop the market in which they were operating. His next major direction was to acquire the distribution rights for prepacked coleslaw on behalf of a major UK food processor who had a manufacturing subsidiary based in Ireland. This acquisition meant that the company was increasing the volume of stores on which it was calling as well as introducing the company to business contracts from schools, hospitals and other institutions.

After five years trading in the marketplace Samuel Geddis and Sons were listed as key suppliers of fresh produce and related products with all the major multiples throughout Ireland. In addition, the catering and institutional side of the business had grown into a substantial share of the total business. Derek Geddis realized that he had a marketing problem. Essentially he realized that he had what was largely a low-value and bulky product. This was difficult to export in a cost-effective manner so he needed to find other market opportunities if the firm was to continue to grow.

Such an opportunity was to arise quite suddenly as a consequence of the relationship with the coleslaw manufacturer running into some difficulties. Derek decided to discontinue the agreement and to commence coleslaw manufacture himself. He already had access to a healthy supply-line of fresh vegetables and only needed to source the oils and mayonnaise. Once he had done this Harry set about designing the necessary manufacturing equipment. Once again this new side of the business flourished and the now rapidly growing factory required further expansion. Regular contact with customers and a sound knowledge of the market indicated to Derek Geddis the need for an expanded product range of prepacked prepared and processed salad lines. Experience and knowledge gained from the manufacture of coleslaw meant that other lines could be added to the product range and a special product range was developed under the 'Nature's Best' range. The success of this range led to many requests from the now thriving grocery multiple chains for own label products. Within a short period of time Samuel Geddis and Sons, now trading under the Avondale Foods name, became the dominant supplier of coleslaws and pot salads in the Irish market. This diversification meant a move into chilled distribution which in itself gave the company a competitive advantage over other players in an increasingly sophisticated market.

Not content with this growth, Derek took stock of his experience, market knowledge and customer trends and identified another market opportunity. He realized that as a consequence of the company's capability to produce top quality coleslaws and pot salads they could now produce salad creams and sauces. He had estimated that the market for these products in Ireland was worth £60 million annually and was dominated by two multinational brand names. Derek did not want to get into competition with the market leaders so opted for what he considered to be a potentially lucrative sector of the grocery market, own labels. Within two years he was producing seventeen own-label products within a product line which had captured 5 per cent of the market. Like other areas of the business the own-label route was once again proving successful.

The fast growth of this sector of the business caused some concern among the market leaders and they put pressure on sauce bottle manufacturers not to supply Avondale Foods. Not to be deterred by this move, the Geddis brothers set about establishing their own bottle manufacturing facility. Not only do they now supply their own bottles profitably, but they also supply bottles to a series of other food processors.

Still not content, Derek Geddis set about identifying another market opportunity. Once again using existing raw material and raw product he identified a potential market for a range of prepared vegetables, salads in a pillow pack form. Using Harry's technical expertise machinery was specifically designed for this product range. Targeting both existing customers and the large catering and institutional customers a profitable market segment was soon established.

Derek continued to search for new market opportunities. He had noticed that sandwiches were quickly becoming a feature of modern food retailing. Sandwiches were being sold at railway stations, airports, supermarkets, forecourt retailers and by institutional caterers. Furthermore, he knew that the quality of these products was variable. In addition, as he was already in food processing, he knew that changing food hygiene regulations would put practically all the existing sandwich manufacturers out of business. To manufacture sandwiches to legal requirements would mean substantial investment beyond the resources of existing suppliers. Derek also realized that his biggest customer, a major multinational food retailer was keen to locate a sandwich manufacturer who could meet their own exacting standards of hygiene. As a result of negotiations with this customer Avondale Foods set up a pilot scheme to manufacture sandwiches for this customer's shops only. The pilot was a major success and a dedicated factory was subsequently built. This new facility was .very successful and now stands as the fastest growing and most profitable sector of the company's business.

Products

Avondale Foods currently supplies 220 product items to the food retailing and catering sectors. The range comprises of the following product lines: prepacked vegetables, loose vegetables, salads and ready prepared salads, pot salads, sauces, mayonnaises, salad creams and sandwiches. When discussing the company's product range Derek Geddis is quick to point out that they have never strayed very far from their core business of procuring, prepacking and supplying the food industry with high quality vegetables. All subsequent diversifications relied heavily on these products and the experience, knowledge and expertise gained from this side of the business. Currently vegetables and ready prepared vegetables account for 41 per cent of the company's business, pot salads account for 37 per cent, sauces, salad creams and mayonnaise account for 11 per cent, and sandwiches 11 per cent.

The customer base has remained largely unchanged in recent years. What Avondale Foods have done successfully is to introduce a stream of new and exciting products to existing customers.

Derek Geddis is modest about the achievements of the company. When asked what he saw as the most important ingredient in his own makeup that contributed to company success, he cited commitment. All other qualities he stressed were important but useless and impotent without commitment. He felt that his brother Harry and he formed a good entrepreneurial team, his own flair for marketing and finance being balanced by his brother's technical brilliance. He feels that the secret to marketing success is grounded in a simple but logical sequence, and his axiom is 'Get the market first and then get the product – as long as it is a quality one'. Viewing his success to date who could argue with that!

Case evaluation

This case again shows the importance of entrepreneurial flair and competence in both manufacturing development and marketing creativity, and the implicit and proactive use of a wide and varied network of key contacts throughout the evolution of this company. This company development is essentially entrepreneurially led and the uniquely situation-specific nature of the highly adapted marketing linked with the concepts of networks and use of appropriate competencies combine to make entrepreneurial marketing.

It should be noted also that while the company has remained close to its core business, the entrepreneurs have been opportunistic and exploited circumstances as they have arrived. It should be noted also that many of these opportunities have led the company into niches as much as the entrepreneurs finding new niches.

4 Next Island Holidays

This company was founded by Tom Allen who had previously been managing director of a large tour operating company in the United Kingdom and prior to that had some ten years' experience in the travel business both in management and as a chartered accountant. Tom founded the company through a desire to operate and develop his own company. He spent the first three months of the company's existence planning and organizing for the forthcoming season. During this time it became apparent that the company was underfunded. Next Island was grossly underfinanced with a starting capital of £20,000, most of which was used to cover operating overheads. It was hoped that advanced booking revenue would be sufficient to pay for accommodation in the various resorts but this proved to be impractical and consequently an overdraft of £20,000 was required to cover these costs. It was obvious that cash supplements were required from somewhere. In an attempt to ease the pressure on overheads the owner worked part-time as an executive director for another tour operator. This arrangement covered the owner's salary and operating overheads of Next Island, but at the same time allowed freedom to run Next Island independently of the larger company. As a result, Next Island's first full year of trading was carried out on a part-time basis by the owner and by two full-time office clerk/administrators.

Products

The product that was used to launch the company can be described as being 'package holidays' incorporating, specialist knowledge of destination; superior service in booking, administration and in-resort service; a good product resort; and a high level of assistance to the customer. The product, while not unique in itself, was presented as an alternative to mass market tour operators, and was to be sold through travel agents with a uniquely planned high level of service and liaison. This approach was intended to be particularly attractive to the independent and smaller chains of travel agents.

Market(s)

The nature of the travel and tourism industry is that of a market-oriented service industry. Because of the relatively low differentiation of holiday packages, companies are highly competitive. They use a wide range of marketing tools and techniques with a brochure as the centrepiece. Many of the characteristics pertaining to services marketing prevail, in particular the intangibility of the service and element of experience quality attached to enjoying a holiday. Tour operators, therefore, devote a lot of attention to the concept of an enjoyable and relaxing time.

While many of the marketing tools and techniques are easily described in general terms, for example, the brochure, price discounting, special offers and promotions, almost all are uniquely adapted to the industry-specific situation. The travel industry has many traditional norms surrounding its marketing approaches:

- Brochures conform to a traditional pattern, incorporating brief descriptions and colourful illustrations of the product. Also, all brochures carry comprehensive price lists and are launched within a three-week period each autumn.
- All companies use colour posters depicting holiday scenes.
- Almost all products represent one or two weeks' duration all-inclusive.

Tom Allen believed that middle-sized operators were being squeezed out of the market and that the best options were to grow big or specialize in particular market niches. In this belief, Next Island have concentrated their market initially on Greece and in particular Greek island destinations.

The characteristics of the market are that tour operators sell holidays by distributing through travel agents or selling direct to the public. Holidays sold through travel agents account for about 80 per cent of the market. Travel agents are mainly multiples, which control about a quarter of the outlets, or small chains and independents. The multiples pursue an intense policy of selection of operators for brochure racking, centring on the major large tour operators. Smaller chains and multiples are much more often open to supporting good quality specialist operators.

Marketing activity

As managing director for one of his previous companies, Tom Allen had been involved in developing and implementing marketing plans. Consequently, it was natural for him to attempt to develop a marketing plan for Next Island. However, as a small company with limited resources he could not hope to invest in the highly structured processes of the formal marketing planning that he had been used to in the past. Instead, Tom confined himself to answering some key questions that would enable him to do successful marketing. With his experience of the industry, he was able to answer many of the external environmental dimensions of the marketing picture and where he did not have answers he was able to call on his many contacts within his industry-wide network. Tom was able to construct a marketing plan that was uniquely adapted to Next Island's circumstances. The main ingredients of this plan included:

1. An overview of the company purpose.
2. A description of the company.
3. Marketing issues, including:
   (a) industry description and outlook,
   (b) target markets,
   (c) competition,
   (d) marketing activities,
   (e) selling activities,
   (f) reaction from perspective customers.
4. Management and ownership.
5. Financial data.
6. Short-term plans for selling and promotion.

The company has broadly followed the objectives and strategies outlined in this first plan. The nature of this kind of business enables a company to follow closely a broad plan. For example, decisions about the product offering and prices have to be made nine months to one year in advance of their being sold. Consequently, the company's products, in terms of resorts and accommodation, must be planned with this kind of lead time.

In addition to this inherent planning culture, much of the first year was taken up with organizing procedures and methods which required a lot of 'What will we need?' and 'What will happen if?' kind of decisions. Also, because actual orders tend to be very seasonal, that is, over an eight-month period from early March until mid-October, the quiet months of November through to February are naturally a time for reflection on what to do for next season.

The focus of the marketing activity was to concentrate on independent travel agents within a broadly defined catchment area. The main thrust of the contact, typical of the industry, was through the use of a brochure. Next Island's brochure was aimed at being fashionable, carrying the image of a friendly professional specialist, providing holidays which the target market would like to take. The design of the brochure was purposefully innovative and aimed at being both attractive and readable.

The brochure was circulated to 640 independent travel agents in the catchment area. A covering letter was enclosed, stating that more copies could be sent but asking that distribution to holiday makers should be discerning, such as offering to customers who could not find anything that attracted them in the brochures of the major tour operators.

Because of the limitation on the owner's time, direct calling with travel agents was severely restricted. Instead, the office staff and, when possible, the owner would take every opportunity to telephone agents and introduce themselves and attempt to explain the benefits of the product.

Pricing policy was aimed at being competitive in terms of being the same as or near the major competitors' prices. The low overheads structure of the company enabled it to offer special prices both to specific customer types and in terms of discounts to travel agents.

The second year of the company's operations saw Tom Allen leave his post with the other company and devote his energies full-time to Next Island. The marketing approach he had devised for the first year had proved quite successful in that the company had achieved its sales targets at peak trading times, although a shortfall in targets had been experienced at off-peak periods. Tom concluded that this was due to lack of on-the-ground support for the product. The company's target for the first year had been 1,500 holiday makers, the actual achieved was 1,150.

The marketing strategy for the second year was simply to concentrate and encouraging the part-time sales people, in this case, the travel agents. Tom devised a sales plan to achieve this by targeting areas, selecting agents who had made a booking the previous year, calling and introducing himself and working out a mutually beneficial strategy with the individual agent. He also selected new agents in the area on a similar basis. He spent four days of every week, from the end of October until the end of the following January, on his 'shaking hands' sales strategy. In addition, one of his office staff did a similar job over the same time period. During the season agents were constantly circulated with information and special offers.

At the end of the second year of operation company sales had grown substantially and achieved the target of 3,500 holidays. The third year of operations consolidated the base of regular agents and expanded the product offering by adding more holiday destinations. A winter season portfolio incorporating 'city-breaks' and 'golf weekends' was introduced to provide revenue during the quiet winter period. The company's steady growth, financed through profits from revenues which benefited greatly from the economies of scale from the larger volumes of sales, allowed the company to develop rapidly so that within five years Next Island had grown to become one of the leading package holiday companies in its market sector.

Case Evaluation

The entrepreneurial competencies of the owner, particularly his knowledge and experience of the industry, coupled with his extensive network of contacts enabled him to overcome many of the difficulties presented by a grossly underfunded new venture. This case is a good example of how to adapt formal marketing approaches to suit the specific SME circumstances. It is also an illustration of the use of a workbook approach, that is, consideration of key questions that need to be addressed in developing a situation specific marketing plan. It can be seen that issues addressed must take account of relevant environmental factors and the particular circumstances of the enterprise. Therefore, the workbook framework is unique to the company in question.

Overall conclusions

In this text we have addressed the fundamental question: 'How can SMEs do marketing?' Such a straightforward question belies a multiplicity of problems. The question is not an academic abstract, it is one that is expressed by most entrepreneurs at some time or other. The fact that such a question exists can only mean that entrepreneurs, and SMEs in general, find it difficult to do the kind of marketing that is touted by academics and business advisers. In addressing this question we have recognized that there is a range of fundamental and inherent characteristics which have an influence on marketing activity in SMEs. We believe that these characteristics must be recognized and taken into account if marketing in SMEs is to be both meaningful and useful.

In our exploration of these characteristics we have tried not to be too radical or revolutionary in our statements. We recognize that there is much to be gained from adhering to the fundamental and frameworks and structures established by both scholars and practitioners over many years. What we have tried to do is take account of these established frameworks but have advocated strongly that these be adapted to suit the SME's circumstance. To this end we have outlined, in the form of a workbook, a marketing approach that is entirely suited to the resource constraints of SMEs.

We have advocated that the best vehicle for performing this adaptation is the entrepreneur, because, we believe, it is the entrepreneur who has the biggest single influence upon the marketing activities of an SME. We have tried to harness the entrepreneurial approach by focusing on aspects which are inherent in every entrepreneur, namely personal contact networks and the latent competencies possessed for decision-making. We have channelled these aspects towards marketing by presenting the concepts of marketing competencies and marketing networks.

By bringing together all these factors we have presented the concept of entrepreneurial marketing. This term, we believe, concisely depicts the kind of marketing for SMEs that is most appropriate. That is marketing which is done, and done comfortably, by the entrepreneur in the context of his or her SME.

Further reading

A fuller description of Eaton & Caron Marketing with academic justification and foundation is contained in the *Proceedings of the American Marketing Association Summer Conference*, Boston, 1993.

A fuller description of Next Island Holidays is contained in 'Some exploratory models for assessing small firms' marketing performance: A qualitative approach', *European Journal of Marketing* 24 (11), pp. 1–51.

Index

Return ⟶ 23rd Feb 2010